Morality, Moral Luck and Responsibility

Also by Nafsika Athanassoulis

PHILOSOPHICAL REFLECTIONS ON MEDICAL ETHICS (*editor*)

THE MORAL LIFE
Essays in Honour of John Cottingham (*co-edited with Samantha Vice*)

Morality, Moral Luck and Responsibility

Fortune's Web

Nafsika Athanassoulis

Lecturer in Ethics, Centre for Professional Ethics,
Keele University

First published in hardback 2005
This paperback edition published 2010 by
PALGRAVE MACMILLAN

Palgrave Macmillan in the UK is an imprint of Macmillan Publishers Limited, registered in England, company number 785998, of Houndmills, Basingstoke, Hampshire RG21 6XS.

Palgrave Macmillan in the US is a division of St Martin's Press LLC, 175 Fifth Avenue, New York, NY 10010.

Palgrave Macmillan is the global academic imprint of the above companies and has companies and representatives throughout the world.

Palgrave® and Macmillan® are registered trademarks in the United States, the United Kingdom, Europe and other countries.

ISBN 978-1-4039-3549-6 hardback
ISBN 978-0-230-24553-2 paperback

This book is printed on paper suitable for recycling and made from fully managed and sustained forest sources. Logging, pulping and manufacturing processes are expected to conform to the environmental regulations of the country of origin.

A catalogue record for this book is available from the British Library.

Library of Congress Cataloging-in-Publication Data
Athanassoulis, Nafsika, 1973–
    Morality, moral luck, and responsibility : fortune's web / Nafsika
    Athanassoulis.
        p.   cm.
    Includes bibliographical references and index.
    ISBN 1–4039–3549–1 (cloth) 0–230–24553–6 (pbk)
    1. Ethics.   2. Fortune—Moral and ethical aspects.
    3. Responsibility.   I. Title.

    BJ1275.A84 2005
    170—dc22
                                                        2004060087

10   9   8   7   6   5   4   3   2   1
19   18   17   16   15   14   13   12   11   10

Transferred to Digital Printing 2010

For ATA and CaK

Contents

Abbreviations, Sources and Translations

Works by Aristotle, cited by abbreviation

EE   *Eudemian Ethics*, trans. Rackham, H. (Cambridge MA: Loeb
        Classical Library, 1935 [1996]).
MM   *Magna Moralia*, trans. Armstrong, C.G. (Cambridge MA: Loeb
        Classical Library, 1969).
NE   *Nicomachean Ethics*, trans. Thompson, J.A.K. (London:
        Penguin Books, 1976). In some places I have used Racham, H.
        (Cambridge MA: Loeb Classical Library, 1926 [1994]) as it
        seemed a more appropriate translation. When this is the case
        it is indicated in the notes.
R   *Rhetorica*, ed. Ross, W.D. (Oxford: Clarendon Press, 1924).
VV   *Virtues and Vices*, trans. Rachham, H. (Cambridge MA: Loeb
        Classical Library, 1935 [1996]).

Citations to Aristotle's works standardly refer to Behher, I. (ed.), *Aristotelis Opera* (Berlin, 1831). So that NE 1147a 35 refers to the sentence in the *Nicomachean Ethics* on line 35 of column A of page 1147.

Works by the Stoics and sources for the Stoics, cited by abbreviation

DF   Cicero, *De Fato*, trans. Sharples, R.W. (England: Aris & Phillips
        Ltd, 1991).
DFin   Cicero, *De Finibus*, trans. Reid, J.S. (Cambridge: Cambridge
        University Press).
DI   Seneca, *De Ira*, in trans. Basore, J.W., *Moral Essays* (Cambridge
        MA: Loeb Classical Library, 1928–32).
DL   Diogenes Laertius, *Lives of the Eminent Philosophers*, vols 1
        and 2, trans. Hicks, R.D. (London: W. Heinemann, 1925).
E   Seneca, *Epistulae*, trans. Gummere, R.M. (London:
        W. Heinemann, 1925).
G   Galen, *The Soul's Dependence on the Body*, in *Galen: Selected
        Works*, trans. Singer, P.N. (Great Britain: Oxford University
        Press, 1997).

HP   Long, A.A. and Sedley, D.N., *The Hellenistic Philosophers*, Volume I: *Translations of the Principal Sources with Philosophical Commentary* and Volume II: *Greek and Latin Texts with Notes and Bibliography* (Cambridge: Cambridge University Press, 1999).

P   Plutarch, *Moralia*, trans. Cherniss, H. (Great Britain: Heinemann, 1976).

SVF   *Stoicorum Veterum Fragmenta*, trans. von Arnim, H. (Leipzig: Teubner, 1921).

Works by Kant, cited by abbreviation

A   *Anthropologie in pragmatischer Hinsicht*
Anthropology from a Pragmatic Point of View (1798), in trans. Gregor, M.J., *Anthropology from a Pragmatic Point of View* (Netherlands: Martinus Nijhoff, 1974).

G   *Grundlegung zur Metaphysik der Sitten*
The Groundwork of the Metaphysics of Morals (1785), in trans. Paton, H.J., *The Moral Law* (Great Britain: Routledge, 1991).

KpV   *Krtitik der praktischen Vernunft*
Critique of Practical Reason (1788), in trans. Gregor, J., *Practical Philosophy* (USA: Cambridge University Press, 1996).

KrV   *Kritik der reinen Vernunft*
Critique of Pure Reason (1781), in trans. Guyer, P. and Wood, A.W., *Critique of Pure Reason* (USA: Cambridge University Press, 1998).

MS   *Die Metaphysik der Sitten*
The Metaphysics of Morals (1797), in trans. Gregor, M.J., *The Metaphysics of Morals* (Great Britain: Cambridge University Press, 1996).

Rel   *Die Religion innerhalb der Grenzen der blossen Vernunft*
Religion Within the Boundaries of Mere Reason (1793), in trans. Wood, A.W. and di Giovanni, G. (eds), *Religion and Rational Theology* (USA: Cambridge University Press, 1996).

Citations to Kant's works standardly refer to *Kants gesammelte Schriften, herausgegeben von der Deutschen, Akademie der Wissenschaften*, 29 volumes (Berlin: Walter de Gruyter, 1902).

Acknowledgements

Many people have supported and encouraged me during the writing of this book and I have accumulated more debts than I could possibly acknowledge here. I am most grateful to John Cottingham for his unfailing patience; to Brad Hooker and Rosalind Hursthouse for their extremely helpful comments; to David Walker, who is the inspiration for my interest in Aristotle; Richard Sorabji for kindly providing me with references on the Stoics; David McNaughton for his unfailing encouragement; Seiriol Morgan for taking the time to comment on my work on Kant; Jonathan Dancy, Philip Stratton-Lake and Michael Lacewing for commenting on earlier drafts; as well as an anonymous reader for Palgrave Macmillan who made some extremely helpful suggestions, especially on the chapters on Kant. Earlier versions of chapters of this work have been presented at conferences at the University of Durham, Michigan State University and the University of Leeds. I am grateful to the audiences at these events for their stimulating comments. Of course any omissions, mistakes and misunderstandings that remain are entirely my own.

In addition I would like to acknowledge with gratitude the financial assistance of the British Academy and the University of Reading in funding the first part of this project and the University of Leeds for funding its completion.

Last, but not least, I would like to thank the CEO of White Nova Corporation for always being willing to drop everything in order to support me.

Introduction

> One's history as an agent is a web in which anything that is the product of the will is surrounded and held up and partly formed by things that are not, in such a way that reflection can go only in one of two directions: either in the direction of saying that responsible agency is a fairly superficial concept, which has a limited use in harmonizing what happens, or else that it is not a superficial concept, but that it cannot ultimately be purified...
>
> – Williams, in Statman, 1993

When Bernard Williams introduced the term 'moral luck' to modern philosophy, he intended it to be an oxymoron[1] because of the contradiction in the implications of the two terms: morality is associated with control, choice, responsibility and therefore praise and blame, whereas luck is about chance, unpredictability, lack of control and therefore the inappropriateness of praise or blame. If there is such a thing as moral luck, then we have to show *both* how it is possible to hold that crucial elements of the moral decision were outside the agent's control *and* how we still want to hold the agent responsible for the act and attribute praise or blame.

The problem of moral luck raises fundamental questions about how we understand ourselves and our moral obligations. On the one hand, even a casual observation of human nature reveals that it is subject to all sorts of contingencies. If we want to give a plausible account of human nature we need to recognize and accommodate all the factors outside our control, which play a crucial role in shaping who we are, what we do and what we are held responsible for. The moral life seems vulnerable to all sorts of influences, even to the point of catastrophic and irreversible disasters befalling entirely unwitting and undeserving agents. On the other hand, the very understanding of morality involves a robust conception of responsibility. There is a sense of unfairness in the suggestion that *moral* matters, and therefore matters of moral praise and blame, can be subject to factors outside the agent's control. Equality in the sphere of morality seems to require an equal footing and an equal chance to do what we are obliged to do and what we will be blamed for not doing.

These two elements are in conflict, exemplified by the possibility of moral luck. Williams movingly draws our attention to how luck has 'captured' agency in a tangled web of factors outside our control and more genuine acts of the will. He finds himself having to accept the possibility of luck and faced with two, equally problematic, options. One option is to accept that agency is a superficial concept. So when we speak of choice, agency and the voluntary we are using these terms in a superficial way, accepting that there are really no such things, as the real influence is the influence of luck. For how can there be real choice if it is not *my* choice? This 'solution' is truly repugnant, as it plays havoc with our understanding of morality. If we still want to make claims of moral responsibility, these are just superficial ones as morality is not really possible. The other option is to accept a concept of responsibility, but admit that it cannot be purified. This would mean that we would have to, at least to an extent, give up on a strong and pure conception of responsibility. This would entirely muddle our understanding of desert and its connection to agency and the voluntary.

The problem is a central one, as it appeals to a fundamental understanding we have of ourselves in terms of what we have done (or more aptly chosen to do) and what we are responsible for. This sense of responsibility is conceptually tied in to agency and choice, and therefore threatened by luck. As a consequence, the only other response to moral luck, one rejected by Williams, is to resist its very possibility. Conceptually, morality is immune to luck, so we need to find a practical way of understanding this as a requirement which can be applied to us as human beings. That is, as beings which are clearly also subject to contingent factors.

The subject of this book is an exploration of the tension created by moral luck: of the requirement for moral immunity from luck, coupled with the need to offer a plausible conception of situated agency subject to contingencies. The discussion will cover two writers whose work is claimed to be at opposite ends of the spectrum on the problem of moral luck. On the one hand, we have the Aristotelian acceptance of the possibility of luck, such that the influence of contingent factors is recognized as a part of the good life. This allows Aristotle to give a plausible account of moral development, accounting for all the factors outside our control which shape us into who we become. On the other hand, we have the Kantian ambition to show how morality as immune to luck is a concept which has an application for human beings. This will allow the Kantian to make strong and pure judgements of responsibility. As we shall see, both these interpretations of Aristotle and Kant are, in part, correct, but also, in part, misleading. Aristotle is more than aware of the demands of reason, while part of the Kantian project involves trying to accommodate a plausible conception of gradual and contingent moral development. I will also consider the Stoics, as their answer to the problem of moral luck shares some of its starting points with Aristotle, while pre-dating some Kantian claims. Finally, I will examine three recent writers, Slote, Hursthouse and Herman, who work in the traditions of Aristotle or Kant, and use their theories to ask whether there really is much of a disagreement between Kantians and virtue ethicists as some commentators would have us believe.

1
Moral Luck

1.1 Introduction

A few decades after Williams' article introduced to philosophy concerns about moral luck, the term remains essentially disputed and the questions raised by it partly unanswered. Part of the problem is that Williams captured a deep unease about responsibility and luck. In the discussions that followed the original paper, commentators have tried to either resolve or discard this sense of unease, or show how it can be accommodated from within their particular theoretical perspective.

This chapter will serve the dual purpose of attempting to explain what is meant by moral luck and throwing some light on why it has been such a perplexing and stimulating philosophical topic. This is important because, although the tension implicit in the term is clear enough, we do not have a clear definition of the term itself, nor do we have agreement over the kinds of examples which are genuine examples of moral luck or how these, genuine examples, might differ from cases of simple bad luck.

1.2 Luck

'Luck' is an unclear term because it can be understood in different ways. In one sense it can be discounted entirely. This is the sense of luck as superstition, that is the sense in which a person may carry a rabbit's foot for 'good luck'. The assumption here is that luck is a property of the rabbit's foot which acts as a magnet, drawing some advantage towards the possessor of the lucky item. This kind of luck is clearly non-existent. Similarly, some people may feel very lucky on a particular day or may take past instances of favourable outcomes as evidence that *they* are lucky. However, luck is not a property, or a force of nature, or a gift of the gods, that attaches itself to certain people and gives them a particular advantage in the way a skill would. Accidental advantages are not merited, nor can we make inferences from previous 'lucky' instances to the possibility of replicating such 'lucky' situations. Furthermore, we cannot take credit for the supposed effects of luck. If by 'luck' we mean something outside anyone's control, then merit, praise or credit for the effects of luck cannot be due to anyone and, further, we cannot predict when lucky situations will occur or do anything to bring them about.

Despite these considerations, the idea that luck rubs off particular objects and people, or the idea that certain actions will bring about good luck as if the phenomenon was somehow consciously controlled, persists. However, the grounds for this persistence are not that such luck exists, but lie rather in the psychological make-up of human beings, that is something along the lines that we are insecure about the future and tend to favour ourselves and tend to rely on supposed occult powers and forces for security and extra help. As far as psychology is concerned, our reactions to luck as superstition can be very interesting, for example it seems that people tend to claim good things that happen to them as related to their own agency, whereas they attribute bad things to luck – a student may think of good essays as the result of hard work, whereas bad essays are due to bad luck. In this sense, then, good and equally bad luck do not exist.

A related way in which we speak about luck involves cases where we accept that there was some chain of causation, but it was so complex and outside our understanding that it appears random. In this sense, it is a matter of luck whether I will win the lottery. There is a chain of events that leads to my winning the lottery, involving physical laws about gravity and the movement of objects which control the spinning of the number balls and so on, but this chain is so entirely outside my ability to predict that it appears random, a matter of luck:

> Causation can be entirely inscrutable – utterly lost in a tangled web of coincidence – and still be causation... when we think of cases of causation we almost invariably think of cases where the relationships are laid bare, where the actuality or at least the practicality of control by an agent is manifest. Some cases of causation are called 'randomizing' processes precisely because of their uncontrollability.[1]

If I have to choose between two options, the reasons behind both being balanced so perfectly that I cannot make a choice, I may leave the outcome to luck by tossing a coin. This does not mean that some peculiar force takes control of the outcome, or that coins are endowed with a peculiar property, rather that the chain of causal events that lead the coin to fall heads or tails is so complex as to be, practically, out of my control. Such cases, of evenly balanced choices, are cases where we actively want to give up control of the decision which we cannot make and toss a coin for precisely that reason.

Cases of luck can sometimes be misidentified as cases of *moral* luck. Williams has illustrated how it is possible for an agent to feel regret for an act for which we would not hold him responsible.[2] The lorry driver who accidentally and *non-culpably* kills a child can feel regret that something terrible happened and that he had a special relation to that happening, but this regret is not evidence of his moral blameworthiness; rather, if anything, it is evidence of his sensitivity. It was the driver's bad luck to be driving at a time and place which meant he was the one who hit the careless pedestrian, but this is not moral luck as the case is set up so that the driver is not morally culpable for what happened. The driver was not negligent, irresponsible, inattentive and so on. If there is fault to be found, it is to be found with the pedestrian, but as he paid for this mistake with his life, this point is not usually dwelt upon. That the driver has moral feeling about what happened, that he feels regret and maybe even guilt, is an understandable reaction to the fact that he was associated with the death of another human being, even if this association was non-culpable. Williams' example seems, to me, to illustrate that one can be the subject of bad luck, and can even have what would be morally relevant feelings about the situation, without this necessarily being an example of bad *moral* luck. This particular kind of regret involves a first-person standpoint, as it is intricately connected with the thought that it was *me* who brought about this event, in such a way that it differs from spectator regret. Also, because of such considerations, it must have a particular kind of psychological content, appropriate to the agent but not necessarily shared by spectators and by-standers. Finally, it also has a particular kind of expression, involving a wish that one had not done the act, even while recognizing that one is not morally culpable for doing it.

Cases of luck, then, involve an outcome which is outside our control (or comprehension) and at the same time involve a certain evaluative status.[3] Cases of moral luck involve a judgement of responsibility, of moral praise or blame. Cases of luck involve some kind of good or bad result in terms of a benefit, a disadvantage, a loss and so on. To borrow Rescher's example, a cloud momentarily shading a passer-by is not an example of luck, since this is indeed a chance but indifferent event. So we, as agents, stand in a specific relationship to cases of luck and an even more complex, and possibly problematic, relationship to cases of moral luck. Even instances of plain luck can have moral overtones. Consider a case where a fairly well-off person wins the lottery; there is a sense in which we feel this outcome is unfair even though everyone else had an equal chance of winning. Sometimes then, we, perhaps irrationally, resent the very 'blindness' of luck, the very fact that lucky outcomes are neither fair nor unfair.

In general, we need to be aware that responsibility, blameworthiness and a desire to make reparations do not always go hand in hand. For example, I may slip, fall and in falling break your beloved vase. I am responsible for breaking the vase, but not necessarily to be blamed as slipping is something that could have happened to anyone,[4] but at the same time I may also feel obliged to buy you a new vase because *I* broke it, even though I did so non-culpably.

Many of the recent discussions on moral luck rely on examples in order to capture what seems puzzling about the phenomenon. However, some of these examples have to be treated with caution as they can be misleading. Nagel seems to misidentify a case of bad luck as one of bad *moral* luck, when he writes:

> Circumstantial luck[5] can extend to aspects of the situation other than individual behaviour. For example, during the Vietnam war even U.S. citizens who had opposed their country's actions vigorously from the start often felt compromised by its crimes. Here they were not even responsible: there was probably nothing they could do to stop what was happening, so the feeling of being implicated may seem unintelligible. But it is nearly impossible to view the crimes of one's own country in the same way that one views the crimes of another country, no matter how equal one's lack of power to stop them in the two cases. One is a citizen of one of them, and has a connection with its actions (even if only through taxes that cannot be withheld) – that one does not have with the other's. This makes it possible to be ashamed of one's country, and to feel a victim of moral bad luck that one was an American in the 1960's.[6]

The American citizens' relationship to their own country, which is perpetrating a moral injustice, may explain their feeling of regret, but this is a case of agent-regret like the lorry driver who stands in a non-culpable way related with a morally regrettable event. It is bad luck that some Americans were citizens of a country which acted beyond their control in perpetrating an immoral act; an immoral act which they rightly disapproved of. However, this is bad luck and not bad moral luck, as we do not hold these individuals morally responsible or treat them as objects of moral judgement in this case. Within a democracy there is limited scope for an objecting minority to influence a government's course of action, so provided that these citizens did what they could within the confines of democracy to voice their opposition, one cannot hold them morally responsible for America's actions. Like the lorry driver, these citizens may still feel guilt and regret for what their country did, but that is because they are decent human beings and regret being associated with such immoral actions even if they could not and were not expected to control them.

Although we ought to be careful to distinguish between cases of luck and cases of moral luck, we must also recognize that sometimes cases of bad luck may give rise to situations of bad *moral* luck. It is bad luck that a particularly anti-social family move into the house next door to yours, but the nuisance they cause and the fact that you live next to them is only bad luck. However, this particular situation may create bad feelings between the neighbours and ultimately result in a situation in which you are tempted to act in an immoral way in order to get your own back at the neighbours. That an agent has found himself in a situation where he is tempted to act immorally has now become a case of bad moral luck.

Finally, related to the concept of luck is the concept of risk. Although this is a topic deserving attention in its own right, it is worth making a few brief remarks on risk. There is a sense in which people are said to 'make their own luck'. The expression relates to managing luck, by managing outcomes which are out of one's control. This can be done by minimizing or attempting to altogether avoid risk. If luck is about one's inability to control a situation, then there may be instances where one can prudently avoid such situations or avoid becoming incapacitated in the first place. Of course, given the nature of luck, such cases will not always be avoidable or even foreseeable, but the point is that some may be, although not in the sense of harnessing luck by possessing a rabbit's foot. By managing risk one can avoid some of the effects of luck. For example, the student who works so hard that he prepares every aspect of the course he will be examined on avoids the unlucky situation where the questions asked are not the ones he can answer. However, even such thoughts on how risk may be partially managed are problematic, giving rise to concerns over how we should understand concepts such as negligence and recklessness.

1.3 Moral luck: Examples

Perhaps the best way to understand what is involved in cases of moral luck is to examine the numerous examples put forward by philosophers as instances of the phenomenon. It is a familiar philosophical picture that reason is what makes us different from animals and gives us the ability to make choices, and therefore it is in virtue of our ability to reason that we are held responsible for who we are and what we do. According to some accounts, luck can even attack this last vestige of independence, as it can influence constitutive factors relating to our ability to reason, the development of our rational faculties, opportunities for exercising reason and so on. The recent revival of interest in the possibility of moral luck started from an article by Bernard Williams, in which he used the possibility of luck to attack an all-powerful conception of reason.[7] In that article, Williams put forward the case of the artist Gauguin which has now become a focal point in discussions of moral luck.

Gauguin is an artist who chooses to abandon his family in favour of a life of artistic creativity that eventually leads him to produce the masterpieces admired by the world today. At the time of the decision he cannot know whether he will succeed or not and Williams argues that:

> the only thing that will justify his choice will be success itself. If he fails...then he did the wrong thing, not just in the sense in which that platitudinously follows, but in the sense that having done the wrong thing in those circumstances he has no basis for the thought that he was justified in acting as he did. If he succeeds, he does have a basis for that thought.[8]

He adds that this justification may not necessarily mean that Gauguin can justify himself to others.

Williams puts this example forward as a case of moral luck, because whether the agent's decision is justified or not depends on the success of the act, which itself is outside the agent's control; that is Gauguin cannot control, at the time of having to decide whether to leave his family, whether he will become a successful artist or not. The example is ultimately an attack on the power of reason to make decisions since in cases of retrospective justification such as this, the agent can never know, at the time of decision-making, all the elements necessary to making a justifiable decision.

In order to understand Williams' example, we have to first discount two ways in which it can be misunderstood.[9] One way in which this

אילו אתה עזרה אל לקוחות ני

can happen is to misidentify the way luck may affect how things turn out. Williams himself is aware of this possibility and draws a distinction between luck external to the agent's project and luck internal to the project. The distinction emphasizes the idea that it matters exactly how the project fails to come off. If Gauguin suffers an injury on the way to Tahiti which prevents him from painting again, his project fails, but this failure does not make the project unjustified. In such a case, Gauguin will never know whether he was right or wrong to leave his wife, and is a case of luck external to the project. What matters is luck internal to the project which has to do with 'how intrinsic the cause of failure is to the project itself',[10] in this case whether he fails as a painter. It is only this kind of internal luck that can unjustify the project.

The second way in which Williams can be misunderstood is to argue that such internal luck could have been avoided had greater care been taken at the time of making the decision. If such an analysis were correct, then the example would not be one of retrospective justification resulting from luck, but rather an example of an agent failing to take due care and attention when making the decision. Williams' point seems to be that it is crucial to the description of a case of retrospective justification that the information relevant to the decision could not, in principle, have been available to the agent at the time of decision-making. In a later postscript to the original article Williams clearly states:

> The third question raised in this article ['Moral Luck'] is that of retro-spective justification, and this is the widest, because it can arise beyond the ethical, in any application of practical rationality. It is the question of how far, and in what ways, the view that an agent retrospectively takes of himself may be affected by results and not be directed simply to the ways in which he or she deliberated or might have better deliberated, before the event.[11]

Thus, the example is important because there is no way in which the agent could or might have deliberated better in order to avoid the influence of luck and Williams is intending to outline a powerful attack on the power of reason to deliberate morally.

The Gauguin example, then, was introduced by Williams in order to illustrate the possibility of moral luck and is frequently referred to by other commentators for the same purpose. I am not sure, however, that it has been correctly identified as an example of moral luck. Williams sees Gauguin as having to decide between the demands of morality, in the form of his obligations to his family, and non-moral considerations based on his preferences as to what sort of life he should live.[12] Moral success for Gauguin's project derives from the good his paintings will yield for the world. I want to argue that there are two moral questions here that Williams is distorting into one. First, I think that initially Gauguin is faced with a moral dilemma, not a dilemma between a moral and a non-moral option. On the one hand, he is confined by the moral demands of his family (we can assume that they have a legitimate and just moral claim on him), however, on the other hand, he is attracted by the moral demand to develop himself and fulfil his potential as an artist. Suppose that Gauguin did not have a family, recognized that he had to move to Tahiti in order to mature as an artist and find the inspiration necessary to exercise his talent, but still contemplated not going because of some trivial reason. In such a case we could argue that he has an obligation to go, and that this is a moral obligation.[13] If this is correct, then in the Williams case, Gauguin has to decide between competing moral obligations.

Secondly, given that Gauguin has to make a moral decision, it is not success or failure that justifies the project, but rather the reasonableness of expecting that one's project will succeed or fail. Gauguin's decision should be judged on the grounds of the reasonableness of his motive and its results. In order to understand why this is so we have to consider two variations on the original example.

In the first case Gauguin has shown great promise as a painter and it is clear to everyone that his project of going to Tahiti has a great chance of succeeding. When making the decision, there is a very small risk of failure, which makes the decision justified at the time. However, although this estimation of risk was and remains correct, Gauguin is unlucky since the 5 per cent chance of failure does actually come about. In this case Gauguin's original decision is still justified despite the ultimate failure of the project, because this was a reasonable project at the time of its conception.

In the second case, Gauguin has, and is aware of having, a very small chance of success. Despite this he still goes to Tahiti. It seems that this decision, at the time it is made, is unjustified because of the great risk taken. However, although the risk was correctly estimated and remains high, Gauguin is lucky and he succeeds as a painter. His original decision remains unjustified despite the success. It was a matter of luck that he hit upon the 5 per cent chance of success. To abandon your wife and family on a slim chance of turning into a great painter is callous, irrespective of whether you succeed by a fluke of luck. The fact that this decision is unjustified is available to Gauguin at the time it is made and there is no element of retrospective justification.

The example can become more detailed if we also consider what is meant by success by distinguishing between two kinds of success: personal and public success. The first has to do with the agent himself. A project will be successful for a person if he achieves his own goals and standards, which may not necessarily be shared by others. Thus, a runner may consider it a personal success that he completed the London Marathon, even though he never came close to being placed. The second kind of success appeals to general standards of success and may not coincide with the first. Thus, a runner may be considered successful by others as he has just won the London Marathon, but he may consider the result a failure for him as he knows he did not try for or achieve his best time. From an Aristotelian perspective,[14] emphasizing the importance of leading a fulfilling life, for example, Gauguin's goal is personal success and he will be in a better position to assess the viability of his project the more self-aware he is. He may be personally successful as, objectively, a terrible painter, as he finds this life fulfilling. If Gauguin is aiming at public success he needs to evaluate his ability as a painter objectively, as well as the market for paintings of this kind. Williams considers and discards as absurd the idea that Gauguin is justified if he is reasonably convinced he is a great artist at the time of making the decision. However, it seems to me that this is because of a misunderstanding of the 'reasonableness' of the project. Williams rightly points out the implausibility of consulting professors of art to establish reasonableness, but this is not the kind of reasonableness I am appealing to here. Self-knowledge, awareness of one's weaknesses and strengths and an understanding of the requirements for individual fulfilment are what is required here and the development of these aspects of one's character is required as part of the moral project.[15]

At this point, one could raise problems with this appeal to probability and indeed Slote does so.[16] One possible objection is that we are making moral blameworthiness dependent on estimations of probability, which in turn may be problematic. Slote mentions problems about subjective versus objective probabilities, and questions whether the probability estimate refers to that made by a reasonable person or whether it is relativized to the individual.[17] These sorts of considerations may need to be addressed if this account of blameworthiness is to work, but they are not as central to the account as Slote assumes. This is because this account of blameworthiness does not essentially rely on probabilities. Although it makes references to probabilities, they are simply a way of determining character traits. It is not the probabilities *as such* which make a difference to the moral judgement of the agent, rather the fact that this agent took a great risk despite the high probabilities against success. To take a great risk with the welfare of others, where the probability of success is low and where only *you* are to gain from success, exhibits callousness and lack of regard for other people. So what the agent is held responsible for is the callousness and recklessness his action exhibits; the probabilities *merely show* why this was a callous act. An understanding of the probabilities involved is necessary in order to understand exactly what was done; we need to appeal to the high probabilities against success to be able to describe the act as 'taking a great risk'. Now if we combine the risk taken with other elements of the act, such as the fact that the risk was taken on behalf of non-consenting others towards whom one has an obligation, then it is clear why this is a reprehensible act. This kind of account of what was done need not appeal to consequences to demonstrate blameworthiness, because the blame is apportioned to the act that exhibits the undesirable character trait, regardless of whether the negative consequences did come about or whether they were avoided due to luck.

It seems, then, that although Gauguin's case can include elements which are down to luck, these elements bear no weight in the moral evaluation of the agent's decision and therefore, this is not a genuine case of moral luck. Luck may enter into the general understanding of what went on in the Gauguin example, but it does not affect the moral evaluation of the agent. Thus, the example, although it is intended to be an illustration of moral luck, has been misidentified as such.[18]

This problem of misidentifying certain examples as cases of moral luck is not uncommon. It seems to stem from an unclarity over what is meant by 'moral luck' and an attempt to explain the term by appealing solely to examples. Williams similarly misidentifies other examples he discusses as cases of moral luck; he sees the case of Anna Karenina as another example of retrospective justification (or unjustification in this case), a project which fails because of intrinsic bad luck. However, it seems to me that Anna Karenina's failure is apparent at the time the decision is taken as a failure in deliberation and in allocating the correct weight to the social considerations and personal character weaknesses which ultimately doom her relationship with Vronsky; again, at least partly, a failure in self-knowledge and understanding of others and one's relationships with them. As such the decision is wrong at the time it is taken, and this is merely illustrated to Anna at a later time, rather than retrospectively unjustified by the outcome of the action. Furthermore, it seems unclear why the failure of the project is a matter of luck in the first place. The relationship fails because of Vronsky's weak character, an evaluation of which is something that Anna did not perform successfully. The only sense in which luck may play a role would be if one were to argue that who Anna fell in love with in the first place was a matter of luck.

An idea that seems to emerge from such examples is that making certain decisions is very hard and may require sophistication in one's reasoning abilities, a great degree of self-knowledge and ability to evaluate one's own motives, as well as experience of judging other people and so on. The idea that certain decisions are very difficult and challenge the all-powerful conception of reason is a very interesting one and one which has been taken up by other writers.[19] However, the idea that reason is not all-powerful is a distinct issue from discussions about the influence of luck. The Gauguin and Anna Karenina examples are misidentified as cases of moral luck and there have been other examples of decisions made under uncertainty which have been misleadingly presented as cases of moral luck.

Nagel puts forward the historical case of Chamberlain's betrayal of the Czechs. It seems to me that our moral characterization of Chamberlain should remain the same regardless of whether bad luck determined that his original act had unexpected, unacceptable repercussions. The act that reveals Chamberlain's character flaws is his betrayal of the Czechs, the direct outcome of which was something that he took into account when he made his decision. The historical fact that this act had further morally unacceptable repercussions does not make Chamberlain a worse person. The reason why he is 'a household name' is because the results of an act that is associated with him affected millions of households. This is more the result of the nature of politics and the accountability of politicians, that is that the public tend to hold politicians more accountable if their acts affect their electorate directly, rather than some faraway and little-known country. Chamberlain is similar to the lorry driver in that he is not morally responsible for what he did as he acted as well as we could have expected anyone to act in order to prevent a disaster,[20] but as the lorry driver was unlucky and hit a child, Chamberlain was unlucky that events turned out badly.

Nagel tries to pre-empt such objections to his example when he argues, 'that these are genuine moral judgements [judgements of culpability or esteem] rather than expressions of temporary attitude is evident from the fact that one can say *in advance* how the moral verdict will depend on the results'.[21] However, the results of the action influence the political verdict and the social condemnation, and these are not necessarily correct moral judgements. Moral responsibility can be distinguished from other kinds of responsibility, for example, legal, emotional, social and political responsibility.[22] These ways of holding people accountable, may have nothing to do with whether they were morally accountable, and praise or blame may be allocated in accordance with different criteria; for example, if the purpose of punishment is deterrence and to protect the social group from individuals who cause it harm, then judgements about legal responsibility may be radically different from judgements about moral responsibility.

Another example of a case where political reality may affect the moral labelling of an act is determining whether a group of soldiers are to be called terrorists or freedom fighters. Should they win the conflict, as the party now in power, they will call themselves freedom fighters. Should they lose, the opposition will call them terrorists. Attempts to define terrorism as the indiscriminate use of violence/terror against the innocent are aimed at avoiding the tangle of political and historical re-definitions and provide a moral (in the sense of justified if not objective) answer to this question.

Chamberlain's action is still a betrayal of trust, whether other factors conspire to push history towards further disasters or not.[23] He would have been responsible for unleashing Hitler on Europe, had there been some mistake of judgement on his part that would otherwise have allowed him to predict the danger. However, such an option is ruled out in the way this case is set up; Chamberlain is not supposed to have made any mistakes in deliberation in Nagel's analysis.

As an alternative to Williams' presentation of Gauguin and Anna Karenina, as well as Nagel's Chamberlain example, consider Jude's speech from *Jude the Obscure*:

'It is a difficult question, my friends, for any young man – that question I had to grapple with, and which thousands are weighing at the present moment in these uprising times – whether to follow uncritically the track he finds himself in, without considering his aptness for it, or to consider what his aptness or bent may be, and reshape his course accordingly. I tried to do the latter and I failed. But I don't admit that my failure proved my view to be a wrong one, or that my success would have made it a right one; though that's how we appraise such attempts nowadays – I mean, not by their essential soundness, but by their accidental outcomes. If I had ended by becoming like one of these gentlemen in red and black that we saw dropping in here by now, everybody would have said: "See how wise that young man was, to follow the bent of his nature!" But having ended no better than I began they say: "See what a fool that fellow was in following a freak of his fancy!"'

'However it was my poverty and not my will that consented to be beaten. It takes two or three generations to do what I tried to do in one; and my impulses – affections-vices perhaps they should be called – were too strong not to hamper a man without advantages; who should be as cold-blooded as a fish and as selfish as a pig to have a really good chance of being one of this country's worthies. You may ridicule me – I am quite willing that you should – I am a fit subject, no doubt. But I think if you knew what I have gone through these last few years you would rather pity me. And if they knew' – he nodded towards the college at which the Dons were severally arriving – 'it is just possible they would do the same.'[24]

Jude's project to educate himself is essentially sound at the time when he critically decides that he ought to pursue it. He has the talent, ability and love for academic pursuits. This is the case at the time the decision is made and remains so to the end. The accidental outcome of his project would neither justify the project itself in the case of success, nor unjustify it in the case of failure. Jude does not accept the possibility of retrospective justification which is central to Williams' Gauguin. Similarly we could argue that the essential soundness of Gauguin's project is what we should evaluate it by and this remains the same regardless of the outcome.

Note that this does not necessitate that either Gauguin or Jude has to be infallibly aware of the essential soundness of his chosen project at the time the choice is made. Jude notes that discovering one's aptness is a critical process and therefore one may make a mistaken decision. Perhaps Chamberlain and Anna Karenina are such examples of people who made the wrong decision;[25] but their decision is still wrong at the time it is made and has no need for retrospective unjustification. Jude also points out that the luck involved in the failure of his project was extrinsic. It relates to the fact that social circumstances made Jude's project impossible. He explicitly rejects an interpretation of his project as having failed due to internal luck when he points out how the crowd's estimation of him would have changed based on the accidental outcomes of his efforts; had he been successful he would be proclaimed wise, but as he has failed he is called a fool. The reason why we should pity Jude then is because he made a wise decision to follow a worthy project, but was hampered by bad luck which resulted in his project failing. However, his project remains essentially worthwhile.

This is what makes the novel so interesting and Jude such a tragic and memorable character.

1.4 Moral luck: A definition?

We have examined some of the examples of moral luck put forward by the philosophers who introduced the topic to recent debate, but we have found them wanting. We are now left with two problems: if we reject these instances of moral luck as genuine cases, we are still left with the question of explaining 'moral luck'. We also have to explain why there are competing interpretations of these examples, some of which question whether these are genuine cases of moral luck. To try to answer these ideas we have to return to the understanding of luck as lack of control and why this poses problems for morality.

The tension highlighted by the idea of moral luck is that between one side of humans, which is passive, vulnerable and delicate, and another which is autonomous, pure and immune to luck. This is the picture of morality elaborated on by Williams. Williams draws a distinction between morality in the restricted sense, a 'local system of ideas that particularly emphasizes a resistance to luck',[26] and the ethical in a more general sense.[27] Morality in the restricted sense is characterized by its reliance on obligations, the idea that blame is directed to the voluntary and that it is 'the characteristic reaction of the morality system'.[28] The particular moral system, discussed by Williams, which most exemplifies this resistance to the idea of moral luck is deontology as developed by Kant. According to the Kantian conception of morality, morality requires autonomy, choice, freedom and so on in order to attribute responsibility. Kant's moral project seems to be driven by this wish to articulate a 'pure' moral theory that escapes the distorting influences of luck. This picture sees luck as being at odds with and ultimately as being a distorting and conflicting influence on the moral project.

However, this is not the only alternative in terms of localized systems of morality. Nussbaum defines luck as follows:

> What happens to a person by luck will be just what does not happen through his or her own agency, what just happens to him, as opposed to what he does or makes. In general, to eliminate luck from human life will be to put that life, or the most important things in it, under the control of the agent.[29]

In her writings, Nussbaum adopts what I shall call an integrationist position. This approach to moral luck integrates the phenomenon into human life and, as we shall see in Chapters 2, 3 and 4, has its roots in Aristotle. According to this position, luck is an inalienable fact of human life. Not only can we not escape luck, because of the human condition, but we should not want to, because hand in hand with luck go all the things that make life worth living:

> That I am an agent, but also a plant; that much that I did not make goes towards making me whatever I shall be praised or blamed for being; that I must constantly choose among competing and apparently incommensurable goods and that circumstances may force me to a position in which I cannot help being false to something or doing some wrong; that an event that simply happens to me may, without my consent, alter my life; that it is equally problematic to entrust one's good to friends, lovers or country and to try to have a good life without them – all these I take to be not just the material of tragedy, but everyday facts of lived practical reason.[30]

For Nussbaum this vulnerability to luck is an essential component of the human life, but we can see why something that threatens the independence of human agency can pose a problem for morality. So luck is an integral part of ethics; the components of a good life are fundamentally the objects of luck. Luck and morality are two sides of the same coin. Nussbaum then seems to be rejecting the idea that there is a tension between morality and luck. Indeed she considers luck a necessary component of the good life.

Accepting this picture of the human condition as vulnerable to luck still leaves open the question of attributing praise or blame. If who we are and how we act is fundamentally a matter of luck and should be taken as a matter of ordinary life, there still remains that question of responsibility. The picture of the moral development of man being like Pindar's young tree, which is of good stock, requires the right soil, proper sustenance, favourable weather, dedicated care and so on, illuminates the vulnerability of the human condition, but it leaves open the more complex question of our individual responsibility for this condition. Human beings, unlike trees, are assumed to have some control over what soil they grow in, favourable weather, dedicated care and so on; that is what influences we accept, what examples we are moved by, which role models we adopt, which attitudes we foster and so on. The most crucial question facing integrationist approaches to morality and luck is one of degree; to what extent is luck an excuse for immoral behaviour, what degree of bad moral luck poses an insurmountable problem and equally how far should our judgements of moral praise be tempered by the recognition that the agent was shaped by good luck.

There seem to be, then, two different approaches to the problem of moral luck as identified by two localized systems of morality. The Kantian picture tries to resist luck, but an Aristotelian approach is not committed to this.[31] This book will serve partly to highlight the two different approaches: on the one hand, Aristotle's acceptance and integration of the possibility of luck within the moral life and, on the other, Kant's rejection of the influence of luck on morality.

As we shall see, both alternatives create problems for moral responsibility. In Chapters 2, 3 and 4 we shall see how the Aristotelian picture of integrating the influence of luck in moral life leaves us with two alternatives with respect to moral responsibility. If luck plays a role in who one is and what one does, then responsibility for these actions is a superficial concept because the agent was not truly in control of what he did. This alternative retains the connection between holding people responsible only for what was under their control, but ultimately there are no cases of true responsibility. Alternatively, if we retain a strong concept of responsibility it must be an impure one, as we have to hold people responsible for things that were outside their control. This alternative rests uneasily with our understanding of justice as fairness and the attribution of responsibility.

Dissatisfaction with these alternatives, and a desire for a pure moral theory, leads Kant to reject the influence of moral luck. However, as we shall see in Chapters 6 and 7, his project is much more detailed and sensitive than it has sometimes been assumed. There is room for a conception of human nature as subject to contingencies within the Kantian project, but its place is specific and has to be understood in the light of other Kantian claims.

Ultimately the two responses to moral luck, the Aristotelian and the Kantian, are not greatly removed from each other as they are both driven by the same two forces: on the one hand, philosophers want to articulate a moral theory with a strong and pure concept of responsibility, but on the other, they want a plausible picture of the human condition as influenced by luck. We shall see how Aristotle emphasizes primarily a plausible picture of the human condition as vulnerable to luck, but cannot avoid considerations similar to Kant's quest for a notion of responsibility. On the other hand, the Kantian focus has been on immunity from luck, but even such an account cannot altogether ignore the plausibility of a picture of morality as influenced by luck. Therefore, the two positions which have been presented as conflicting alternatives are actually concerned to satisfy the same two requirements, each emphasizing one more than the other.

The discussion of the two responses will also serve to clarify what is meant by the cluster of phenomena that are discussed under the term 'moral luck'. Williams' and Nagel's articles were crucial in reviving the recent interest in moral luck, and their examples are taken up by most philosophers who have subsequently written in the area, but, as we have seen, these examples can be and have been challenged. I have argued that some of these examples are not genuine cases of moral luck, whereas others have been misinterpreted. What I have done in the preceding discussion is to re-describe the examples and show that what these agents did was, or could have been – had they deliberated better – under their control, so that when we hold them responsible for it, there is no tension (e.g. Gauguin and Anna); or I have argued for narrowing the description of what it is we are holding them responsible for (e.g. Chamberlain). Our conception and understanding of the power of reason to guide deliberation is crucial in explaining these examples. In many ways, as we shall see in the contrast between the Aristotelian and the Kantian use of reason, how we conceive of the power of reason brings about a crucial difference in the understanding and importance of moral luck.

These examples of moral luck have proven to be so controversial because there are a number of different ideas that are raised by the concept and a cluster of different cases that all lay claim to this term. Furthermore, how we should respond to particular cases of moral luck seems to be determined by the theoretical framework through which we understand morality. Thus, instances claimed to be cases of moral luck will remain controversial. The only possible definition that we can come up with for moral luck, then, has to be a fairly innocuous one, such as the one given by Nagel:

> Where a significant aspect of what someone does depends on factors beyond his control, yet we continue to treat him in that respect as an object of moral judgement, it can be called moral luck.[32]

This definition is successful in that it highlights the tension inherent in the concept of 'moral luck', but it is not very informative in terms of resolving disagreements about whether particular cases are genuine cases of the phenomenon. Since particular examples have proven to be so controversial and have tended to obscure rather than clarify the discussion, rather than rely on specific examples, it will be helpful to follow Nagel in identifying three ways in which an agent and his actions may be affected by luck:

1. *Constitutive luck*: What kind of person one is, including inclinations, capacities and temperament.
2. *Situational luck*: The kinds of situations, of varying degrees of temptation or difficulty, one comes across.
3. *Resultant luck*: Regarding how the effects of one's actions turn out.[33]

Cases of constitutive luck seem to pose the most extreme problems for our notions of responsibility and equality. The influence of constitutive luck plays havoc with our intuitions that we all at least start off equally with respect to the moral sphere, and that everyone has an equal footing from which to make the moral decisions we hold them responsible for. If constitutive luck cannot be discounted, then we have to accept that we all are not equal, that some people have an innate advantage or disadvantage when it comes to acting morally and this realization about the inevitability of some of our moral decisions must have implications for responsibility and blame.

The discussion of constitutive luck will bring up the importance of the relationship between nature and morality. The Aristotelian approach draws a distinction between natural tendencies, the object of luck, and rational choices and developed dispositions, the objects of morality. However, as we shall see, it is not that easy to escape the charge that deep down humans are restricted by their make-up. What makes some of our positive natural tendencies into affirmed dispositions and leads us to abandon other less-favourable tendencies is our reason. However, why should we suppose that reason is immune to luck? We saw that Williams' attack on reason can be called into doubt, but this attack is much more serious. Why is our ability to reason itself not subject to constitutive luck? The relations between reason and morality will play a major role in how different theories respond to the possibility of luck. For Kant, our ability to reason as autonomous human beings is entirely immune to luck, that is available to all equally, no matter what their constitution, background or experience, available at any moment in time, despite previous history or entrenched character traits, and offering a solution to any moral problem, no matter how difficult.

Situational luck, discounted by Kant, plays an important role in the Aristotelian moral picture. The problem posed by situational luck was highlighted by Nagel:

> What we do is also limited by the opportunities and choices with which we are faced, and these are largely determined by factors beyond our control. Someone who was an officer in a concentration camp might have lead a quiet and harmless life if the Nazis had never come to power in Germany. And someone might have become an officer in a concentration camp if he had not left Germany for business reasons in 1930.[34]

We shall see how situational luck and the wider idea of developmental luck[35] play a significant role in Aristotelian moral theory. The Aristotelian model of gradual development, open to influences from a good teacher, favourable examples, opportunities for practice and habituation and so on, is inherently vulnerable to situations one finds oneself in. In brief, the vulnerable student of virtue may find certain moral tests more difficult than the established virtuous agent, or having been subjected to great temptation at an early stage of moral development, he may lose any chance of becoming virtuous. Again the role assigned to our power to reason is crucial here. We shall see that there is no easy answer to the question of how great a temptation is it reasonable to expect the moral agent to overcome, or how long we can expect the student of virtue to stand in the face of difficulty. The answer to such questions will remain imprecise, perhaps because of the imprecise nature of ethics, but recognizing this may still remain Aristotle's greatest insight.[36]

In contrast, the Kantian picture leaves no room for the influences of situational luck. The moral agent can turn to virtue at any time in his life, no matter how many contrary influences he has been subjected to or how many times he has acted viciously. Virtue is the result of an instantaneous revolution of the will, which can take place in any agent at any time. This picture, as we shall see, is compelling in that it offers an equal chance at the virtuous life to everyone.

Cases of resultant luck, or luck in how the effects of one's actions turn out, pose the least problems for either Kantians or Aristotelians. For Kant, it is clearly the act of the will that is the object of the moral judgement, and should the will be prevented from acting by external factors, this should make no difference to the evaluation of the agent (of course outside observers can never be sure of the purity of a will that is always prevented from acting, but this is an epistemological obstacle to the evaluation of the agent by others). Aristotle's answer to cases of resultant luck is intimately connected with his thoughts on voluntary actions and choice. As Aristotle's thoughts on this are quite extensive I shall postpone their discussion until Chapter 3. What is important to note here is that, as with other examples of cases of moral luck, when we discuss examples of resultant luck provided by recent writers we may find that they are not truly genuine cases of moral luck. Aristotle's thoughts on responsibility will clarify the importance of the idea that some of the effects of our acts appear to be out of our control.

In this discussion, then, I will make use of Nagel's broad division of cases of moral luck into constitutive, developmental (situational) and resultant, as this classification seems to avoid some of the problems of dealing with particular examples. I will use this understanding of moral luck to examine the different answers to the problem presented by Aristotle and Kant and question to what extent these should be seen as rival and conflicting responses. In Chapter 8 I will go on to examine some recent developments in Kantian and Aristotelian ethics and see whether these give a more satisfactory account of moral luck and how far they in fact follow the spirit of Kant and Aristotle. As we shall see, there is much less opposition between these two ways of doing ethics (Aristotelian and Kantian) than many of the proponents of the theories would like us to believe. Ultimately Aristotle and Kant give the same answers to the problem of moral luck, but focus on different elements of the answers. Meanwhile, Chapter 5 will be an interlude from the main discussion, putting forward the Stoic answer to the problem of moral luck. The Stoic answer is examined because in many ways it prefigures the Kantian approach, while sharing many crucial features with Aristotle's theory.

1.5 Conclusion

The possibility of moral luck raises a large number of complicated and interconnected issues which relate to fundamental questions about what it is to be human. This introductory chapter has tried to raise the possibility of these questions and this book will try to show how certain theories provide different answers to them. Questions about how we should deal with moral luck relate to our fundamental understanding of what it is to be human and what it means to be a moral being. Is luck an inalienable and unavoidable part of human life? A part which also makes life rich and fulfilling? Or is it an attack on our independence and essentially human autonomy? Does luck make the moral project richer or should we strive to understand morality as immune to luck?

Fundamental to these questions is our conception of reason and its power to overcome adversities and contrary influences. Is reason our refuge from the influence of luck or is it itself shaped and controlled by luck? And how should the answers to all these questions affect responsibility?

These questions are fundamental philosophical questions centering on problems with which philosophers have always grappled and to which perhaps there are no definite answers. This book does not aspire to answer them in their entirety, but rather is aimed at using the discussions on moral luck as an introduction to some of the different ways there are to approaching these questions. The possible answers to these questions are many and diverse, and I cannot hope to provide a comprehensive account of all of them. Rather, I will concentrate on elaborating the contrasts and similarities between two different approaches, that of Aristotle and that of Kant (purposefully ignoring any further questions raised by the theory usually presented as the third alternative, consequentialism).

As to how this will be done, we have already seen the problems associated with providing examples in order to explain what is meant by moral luck. I have tried briefly to identify some of the ways that one can go wrong in using examples. We must be careful not to confuse cases of bad luck with cases of bad moral luck, or cases where some of the elements of the example are subject to good or bad luck with moral luck. A broader characterization of types of moral luck into constitutive, developmental (situational) and resultant may be of more use. Ultimately, we shall see that although resultant luck can be explained and accommodated for, developmental (situational) and constitutive luck pose more fundamental problems. This is slightly surprising as constitutive luck in particular tends to be generally side-stepped in recent discussions of moral luck. However, this may be because the possibility of constitutive luck goes to the core of the fundamental questions discussed above and raises the greatest challenges for our conception of humanity and morality.

1.6 A note on style

A final word on the combination of literature and philosophy, which I have already used to illustrate points and which I shall continue to employ in what follows. Why use literary examples to illustrate philosophical issues? This approach is not entirely unusual, its best known advocate being Martha Nussbaum.[37] Such an approach has its roots in Ancient Greek philosophy where extracts from poems and tragedies are often used to make points. Plato uses Pindar's poetry to talk of the man who has led a just and god-fearing life:

> sweet hope,
> Who guides men's wandering purpose,
> Treads at his side, gladdens his heart,
> And comforts his old age.[38]

Aristotle recommends Hesiod's advice:

> Best is the man who can himself advise;
> He too is good who hearkens to the wise;
> But who, himself being witless, will not heed
> Another's wisdom, is worthless indeed.[39]

One reason for using such a method can be traced back to Aristotle. Early on in the *Nicomachean Ethics* he points out that '[o]ur account of this science [politics] will be adequate if it achieves such clarity as the subject-matter allows'.[40] And later on,

> [n]ow questions of conduct and expedience have as little fixity about them as questions of what is healthful; and if this is true of the general rule, it is still more true that its application to particular problems admits of no precision. For they do not fall under any art or professional tradition, but the agents are compelled at every step to think out for themselves what the circumstances demand, just as happens in the arts of medicine and navigation.[41]

Now, given this inherent imprecision, perhaps the best way to approach such questions would be to point to specific examples instead of trying to provide an exhaustive characterization of the virtuous agent, which would attempt to describe all eventualities and highlight all possibilities. This is exactly what works of literature help us do. It is no coincidence that great writers from a variety of traditions, and I am thinking here of people like Henry James, Thomas Hardy, Alexander Tolstoy, Fyodor Dostoyevsky, are studied exactly because of their detailed and illuminating portrayal of moral characters. What better way to understand the moral dilemmas of women on the topic of love, for example, than to follow the fortunes of Tess of the D'Urbervilles, Isabel Archer or Anna Karenina. Perhaps then, the best way to understand the virtuous, or vicious, person is to follow him or her in action. Aristotle's own frequent references to historical and literary examples which the average Athenian was likely to recognize, and his admiration of tragedy in the *Poetics* are an indication that he would favour such an approach.

2
Aristotle on Constitutive Luck

2.1 Preliminaries

One way of distinguishing between different moral theories, which has been popular in recent years, is to distinguish between theories that are outcome-based (the chief example being consequentialism), agent-based (e.g. deontology) and character-based (referring usually to Aristotle and virtue ethics). Whether this distinction is viable and/or useful is an issue which will be discussed within the wider context of moral luck.[1] However, for our present purposes we can start by accepting that Aristotelian theory is indeed character-based and proceed from there to see how this affects the Aristotelian answer to the problem of moral luck. The process of answering this question will also eventually explain what is meant by a character-based theory and how, if in any way, such a theory differs from other alternatives.

Aristotle's approach to ethics makes use of the notion of 'character', and as such his account of what is morally important cannot be just about a state of being.[2] This is because having a certain character is not only about being in a certain state, but being disposed to act in accordance with that state. Character is being as doing;

> no doubt it makes a great difference whether we conceive the supreme good to depend on possessing virtue or on displaying it – on disposition, or on the manifestation of a disposition in action. For a man may possess the disposition without its producing any good result, as for instance when he is asleep, or has ceased to function for some other cause; but virtue in active exercise cannot be inoperative – it will *of necessity* act, and act well.[3]

This 'of necessity' is of importance here. It is part of a virtuous disposition that it will involve action; it cannot be merely an inactive disposition. The realization that kindness is the appropriate response to a particular case, for example, cannot remain simply a disposition to act without a corresponding attempt, at least, at acting. I say 'attempt at acting', because acts may be, on occasion, thwarted by factors outside the agent's control.[4] Although, then, an agent may, on occasion, be prevented from acting in accordance with his character, the idea of someone having a certain character but never, on principle, acting from it would be unintelligible.

A character trait is a stable, fixed and reliable disposition to act in a certain way. It is possible to imagine the case of a person who has a certain character but is prevented from acting in accordance with it because of unfavourable circumstances. For the sake of the example let us assume that courage is defined as displaying the appropriate amount of fear in situations of just war and a certain agent, although he is courageous, never has the opportunity to act as there are no just wars during his lifetime. This agent is still courageous as he has the appropriate settled disposition with respect to fear and this disposition would manifest itself in the right circumstances. It is simply unfortunate that this agent never comes across the right circumstances for acting courageously because of external factors.[5] However, such examples are extreme and, to an extent, contrived. For the most part a theory based on character will be a theory of action, and claiming that it is possible for a theory to place great importance on the notion of 'character' without ever involving the idea of the person in action displaying his character is misusing the notion of character. This is why it has been argued that Aristotle is concerned with how one should live,[6] and one cannot be concerned with this question without considering how one should act.

Aristotle does not actually use a word that corresponds to 'character', but rather uses what is translated as 'disposition'. If we understand one's character as the collection of one's dispositions, we can see why commentators link the use of character in moral philosophy with Aristotle. I need to say a few things to explain what I will mean when I use the words 'character' and 'disposition'.

The word 'character' derives from the Ancient Greek for carving, also meaning a stamp or mark (as well as an image or representation). This gives us a good indication of what 'character' is intended to mean. A carving in stone is a very permanent and indestructible way of pre-serving what one wants to write, and similarly one's character is the set of well-established and persistent characteristics. The particulars of one's character are well established as they tend to persist over time and manifest themselves in different circumstances, including cases where there is a great degree of temptation to act contrary to one's character or a great degree of difficulty in acting in accordance with one's character. One should not assume that only good characteristics are well entrenched; bad characteristics can equally persist over time. Character traits, relating to particular characteristics of people, once formed are well established, but, perhaps because of this, they take a long time to form and be developed. A developmental picture of morality plays a central role in Aristotelian ethics.

People are born with certain natural tendencies. These are encouraged and developed, or discouraged and thwarted, partly because of the influences one is exposed to when one is growing up and partly as a matter of choice by the moral agent himself. There are a number of factors which may affect one's character development, such as one's teachers, peer group, role models, the degree of encouragement and attention one receives, exposure to different situations and situations of varying degree of difficulty and so on. Again it is important to remember that all these factors, including the 'raw material', that is the natural tendencies one is born with, may work towards promoting bad as well as good characteristics.

Aristotle's picture of character development, then, is a gradual one, which only eventually leads to settled and strong dispositions. It is only once an agent's character is firmly established that we can depend on him to act consistently and predictably in a variety of situations. The person with the morally developed character is the virtuous agent. We can expect of the virtuous agent that he will have settled dispositions to act in accordance with the virtues and do so in the face of great difficulty and temptation. However, it is crucial to note that most moral agents will not become virtuous and most virtuous agents will not be virtuous for the greatest part of their lives. The road to virtue is long, complicated and fraught with difficulties.[7] As a result most of us will spend most of our lives in a state that corresponds not to perfect Aristotelian virtue,[8] but in one of the lesser states he calls 'continence' or 'incontinence' or even vice.[9]

The distinction between virtue, continence and incontinence occurs in Book VII and is one of the most complicated discussions of the *Nicomachean Ethics*. There are six possible states of character: superhuman virtue, virtue, continence, incontinence, vice and bestiality. Superhuman virtue commonly belongs to the gods and bestiality to animals, and as these states are rare amongst humans, we can set them aside (we will come back to bestiality later). A state of virtue and a state of vice are complete opposites in respect of what is excellent, noble and just, but they are similar in that they both are extremes in the sense that they are settled, enduring and persistent dispositions. Virtue involves a conscious choice of what is good, and a habituation in doing good acts until these acts become 'second nature'. Vice is similar in its nature and development; indeed it is so similar that when discussing vice, Aristotle refers the reader to his earlier discussion of the development of virtue.[10] More interesting for our purposes is the distinction between continence and incontinence.

The continent and the incontinent agents are similar in that they both see the right thing to do, but although one succeeds in acting, the other one does not. The question posed by the possibility of incontinence is, how can one have knowledge of what is good, but fail to use it in order to act? Aristotle sees a number of possible explanations:

1. The agent may have knowledge, but may not be conscious of it, or be consciously reflecting on it.
2. The agent may be exercising his knowledge of the universal premise, but not of the particular; and as actions concern themselves with particulars, he fails to act.
3. An agent may both have and not have knowledge because of the influence of the passions, in the same way as someone who is asleep or drunk has and does not have knowledge.
4. Desire can affect the practical syllogism, so that incontinent action is an action 'in a sense under the influence of a principle or opinion, but an opinion not in itself but only incidentally opposed to the right principle (for it is the desire, and not the opinion, that is really opposed)'.[11]

These passages in the *Nicomachean Ethics* are particularly complicated and the subject of intense speculation, but I want to take the following idea from them: knowledge of what is right comes gradually and increases in strength with the passage of time and the accumulation of experience. As this knowledge becomes more entrenched it can better withstand the contrary influences of desire. Thus, the virtuous, continent and incontinent agents all possess knowledge of the good, but to different degrees. The virtuous agent has fully understood the good and appreciated its force to the extent that desires for contrary actions have been extinguished. The continent agent appreciates the force of the good as creating an obligation for him to act in a certain way, but cannot help still having contrary desires, which he nonetheless manages to overcome.

The incontinent agent is similar to the continent agent, but cannot overcome his desires. In interpreting these passages we must resist the implication that practical thought flows smoothly into action. Evidence of practical thought failing to *flow* into action is the existence of the incontinent agent, whereas evidence of practical thought failing to flow *smoothly* into action is the continent agent.[12] Thus, according to this picture, when reason speaks in favour of a certain action, we should be motivationally swayed to act, but the strength of this motivation can vary. It seems to me that although the continent agent possesses knowledge of the good, this knowledge must be in some way defective, or incompletely internalized, as it leaves room for contrary desires to operate. To borrow an argument from Platts,[13] it may be that moral concepts exhibit semantic depth and we are 'inadequate epistemic creatures'; thus weakness of will is possible not because our appreciation of these concepts is shallow but because it has to deal with deep concepts.[14]

The above thoughts may give the false impression that for Aristotle moral development is solely a matter of intellectual development. This is not the case. Moral development involves two things: on the one hand, an increase in the agent's understanding of the good and the moral obligations it imposes on us, on the other, a weakening of contrary desires which is produced by this understanding plus habituation; in the words of Burnyeat, '[w]hat is exemplary in Aristotle is his grasp of the truth that morality comes in a sequence of stages with both cognitive and emotional dimensions'.[15] Moral development is the process of moving from incontinence, to continence to full virtue.

Of course, not all desires are contrary desires. As Aristotle's doctrine of the mean states, virtue involves appropriate desire. The discussion of weakness of will refers to a particular moral phenomenon, that of being overcome by contrary desires. However, one can go wrong with an *exaggerated* response with respect to the *right* desire. It is easier to illustrate this point with the concept of fear rather than pleasure. Some fears are *right* fears, like the fear of pain or death, in that one should rightly be afraid of these sorts of things. To be entirely unafraid in the face of pain or death is a sign of rashness. Equally, to be entirely overwhelmed by one's fear of these things will lead to cowardice. However, the appropriate response requires a 'healthy' appreciation of pain and death, along with which comes a certain amount of respectful fear.[16] Fear of pain or death is the right desire with respect to courage, without necessarily being a harmonious desire. A harmonious desire entirely affirms and promotes the dictates of right reason, temperance being a good example of such a desire. Contrary desires pull away from the right reason resulting in the tension of continence or the failure of action of incontinence. At the same time, some affective states, like fear of pain, act as appropriate restraints within which virtue should be exercised. Without the restraint of an appropriate amount of fear, courage would become rashness, so fear is the right desire in this case.

Presumably there are many other ways one can fail on the road to virtue. For example, developing certain emotional responses, such as empathy towards the concerns of others, may make it easier to perceive morally relevant features of situations. Deficiency in such emotional responses may lead to a lack of awareness of the fact that a moral response is required of the agent. Faculties such as moral imagination may also be required for the correct grasp of situations. However, this is a whole topic in itself and all we need to take from this discussion is a specific understanding of virtue.

Full virtue, then, represents a plateau in one's moral development; once reached, the agent has fixed and firm virtuous dispositions. The fully virtuous agent appreciates the dictates of reason, feels their full motivational force and has eliminated all contrary motivational pulls. For the virtuous agent, virtuous actions follow easily, predictably and reliably from firm and fixed dispositions. Virtue and vice are stable states of character, whereas continence and incontinence are less stable states of character, as they are swayed by the influence of desire. 'For vice resembles diseases like dropsy and consumption whereas unrestraint is like epilepsy, vice being chronic, unrestraint an inter-mittent evil.'[17] Incontinence, like epilepsy, comes and goes in fits, whereas vice is settled and ever present. An agent may progress from incontinence to continence, but it is important to note that the same agent may be continent with respect to some virtues, but incontinent with respect to others, as well as that continence can collapse into incontinence again in the face of great temptation or difficulty. For example, a particular agent may be continent with respect to kindness, perhaps aided by natural tendencies, exposure to correct role models, opportunities to practice kindness and so on, while remaining incon-tinent with respect to courage. Equally, as this agent works on strengthening his resolve to be more fearless as he is prone to cowardice, he may find he makes progress in the face of moderate difficulty, but re-lapses into cowardice in the face of particularly fearful situations. This is because

a person who is continent or incontinent can achieve at most an imperfect approximation to the 'situational appreciation' of a person who is temperate in the strict sense, in a situation where temperance requires refraining from an opportunity for pleasure. The picture is that full achievement of that 'situational appreciation' would prevent the attractions of competing courses from actually exerting any motivational force. If the attractions of competing courses do exert a motivational force, as they do in cases of incontinence or continence, it follows that the 'situational appreciation' that is characteristic of fully-fledged practical wisdom cannot have been achieved. The most we can find in such cases is something less: something that yields a similar selection of what matters about the situation, but without the singleness of motivation that fully-fledged practical wisdom would achieve.[18]

It is interesting here to note that these thoughts may offer an explanation for at least some instances of the phenomenon of acting out of character. The possibility that people act out of character is put forward as a criticism of virtue ethics.[19] For example, a kind and compassionate person may perform a callous act while acting under the pressure of orders which seem to distort his usually good moral sense.[20] In such a case we would not want to attribute a callous character to this person on the basis of one act, but we still want to call that particular act callous and retain some sort of connection between act and character, of the kind which is central in virtue ethics. The way out of such problems is to re-describe what is going on in such cases and, in doing so, show that, in many instances, there is no such thing as acting out of character.

We judge a person's character by observing their responses to various situations and making inferences about their reasons, beliefs, motives and intentions. The reason why people appear to be acting out of character is, often, because we only have limited information about their character. Complete character assessment requires information not only about the external manifestation of dispositions, that is actions, but also about the reasoning and desires behind the choice to act. Character formation is an ongoing process of trying to form fixed and permanent dispositions, and part of this process will involve behaviour which is inconsistent with previous behaviour. What we call acting out of character are cases where agents lapse from continence into incontinence under unusually difficult or tempting circumstances (and vice versa from incontinence to continence due to extremely favourable circumstances). So what is called acting out of character is actually a manifestation of the struggle for the formation of one's character. Acting in character, in the full sense of predictable, stable, fixed and so on behaviour, is only open then to the virtuous agent.

An example of how these thoughts work out in practice are the Milgram experiments. The Milgram experiments were carried out after the Second World War in an attempt to explain the behaviour of the German soldiers involved in the genocide of millions of people. They were designed to test whether the excuse that one was only obeying orders is one which had any force, and whether most people would follow the dictates of morality or follow orders to the contrary. At the time of the Nuremberg trials the general feeling was that obeying orders was no excuse for committing such violent crimes against other human beings. Amongst non-Germans the feeling was that had they been in a similar situation as the German soldiers they would have resisted obeying the orders at the cost of abhorrently immoral behaviour. The surprising result of the Milgram experiments was that most people, it is assumed like the German soldiers, would follow orders at the cost of what they would normally consider unacceptable moral behaviour, that is inflicting considerable pain on others.

The Milgram experiments were designed to test the hypothesis that most people would remain compassionate or refrain from being cruel even when under pressure from orders to do otherwise. In the terms of this discussion the experiments supposed that most people were fully virtuous with respect to compassion and that they had a firm and stable disposition to act this way even under great pressure and difficulty. What the experiments uncovered was that most people were not compassionate under orders to do otherwise, as was previously commonly assumed, but rather their actions were the results of 'destructive obedience'. What this conclusion shows is that people tend to be over-optimistic in attributing good character traits to others and even to their own selves. Most people are not compassionate, even if they like to think that they are, and we should not assume that they possess the stable virtue of compassion. Most people are only continent with respect to compassion, that is they can behave compassionately under moderately difficult conditions, but once the temptation to do otherwise becomes strong enough, most people re-lapse into incontinence.[21] Thus, what appears to be an instance of 'acting out of character' is an instance of the agent lapsing from his usual continent state to incontinence due to a particularly difficult or tempting situation. In the words of another writer borrowing an observation from Schopenhauer, 'the Lord's Prayer's petition "Lead us not into temptation" could be regarded as a plea for matters so to arrange themselves that we need never discover the sorts of people we really are'.[22]

Furthermore, virtue requires the opportunity for the display of virtue. Hursthouse discusses another type of case where we mistakenly say that someone has acted out of character. An otherwise ordinary person performs a particularly courageous act and is described as acting uncharacteristically as her behaviour is unexpected of an otherwise unremarkable person. However, the judgement that this one act is uncharacteristic may well be mistaken. It may well be the case that this is the very first instance where this agent acts courageously in such a spectacular manner, but her thoughts and attitudes up until now could well conform with those of a courageous person. Indeed we would be surprised to find out that she had displayed every characteristic of a coward up until the moment when she suddenly 'converts' to courage and performs this one act because it is right.[23]

Finally, there are cases in which the virtuous agents act 'out of character', such as 'when they are exhausted, dazed with grief, ill, drunk (though no serious fault of their own, we must suppose), shell-shocked and so on'.[24] However, we have already seen how situational factors affect dispositional factors. Situational factors affect the development, strengthening and exercise of dispositional factors, and surely these are examples where situational factors outside the agent's control have an effect on the instantiation of character traits in action. If a virtuous agent is incapacitated because he is intoxicated, but he is not responsible for having become intoxicated, we should not interpret his failure to act as an uncharacteristic failure of virtue. However, we will return to the implications of some of these extremely unfavourable external factors in the next chapter when we discuss the misfortunes of Priam.

In summary then, these preliminary thoughts relate to moral luck in a number of ways. First, constitutive luck will affect the 'raw material' one is born with and it remains to be seen to what extent it affects one's ability to reason. Secondly, a virtuous state of character will be less vulnerable to luck than a continent or incontinent one. As virtue is more stable, fixed and well developed, it will be more immune to outside influences, temptations and difficulties. Luck which affects one's development will be more likely to affect continent or incontinent agents. Finally, I will also explain how Aristotelian theory deals with the problems posed by resultant luck. The remainder of this chapter will concentrate on the issues raised by constitutive luck, whereas Chapter 3 will consider cases of developmental, situational and resultant luck.

2.2 Constitutive luck

Cases of constitutive luck seem to pose the most extreme problems for our notions of responsibility and equality. The influence of constitutive luck plays havoc with our intuitions that we all at least start off equally with respect to the moral sphere, and that everyone has an equal footing from which to make the moral decisions we hold them responsible for. Constitutive luck affects who we are and poses the most fundamental questions for responsibility, for how can we be responsible for what we do if who we are is not up to us? If constitutive luck cannot be discounted, then we have to accept that we all are not equal, that some people have an innate advantage or disadvantage when it comes to acting morally and this realization about the inevitability of some of our moral decisions must have implications for responsibility and blame.

2.3 The case of Billy Budd and his Claggart

One case of constitutive luck involves a person who has been born with a tendency towards certain virtuous or vicious behaviour. An agent may find it particularly easy to act virtuously with respect to a particular virtue because he has been born with a tendency towards such acts. In this case it does not seem appropriate to praise this person for what comes so naturally to him and blame someone else for not acting similarly. This is because moral praise is due to actions which are the result of conscious choice and not just chance and natural inclination. Equally, an agent may be naturally disposed to evil to such a great and ingrained extent that we cannot see how he could easily escape his nature. For example, in Herman Melville's short story 'Billy Budd',[25] Budd's enemy, Claggart, is described as having 'a *natural depravity* – a depravity according to nature'.[26] 'Now something such was Claggart, in whom was the mania of an evil nature, not engendered by vicious training or corrupting books or licentious living, but born with him and innate, in short, "a depravity according to nature".'[27] Significantly, Claggart's evil nature could not be diverted by an appeal to reason:

> the thing which in eminent instances signalises so exceptional a nature is this: though a man's even temper and discreet bearing would seem to intimate a mind peculiarly subject to the law of reason, not the less in his soul's recesses he would seem to riot in complete exemption from that law, having apparently little to do with reason further than to employ it as an ambidexter implement for effecting the irrational.

That is to say: towards the accomplishment of an aim which in wantonness of malignity would seem to partake of the insane, he will direct a cool judgement, sagacious and sound.[28]

But this reason cannot be appealed to in order to make him see the essential unsoundness of his project. His ability to reason is not the ability to reason morally but seems more like the Aristotelian understanding of cleverness, that is the capacity for finding the means to the aim we want to achieve, but which does not give its possessor the ability to evaluate ends.[29] Claggart is doomed by his nature, over the choice of which he had no control, and lacks the power of reason to overcome this evil nature:

> With no power to annul the elemental evil in himself, though he could hide it readily enough; apprehending the good, but powerless to be it; what recourse is left to a nature like Claggart's, surcharged with energy as such natures almost invariably are, but to recoil upon itself, and, like the scorpion for which the Creator alone is responsible, act out to the end its allotted part?[30]

This description of Claggart's fate as unavoidable, of the evil in his nature as irresistible and not the result of his choice, raises troubling questions about the appropriateness of holding him responsible for his acts. In one sense, he is the author of his evil acts in that he causally brought them about: however, in another sense he is not the author of his acts, since he lacks the power to resist them and they proceed from factors not of his own making.[31]

One of the interests of the story is that Claggart's object of irrational hate, Billy Budd, is the complete opposite to him:

> Billy in many respects was little more than a sort of upright barbarian, much such perhaps as Adam presumably might have been ere the urbane serpent wriggled himself into his company. And here be it submitted that, apparently going to corroborate the doctrine of man's fall (a doctrine now popularly ignored), it is observable that where certain virtues pristine and unadulterate peculiarly characterise anybody in the external uniform of civilisation, they will upon scrutiny seem not to be derived from custom or convention but rather to be out of keeping with these, as if indeed exceptionally transmitted from a period prior to Cain's city and citified man.[32]

Billy's goodness comes directly from his natural make-up. He is completely lacking in knowledge or sophistication, so much so as to be practically 'a barbarian'. His virtue is not the result of thought and choice, or even the desire to conform to social rules, but proceeds from his fundamental state of being.

Both Billy and Claggart pose problems for moral praise and blame. It is perhaps more evident why blaming Claggart for who he is, when this is entirely outside his control, is problematic. This blame is entirely undeserved and in a sense blaming Claggart would be to perpetrate a further moral wrong. However, Claggart's evil nature leads him to perform great moral wrongs, which seem to demand some sort of moral response. The correct moral appraisal of Billy is not so pressing, as his actions happen to be virtuous. At least, what Billy does *naturally* happens to coincide with what we would want him to do morally. However, attributing praise to Billy for doing what comes naturally is as problematic as attributing blame to Claggart. That one naturally does what is good and the other what is evil is not of primary importance when it comes to responsibility, given that we want to hold people responsible only for what is under their control. If such acts proceed from a naturally virtuous and irresistible nature, then this virtuous agent is not truly deserving of praise in the same way that Claggart is not truly deserving of blame. However, the alternative, that praise and blame are not appropriate responses, is an uneasy option. This is the essence of problems of moral luck: both alternatives seem unacceptable. Is there an Aristotelian answer to such a problem?

2.4 Natural tendencies and cultivated dispositions

One response to such a criticism is to accept that there is a certain amount of luck involved in constitutive make-up and some people may be born with a tendency to go in one direction rather than another. When discussing the doctrine of the mean, Aristotle points out that the mean has two extremes, but that we sometimes oppose one extreme to the mean because one extreme seems further from it than the other. For example, cowardice seems further from courage than rashness; he argues that

> [i]t is the things towards which we have the stronger *natural inclination* that seem to us more opposed to the mean. For example, we are *naturally more inclined* towards pleasures, and this makes us more prone towards licentiousness than towards temperance; so we describe

as more contrary to the mean those things towards which we have the stronger tendency.[33]

So we could accept that we all have natural tendencies, due to luck, towards virtues or vices, but that no one has a natural tendency towards all the virtues, so in the end all these differences are ironed out, since I may have to work harder at being courageous, but you have to work harder at being truthful. Such an explanation, however, might not be entirely convincing. It is entirely possible that someone, like Billy, may be naturally gifted with all the appropriate tendencies, in which case all virtues come easily to him and another agent is naturally hampered by all the vices, and this seems unfair. Although it may be possible to overcome one contrary inclination, a character which is naturally made up of all the vices, like Claggart, seems doomed to a life of vice.

To understand the possible Aristotelian answer to this problem, we need to examine further what is meant by having a virtue. It is true that someone may have a natural tendency to be kind, which is the result of luck, but this does not mean that he possesses the virtue of kindness. The virtue of kindness is not merely a tendency to be kind, but

a purposive disposition, lying in a mean that is relative to us and determined by a rational principle, and by that which a prudent man would use to determine it.[34]

Dispositions, inclinations and tendencies are used interchangeably to refer to the make-up of people's characters, but I would like to draw a distinction between natural tendencies and cultivated dispositions. Natural tendencies include all the propensities towards certain emotions and actions which we have by virtue of our natural constitution. For example, a person can be born irascible or immune to fear. These natural tendencies may have a strong hold over an individual, in the sense that they are not easy to resist, they persist over time and lend a degree of predictability to his behaviour. Cultivated dispositions, on the other hand, differ from natural tendencies in that they do not just naturally occur in individuals. Rather, they are the result of deliberate choice and their gradual development requires effort. Once established they can also be settled, strong and lead to persistent and reliable behaviour patterns.

An individual's natural tendencies are a matter of luck, as they form a basic part of his constitution which is outside his control. Some natural tendencies may reinforce behaviour which is characteristic of virtue, such as a natural resistance to fear, or behaviour which is characteristic of vice, such as irascibility. In that sense some people are luckier in terms of their constitution than others, since their natural tendencies happen to accord with virtue. However, true virtue is not a natural tendency, but a reflective and deliberately cultivated disposition. A virtuous disposition must be chosen, for its own sake and knowingly.[35] Unlike natural tendencies, virtuous dispositions, as we have redefined them, cannot be engendered in us by nature, rather:

> we are constituted by nature to receive them, but their full development in us is due to habit. Again, of all the faculties with which nature endows us we first acquire the potentialities, and only later effect their actualisation.[36]

Another important distinction between natural tendencies and cultivated dispositions to virtue is that a particular agent may have some of the former, but not others, whereas a fully virtuous agent possesses all the virtues. The unity of the virtues is derived from the fact that they are all underlined by the same principle: prudence or practical wisdom.[37] The virtuous agent who is prudent will share in all the virtues, whereas the naturally gifted agent may be gifted in some respects, but not in others;

> These considerations therefore show that it is not possible to be good in the true sense without prudence, nor to be prudent without moral virtue. (Moreover, this might supply an answer to the dialectic argument that might be put forward to prove that the virtues can exist in isolation from each other, on the ground that the same man does not possess the greatest natural capacity for all of them, so that he may have already attained one when he has not yet attained another. In regard to the natural virtues this is possible; but it is not possible in regard to those virtues which entitle a man to be called good without qualification. For if a man have the one virtue of prudence he will also have all the moral virtues together with it.)[38]

Natural tendencies are related to true virtue in the same way that cleverness is related to prudence. Cleverness is merely the capacity to achieve a certain aim, but it can be put to good or bad uses, achieving good or bad aims. As such it is different from prudence, which relates only to good aims, since it goes hand in hand with virtue.

The fact is that the case of virtue is closely analogous to that of prudence in relation to cleverness. Prudence and cleverness are not the same, but they are similar; and natural virtue is related in the same way to virtue in the true sense. All are agreed that the various moral qualities are in a sense bestowed by nature: we are just, and capable of temperance, and brave, and possessed of the other virtues from the moment of our birth. But nevertheless we expect to find that true goodness is something different, that the virtues in the true sense come to belong to us in another way. For even children and wild animals possess the natural dispositions [natural tendencies, following the terminology I have used so far], yet without intelligence these may manifestly be harmful.[39]

We may have natural tendencies which facilitate or frustrate our aim to become virtuous, but in order to become truly virtuous we have to actively affirm these natural tendencies by turning them into settled and strong dispositions.[40] In short, we have to develop the right, strong and unchangeable character.

It is important to pause here and examine in greater detail the process by which natural tendencies are turned into cultivated dispositions. Burnyeat[41] points out that

A wide range of desires and feelings are shaping patterns of motivation and response in a person well before he comes to a reasoned outlook on his life as a whole, and certainly before he integrates his reflective consciousness with his actual behaviour.[42]

We are agents who act, long before we are fully rational moral agents, and the acts we perform before reaching mature moral agency, as well as the desires and feelings that motivate those acts, go towards shaping who we become. Moral agents are first, children, who are susceptible to different influences. Such influences go towards shaping one's moral character long before it is reasonable to expect one's reasoning faculties to take over moral deliberation. This is why early learning, practice, habituation, role models and so on are so important for Aristotle. All these influences can go towards making or breaking the raw material that will eventually constitute the fully developed moral agent.

Such considerations can explain seemingly perplexing passages in Aristotle, such as the following:

Anything that we have to learn to do we learn by the actual doing of it: people become builders by building and instrumentalists by playing instruments. Similarly we become just by performing just acts, temperate by performing temperate ones, brave by performing brave ones.[43]

How can it be possible to become just by doing just acts, since it is only when one becomes just that one knows which acts are just? This passage seems circular. However, the explanation for this apparent circularity is simple. One can perform just acts by following the example of someone who knows better or is doing so in a habitual, non-reflective way. These acts are just, but they do not proceed from a just character, yet they do go towards making the character just. They do not proceed from a just character because they are not the result of fixed and firm dispositions, chosen for their own sake. One can know 'the that', and this is the beginning, but an agent needs to come to appreciate 'the because' before he can be truly virtuous[44] ('the that' and 'the because' are also translated as the fact and the reason). 'The because' is the understanding of why the act is just, which leads to the choice of the act itself. Habituating oneself in 'the that' will lead to a character that is more inclined to perform virtuous acts and less inclined to be diverted by contrary inclinations. Understanding 'the because' will lead to the development from natural tendencies to cultivated dispositions. This is why it is important to associate with virtuous role models, who can point out virtuous actions. The student of virtue can then perform such acts and habituate himself in such acts, long before his reason comes to choose and affirm them for their own sake. Complete and mature virtue comes with understanding why such acts are virtuous and choosing them for their own sake.

Natural tendencies, then, can lead to vice and virtue, but this is not true vice and virtue as they are not chosen knowingly and for their own sake. The outcomes of actions resulting from natural tendencies may appear indistinguishable from the outcomes of actions resulting from cultivated dispositions. Aristotle seems to be accepting such a possibility when he says in the *Eudemian Ethics*:

If, then, some have a fortunate natural endowment as musical people, though they have not learned to sing, are fortunately endowed in this way – and move without reason in the direction given to them by their nature, and desire that which they ought at the time and in the manner they ought, such men are successful, even if they are foolish and irrational, just as the others will sing well though not able to teach singing. And such men are fortunate, namely those who generally succeed without the aid of reason. Men, then, who are fortunate will be so by nature.[45]

and further on

And for this reason, as I said a while ago, those are called fortunate who, whatever they start on, succeed in it without being good at reasoning. And deliberation is of no advantage to them, for they have in them a principle that is better than intellect and deliberation, while others have not this but have intellect; they have inspiration, but they cannot deliberate.[46]

So, it seems possible that people may perform, because of luck, acts which appear indistinguishable from virtuous acts, but are different. The difference lies in that virtuous acts are done in a certain state, that is chosen knowingly, for their own sake and from a fixed and permanent disposition, but despite this difference it may appear to an observer that the virtuous act and the act performed because of luck are indistinguishable. The crucial difference between natural tendencies and cultivated dispositions is the role of reason. Deliberation is crucial for true virtue. Without deliberation and understanding of 'the because', virtue is just a habit. Since habits are unreflective and not consciously controlled, it seems odd to expect virtue to be a habit. For how can we attribute moral praise or blame to something that is unreflective and not consciously controlled? The answer is that habituation is not virtue, but is part of the road to virtue.

It is interesting to note that since acts performed from natural tendencies and those performed from cultivated dispositions are indistinguishable in their manifestations,[47] we may not be able to tell apart true virtuous agents from those who are merely naturally virtuous (the same goes for vice). The virtuous agent can be relied upon to act virtuously in all manner of difficult and tempting situations, but the same can be said of the naturally virtuous person. Where the virtuous agent's behaviour can be relied upon because of his understanding of the right reason, the naturally virtuous is motivated by his own sympathetic nature. Natural sympathy, of this extreme kind, can be as effective as understanding the right reason in producing reliable behaviour. This epistemological problem will become apparent again and again in Aristotelian theory.

This is because we can only make inferences about an agent's internal world and his dispositions from the external manifestations of these dispositions. However, if these external manifestations can correspond to more than one state of character and it is not easy to have access to the internal world of agents, in practice it may be difficult to tell the difference between naturally virtuous agents and those who have true, chosen, deliberative virtue. Perhaps one way out of this problem is to expect those with true virtue to be able to rationally account for their actions, as deliberation is crucial to virtue, but I am not sure whether such a suggestion would be useful.

2.5   Conclusion

The distinction between natural tendencies and cultivated dispositions has allowed us to partially account for the influences of constitutive luck. Good natural tendencies are undeserved and the result of contingencies outside our control, but they do result in actions that are similar to true virtue. Although the external manifestations of natural virtue and true virtue are the same, the characters they proceed from differ. The truly virtuous agent is the object of real moral worth, as he has consciously chosen virtue, whereas the naturally virtuous agent is good simply due to luck. Thus, Billy Budd is not truly virtuous. As to how this should affect our moral evaluation of him, Aristotle is not entirely explicit, but he seems to say that although natural virtue is not as valuable as true virtue, it is still a good state of character that results in good actions. Whether natural virtue deserves true praise or some sort of qualified praise is not entirely clear.

These thoughts may partly account for the case of Billy Budd, but they do not necessarily accommodate the case of Claggart in a similar way. So far I have argued as if the same thoughts that apply to the possibility of natural virtue apply to the possibility of natural vice. However, all the quotations so far relate to the possibility of natural virtue and thus only explain Billy Budd; what should we make of Claggart? In many passages, Aristotle likens virtue to vice, for example in that they are both stable, permanent dispositions, both involve choice and so on, so perhaps we should assume that what has been said with respect to natural virtue also applies with respect to natural vice. However, I do not think this is entirely correct.

In one of the few places where Aristotle discusses natural depravity as opposed to vice, he likens natural depravity to bestiality.[48] This is important since bestiality is below vice in the order of character states,[49] and is so close to an animal state that it does not merit proper praise or blame or the attribution of responsibility:

> These practices [e.g. cannibalism, sexual perversion] result in some cases from natural disposition [tendency], and in others from habit, as with those who have been abused from childhood. When nature is responsible, no one would describe such persons as showing unrestraint, any more than one would apply that term to women because they are not active in sexual intercourse...[50]

If such characters were incontinent, they would know what is right but fail to do it. As a result we could hold them responsible for their actions, but bestial states of character, unlike incontinent states, are outside the scope of responsibility. The state of bestiality is associated with animals, which have no choice in their actions and therefore cannot be held responsible for them. Bestial individuals act out of a state of natural necessitation. Natural vice, then, leads to a state of bestiality; a state so depraved and almost outside the scope of human experience that our normal notions of blame have no application.

It seems then that Billy and natural virtue get a different treatment from Claggart and natural vice. It is also peculiar that although a number of passages are dedicated to examining the possibility of natural virtue, natural vice is hardly discussed at all. Perhaps this is because natural vice poses much greater problems than natural virtue. Natural virtue is significantly – in terms of our evaluation of the agent – different from true virtue, but ultimately it does not pose such a great problem as natural vice as the actions of the naturally virtuous man correspond with the actions of the truly virtuous man. Of course, this correspondence is incidental and this should affect how we attribute responsibility for such acts, but in practical terms, in the naturally virtuous agent we are faced with a person we can easily live with. At least the naturally virtuous man acts in desirable ways, even if we cannot truly praise him for doing so. The naturally vicious man acts in problematic ways and it seems that we cannot truly blame him for it. So natural vice is doubly problematic.

In conclusion, the positive feature of Aristotle's account is that it allows us to differentiate between natural virtue and true virtue and correspondingly between good actions and good actions deserving of praise. Thus, it clearly marks out the appropriate domain of moral praise. However, Aristotle finds cases of natural vice more problematic.

Ultimately, his best response seems to be to liken natural vice to a state that is barely human and assume because of that that the attribution of responsibility to the bestial agent is not an appropriate response. The next chapter will now consider the Aristotelian answer to the problems of developmental, situational and resultant luck.

3
Aristotle on Developmental, Situational and Resultant Luck

3.1 Introduction

Admittedly, the cases of Claggart and Billy are rather extreme examples. By far more common examples are those of agents who have a mixture of good and bad natural tendencies and could develop in either good or bad ways depending on the influences they receive. Developmental luck relates to all the contingencies encountered which affect factors leading to an agent's moral development.

As we have already seen, the road to virtue is long and requires effort. Moral agents have to develop their character and progress through different stages of moral maturity. A number of factors such as the quality of one's education, the availability of role models, opportunities for practice, the encouragement of habits, the influence of peers and so on will affect, in good or bad ways, an agent's moral development. The availability and quality of all these factors, however, is subject to luck.

It seems plausible that most of us are born with a collection of natural tendencies, some facilitating and some discouraging virtue. Let us also suppose that these natural tendencies are evenly balanced so that most people start off their moral life with as many advantages as disadvantages. In such cases we presume the minimum of influences from constitutive luck; with regard to make-up, such agents could become either virtuous or vicious. What will play a crucial role in most people's development then are factors relevant to character formation. If the agent is exposed to influences that encourage virtue and discourage vice he will be subject to good developmental luck, if he is exposed to influences that encourage vice and discourage virtue he will be subject to bad developmental luck. The problem posed by developmental luck, however, is that agents do not have control over the quality and availability of such factors. Thus, the agent's resulting character has developed due to factors outside his control, while we may still want to hold him responsible for the actions that proceed from that character.

A specific instance of developmental luck is situational luck, which relates to the situations one finds oneself in which require moral decision-making. Situational luck is particularly important as it forms a crucial part of general developmental influences. The problem it poses was highlighted by Nagel.[1]

The influence of situational luck will vary depending on the stage in the moral development of the agent. We have already seen how moral development for Aristotle is gradual. The virtuous agent has reached a plateau in moral development; his dispositions are firm, well established, fixed and persist over time. He is disposed to act virtuously under conditions of difficulty and temptation, for real virtue is not simply to act well when it is easy to do so, but to act well when it is difficult to do so and there is extreme temptation to do otherwise. The virtuous agent has reached such a stage of moral maturity that what appears to others as temptation to do other than the virtuous act is of no importance to him. His virtue is so well entrenched and flows so smoothly from his character that perceived difficulties and temptations are not real difficulties and temptations for him. The continent and incontinent agents, however, are much more open to the temptations of vice and more likely to be put off by circumstantial difficulties in persisting in virtue.

Situational luck is crucial because if its influence is strongly felt at a time when the agent is at a vulnerable, immature state in his moral development, it can ruin their character. Situations, such as the decision to fight the Nazis, which may be easily dealt with by the virtuous agent will sometimes pose insurmountable problems for the continent agent. For example, consider two moral agents at the same point in their moral development, and both are mostly continent with respect to virtue. One lives in England and develops on the road to virtue. The other lives in Germany and is faced with a serious moral decision in the face of the Nazis. The prospect of standing up to popular opinion and the government of the day at the risk of his life proves too much for him and he fails this moral test. Because he has failed a serious moral test, his moral development suffers a serious setback. His English counterpart is lucky because he altogether avoids this moral test, simply by living in another country. Of course, the English agent is likely to come across other moral tests in his life, but by then he may have developed to a more stable and unshakeable stage of character and as such be better able to deal with moral problems. One agent fails in the greater moral project, which is the formation of a virtuous character over the period of one's life, where the other agent succeeds, because of the influence of one moral test presented at the wrong time. Where one lives, what kinds of moral problems one encounters, what temptations come across one's way and so on, that is the situations under which one is called upon to act, are all a matter of luck, and the influence of situational luck on moral life is significant.

Finally, cases of resultant luck are cases where the results of one's action are under the influence of luck. For example:

> [c]onsider two similar cases, in which one is negligent in not putting out a fire one lights. In one case the fire is fortunately put out by rainfall, and thus nothing regrettable happens, whereas in the other a nearby house is set on fire and a child is burnt to death. It is obvious that the outcome in both cases is beyond one's control, in the sense that it was not within one's control to make it the case that a rainfall occurred or did not occur, or that a child was or was not in the house nearby. In this sense, the outcome was a matter of (good or bad) luck.[2]

Questions about resultant luck raise questions about our understanding of negligence, the degree to which the results of actions are foreseeable, reasonable expectations and so on. They are similar to cases of situational luck, in that we expect mature moral agents to be more adept at the kind of reasoning relating to the results of one's actions than immature moral agents. The question posed by resultant luck is very often one of degree: how much can we expect agents to know/predict/expect, how far do we expect them to go in order to find out and so on; and sometimes it can also be a question of which action we can reasonably attribute to the agent, for example the lighting of the fire or the burning of a child.

This chapter will attempt to collect together all of Aristotle's relevant remarks on the questions posed by developmental, situational and resultant luck, and use them to elaborate on the Aristotelian response to the problems they raise.

3.2 The case of Raskolnikov

A particularly poignant example of a moral agent influenced by developmental and situational luck is the example of Raskolnikov,[3] brought up to expect a certain lifestyle for himself, one of relative wealth and independence to pursue academic interests. However, circumstances conspire to put him in great temptation. Raskolnikov murders the old woman for her money and he does so of his own choice, but the circumstances that lead him to become a murderer are complex and not necessarily under his control. One of the reasons for the novel's great success is the appeal of the central character's moral test. Raskolnikov has been brought up to value money and social status more than moral behaviour. He is also placed in extremely tempting circumstances, having to survive on very little money – '[h]e had been crushed by poverty'[4] – and coming into contact with an 'easy' potential victim. Raskolnikov's poverty is extreme and it overwhelms him; in the words of another character:

> When a man is poor he may still preserve the nobility of his inborn feelings, but when he is destitute he never can. If a man is destitute he isn't even driven out with a stick, he's swept out of human society with a broom, to make it as insulting as possible...[5]

His own sister is forced to 'sell herself for those who are dear to her'[6] in an arranged marriage with an older man, in order to find money for the family, while he is a complete failure and has not even been able to reveal to his mother that he is no longer a student. The intended victim, his friends say, 'doesn't deserve to live'[7] and her money could be put to good use after her death (to Raskolnikov's own 'deserving' ends, rather than being hoarded by an old woman).

Each of these circumstances on its own is not enough to push Raskolnikov into murder, but combined they lead him to kill the old woman. They also provide an explanation as to why he was driven to this abhorrent act. Raskolnikov is ashamed that: 'he had gone to his doom so blindly, hopelessly, in deaf-and-dumb stupidity, following the edict of blind fate...'.[8] But we can see why fate pushed him in the direction it did: all his influences were negative, all his expectations unrealistic, all the temptations present.

The novel also takes us through Raskolnikov's thoughts and feelings following the crime. His constant changes of heart about whether he should confess or not clearly show his internal struggle. Ultimately, Raskolnikov is 'saved' by his own self-renunciation, so that the novel ends on a positive note. In the end, Raskolnikov has the strength of character to recognize the evil in what he has done and confess to the police and, more importantly, to his own self the viciousness of his crime; '[b]ut at this point a new story begins, the story of a man's gradual renewal, his gradual rebirth, his gradual transition from one world to another, of his growing acquaintance with a new, hitherto completely unknown reality'.[9]

However, we can easily imagine an alternative ending, where circumstance and temptations thoroughly overcome the main character and he is unable to free himself from the influences of his environment. More recently, Irvine Welsh[10] has portrayed such an ultimately lost main character. Roy is subjected to the most depraved upbringing and the worst influences; like Raskolnikov he gives in to them, but he is incapable of admitting, even to himself, the extent of his depravity. Roy, as a child, is to be deeply pitied. As a young child he is no better or no worse (in terms of moral potential) than any other child. However, he is brought up in an abusive, neglectful environment, which pushes him towards everything that is wrong. Roy as an adult is evil and cannot even admit this to himself. In the end, where Raskolnikov is saved, Roy is lost, for Roy fails to see that what he has done is wrong.

The question posed by Raskolnikov and Roy is to what extent, if at all, we should take developmental influences into account when deciding on whether to hold agents responsible for their actions. Bundy, the British serial killer, talking in the third person about his attempts to understand himself said:

> It's like trying to examine what's in the medical cabinet by, in great detail, examining what's in the mirror...he wasn't seeing through perhaps, the morass of justifications and obfuscations that he'd created and indulged in – and what he was closely examining was the reflection in the mirror, not what was behind it.[11]

The implication here is that there is something beyond or beneath what is on the surface, something for which the agent is ultimately responsible, and the process of redemption is a process of seeing through the mass of excuses to recognize one's own responsibility. The question then is whether we should accept that the influence of developmental factors plays an overwhelming role in determining actions with the implication then that agents are not entirely responsible for such actions, or whether we should expect agents to 'see through' to an essential core of themselves for which they can be held responsible. We shall now see whether Aristotelian ethics can help us answer this question.

3.3   Developmental, situational and resultant luck

It is, almost certainly indisputably, the case that Aristotle attaches great weight to character formation. He makes a number of remarks explaining how the child develops its moral character through education, habituation, role models and so on. If then 'we are constituted by nature to receive them [the virtues], but their full development in us is due to habit'[12] a crucial part of an adult's moral character is determined by early influences and guidance; indeed: '[i]t makes no small difference whether one is brought up in these or those habits from childhood, but a very great difference; or, rather all the difference'.[13]

However, the problem is that the quality of the influences and guidance we receive in childhood is entirely a matter of luck. In the *Rhetoric*, Aristotle argues that the young have certain characteristics, of which the elderly are no longer capable, which, if developed properly and encouraged, can lead to virtue. The young are open, guileless and trusting because they have not yet been cheated, they have no concern for money because they have no need for it, they are optimistic about their fellow men because they have not yet seen wickedness, they are sanguine and have high expectations because they have not suffered any disappointments, they are courageous and confident because they have not been humbled by life, they form friendships easily, are prone to laughter and they feel pity out of laughter. In short, it seems that they are capable, in the short run, of certain high and noble things, and, in the long run, of becoming virtuous, because they have not suffered in life. This may be an idealistic and sheltered view of childhood, but even if this is an ideal, some lives can fall very short of it. The crucial point seems to be that at childhood we have unique qualities which may facilitate moral development, which are not available to us later on in life. To put the point more simply, we could just consent to the fact that children are more open to suggestion, guidance, change and so on whereas adults are more set in their ways, find it difficult to accept change and so on.

The quality of such influences, guidance, education, role models and in general the environment within which children grow will determine the direction which they take. If everything that is good in them is encouraged, nurtured and promoted there is a great chance that they will grow up to be good. If every contrary impulse is promoted and every good thwarted, then children will become vicious. So, even if we accept that the majority of people will be born with a collection of good and bad influences, such that they could develop in either way, early influences play a crucial role in future character development:

Again each man judges correctly those matters with which he is acquainted; it is on these that he is a competent critic. To criticize a particular subject, therefore, a man must have been trained in that subject: to be a good critic generally, he must have had an all-round education.[14]

Perhaps then for us at all events it is proper to start from what is known to us. This is why in order to be a competent student of the right and the just, and in short of the topics of politics in general, the pupil is bound to have been well trained in his habits.[15]

All these early influences, however, are the subject of luck. Such influences are not under the direct control of children and they play a crucial role at a time when children are far too immature to be expected to recognize and seek out good influences while avoiding bad ones.

As the road to virtue is a long and complicated one, these considerations do not apply exclusively to children. Any moral agent who has not yet reached full virtue is open to such influences. Anyone less than fully virtuous will not have the ability to clearly see the road to virtue every time, especially under conditions of extreme difficulty and temptation. This is why situational luck is particularly important, as it arbitrarily tests some agents while sparing others.

Aristotle did not make direct references to the question of situational luck, but there is one place where he seems to be dealing with its influence:

For we believe that the truly good and wise man bears all his fortunes with dignity, and always takes the most honourable course that circumstances permit; just as a good general uses his available forces in the most military effective way, and a good shoemaker makes the neatest shoe out of leather supplied to him, and the same with all the other kinds of craftsmen.[16]

Aristotle seems to be considering and overcoming the problems created by situational luck[17] with respect to the virtuous man, who is truly good and wise. A virtuous man is singled out from the other states of character as his character has reached a high degree of sophistication, maturity and stability which will enable him to deal with extraordinary circumstances. The virtuous man will possess the moral perception or situational appreciation necessary to identify the relevant moral features of this case, as well as the practical wisdom necessary to see the virtuous course of action amongst conflicting alternatives. In cases of bad situational luck, the virtuous person will make the best he can out of a bad lot, in the same way that a good craftsman will make the best use of substandard material. The virtuous agent cannot be held responsible for elements of the situation which are not under his control, but should be praised for performing the best possible action, under the circumstances. Perhaps a contemporary example of the good craftsman faced with bad material is that of Oscar Schindler.[18] Schindler found himself in a morally demanding situation; he needed determination and commitment in order to carry through the demands of morality. In addition he had to work with 'bad' material in that there was no possible way he could save all the Jews who were equally at risk from the Germans and he could not even save all the Jews he came across. The reason he is to be praised is for, first, responding to the moral demands, and secondly for making the best out of a bad situation, that is saving as many people as possible.

However, the same ability to deal with 'bad material' cannot be expected of the less sophisticated continent and incontinent agents. An apprentice craftsman may find that the difference between success and failure lies in the quality of the material he uses. A good way of identifying an excellent craftsman is to test him with a particularly difficult task. Similarly, when the moral action is obvious and easy to execute, both the virtuous and the continent agents will act appropriately. However, a greater test of moral resolve will separate true virtue from mere continence.

In terms of one's development then, coming across moral decisions of great difficulty, that is where the correct answer is not clear, or great temptation, for example a strong contrary desire, or actions where one has to make the best of a bad situation, at a time when the agent is immature can be disastrous. What kinds of moral situations one comes across is obviously a matter of luck and not under the control of the agent, so the influence of situational luck is considerable and significant. Incontinent agents have knowledge of the right principle, even though it is not being exercised or it is being overwhelmed by the contrary desire. This would lead us to think that, in retrospect and with some effort, they should be able to recognize their own incontinence. Situations which provoke great lapses into incontinence are likely to, therefore, affect one's overall moral development. Recognizing that one's incontinent non-action in the face of Nazi oppression contributed to the death of millions may well have devastating results for the agent, that is for the possibility that he develops virtue in the future, in the same way that facing a moral dilemma may devastate one's virtue. However, we will return to this when we discuss moral dilemmas.

The actual process of making moral decisions is something that the virtuous agent will be better at than those less than virtuous because of his ability to perceive the morally relevant features of situations and his practical wisdom in judging their relative weight. A popular way of distinguishing Aristotelian moral theory from other alternatives, that is deontology and consequentialism, is to say that it is not principle-based. Some moral theories arrive at correct decisions by appealing to predetermined moral principles. This does not seem to be the case for Aristotle. In a famous passage he cautions us not to expect more precision from ethics than the nature of the subject permits. If ethics is an inexact science, its essence cannot be captured by inflexible, rigid rules. What one must do is pay attention to particulars, develop the ability to 'see' relevant particulars, that is moral perception, as well as the ability to see the importance different elements of a situation have in each context, that is practical wisdom. The virtuous agent has perception and practical wisdom to the fullest, but for other agents it is not always easy to decide what to do.

The virtuous agent's perception and practical wisdom will help him judge the consequences of his actions and predict, with a reasonable degree of accuracy, the results of his decisions. However, what constitutes reasonableness in such a context is open to discussion. Aristotle seems to be aware of the questions raised by negligence and degrees of liability. For example, he argues: 'When the injury occurs contrary to reasonable expectation it is a Misadventure; but when it occurs not contrary to reasonable expectation but without malicious intent it is a mistake.'[19] Agents are responsible for finding out the consequences and particulars of their actions where it is in their power to do so, otherwise we call them negligent and hold them responsible. The discussion of voluntary and involuntary actions is relevant in clarifying the notion of 'reasonableness', which seems to be playing such a crucial role here.

Actions are involuntary if performed under compulsion or through ignorance. Whether someone is forced to act under compulsion may be a matter of situational luck. The cases of the man whose children are held by a tyrant and the captain who is forced to throw his cargo away in bad weather are cases that have been brought about due to bad luck, in the sense that the agent is not in any way culpable for finding himself in a situation that forces him to make an unpleasant decision. Aristotle concludes that

> the terms voluntary and involuntary should be used with reference to the time when the actions are performed. Now in cases like the above the agent acts voluntarily; because the movement of the limbs that are the instruments of action has its origin in the agent himself, and where this is so it is in his power either to act or not. Therefore such actions are voluntary; but considered absolutely they are presumably involuntary, because nobody would choose to do anything of this sort in itself.[20]

In a sense, the examples of the captain and the man whose children are held by the tyrant are similar to the good craftsman who makes the best of bad material, since they find themselves, through no fault of their own, in situations where they have to do something they would not choose to do. It is not the craftsman's fault that he has been given bad material, and it is a testimony to his skill that he makes the best object out of them. Similarly it is not the captain's fault that he finds himself in a storm and is forced to jettison his cargo.[21] Although we must be careful not to draw this analogy between the craftsman, as similar to the virtuous man, and the captain, as an example of a mixed act, too far. The craftsman, similarly to the virtuous man, chooses the right act, but is constrained in its exercise by the poor materials that he has; nevertheless he makes the best of a less-than-ideal situation. The captain of the ship is forced into the action and in a sense does not choose it, as no one would voluntarily choose to jettison their cargo.

Aristotle also accepts that ignorance may make an act involuntary and its agent a possible subject of pity and pardon. Acceptable ignorance is ignorance of particulars rather than ignorance in choice or of the universal.

> All these particular circumstances of an action admit of ignorance, and anyone who is ignorant of any of them is considered to have acted involuntarily, especially in the case of the most important of them, which are supposed to be the circumstances of the act and its effect. Further, for an act to be called involuntary in virtue of this sort of ignorance, the agent must also feel distress and repentance for having done it.[22]

The case of the captain is also relevant to the above considerations, because the captain, presumably, was not aware that he was heading for a storm and could not reasonably be held responsible for not being aware of this. Aristotle accepts that there are cases of unavoidable ignorance which excuse the agent from responsibility.[23] If the captain was aware of the impending storm and had steered for it regardless, then he would be negligent for an act performed voluntarily (steering a ship into the storm), and jettisoning the cargo would no longer be involuntary in any sense since the bad situation he found himself in was the result of his bad judgement, rather than bad luck. Agents are punished for their ignorance if they are responsible for it, for example ignorance of the law and ignorance caused by drunkenness,[24] but again this depends on the circumstances of the case:

> Indeed the fact that an offence was committed in ignorance is itself made a ground for punishment, in cases where the offender is held

responsible for his ignorance; for instance, the penalty is doubled if the offender was drunk, because the origin of the offence was in the man himself, as he might have avoided getting drunk, which was the cause of his not knowing what he was doing.[25]

The habitual, violent drunk is responsible for choosing to drink yet again and is therefore to blame for the consequences of the actions he performs while under the influence. When sober, this person knows from past experience the negative effect alcohol has on him, so he should avoid all exposure.[26] Whereas the first time drinker who becomes violent after his drink has been spiked cannot be held responsible. He is not responsible for his drink being spiked or for his actions which were the result of this. Similar thoughts apply to virtue and vice in general: '... the unjust and the profligate might at the outset have avoided becoming so, and therefore they are so voluntarily, although when they have become unjust and profligate it is no longer open to them not to be so'.[27]

So, although when the agent is truly vicious he is no longer able to change his life and his actions, if the decision to take this path was up to him, then his character and the actions that follow from it are voluntarily chosen. He is then responsible for what he does, even if he no longer voluntarily chooses to do the acts that proceed from his character, just like the habitual drunk who has chosen to drink when sober, but who can no longer control either himself when drunk or his now habitual desire for drink.

Aristotle's thoughts would give definite answers to contemporary questions relating to moral luck. A case, presented in recent literature as an example of moral luck, is the question of why we punish and blame to different degrees the drunk driver who kills a pedestrian and the drunk driver who gets caught before he does any harm or even gets away with it.[28] Following Aristotle's observations previously, we would have to establish whether the driver was responsible for getting himself drunk and whether he knew before he got drunk that there was good reason not to (i.e. that he would drive when drunk). If the driver was not acting as the result of any kind of relevant ignorance then he is to be blamed for putting other people's lives at risk while driving. The blame for this act should be the same whether he kills someone or not. This is because the agent has voluntarily placed himself in a situation where the unacceptable results of his act are at the mercy of luck. When sober, the driver knows that if he drinks he will drive drunk and if he drives drunk he will be putting other people's lives at risk. He has, therefore, already performed the vicious act in deciding to drink, regardless of whether, due to circumstances out of his control, a pedestrian is around on his planned route. Whether he hits someone or not, should not matter in our moral appraisal of his act.[29]

The cases of the drunken driver and the unfortunate drunken driver are similar to the case of the attempted murderer and the actual murderer. Both agents choose and fully intend to kill their victim, but due to circumstances out of his control one agent fails in his aim because his gun jams. The attempted murderer differs from the actual murderer only in that, due to luck, his act did not have the consequences he intended it to have. As before, we can argue that the attempted murderer chose the act, fully aware of its consequences and fully intending to bring them about. As a result he should be blamed as severely as the actual murderer, as it was a matter of luck, out of his control, that the 'desired' result did not come about.

The two drivers are equally to blame because they have similar character traits which make them irresponsible and likely to disregard the danger they put other people in by driving drunk. The character traits, relevant to the moral evaluation, have already been displayed in the act of choosing to drive while drunk (or choosing to drink when one can reasonably foresee that one will then drive), and whether this act ends in the death of another person or not is not a relevant factor when assessing this character. Both drivers are guilty of gross negligence and disregard for the safety and lives of other people.[30] According to this analysis, this case is not a genuine case of moral luck, as the element that is subject to luck, whether there is a victim or not, should not be taken into account when making a decision about moral responsibility. What is taken into account is what is under the agent's control, that is whether to exhibit this particular character trait and drive drunk. Since this character trait involves an irresponsible attitude with regard to the safety and lives of other people, we can also predict that those who possess it will display it in a number of different ways, not just by drunk driving. By this I mean that drunk driving is just one instance of the general character trait of showing disregard for the welfare of others and how this is affected by one's actions. We should not be surprised if we find that habitual drunk drivers are likely to value their own convenience over causing harm or risk of harm to others, in situations other than driving.

A similar case could be made for attempted and actual murders. The two people who merely attempt and actually succeed in committing murder possess and display a similar vice. The flaw in their character which leads them to take the lives of others is apparent in the mere attempt to murder. Whether this attempt is successful or not does not do much to either reinforce or lead us to abandon the belief that they have this vice, since it is the result of forces outside their control. Again, whether the murderer is actually successful or not is irrelevant to the moral evaluation of the character of these two agents.[31] As with the previous case, this is not a genuine case of moral luck, since although there are elements of the case that are outside the agents' control, these elements are not relevant in the moral evaluation of their characters.

Although Aristotle did not comment on the cases of the drunken drivers and the attempted murderers directly, it seems that his remarks elsewhere support such an analysis of the two examples. Such an approach to the characterization of acts is not entirely without support from modern writers. Consider Nussbaum's account of Oedipus. In this case there are important extenuating elements in the description of what has happened, namely Oedipus' excusable ignorance of his family relationships. If this particular element in this case is taken into account, then Oedipus is not guilty of patricide because 'the act that he intended and chose was not the act that we have judged him to have performed'.[32] Nussbaum's appeal is a personal appeal to her readers to see the situation from the point of view of the person involved in it, as this is the only way one can appreciate the difficulties involved. She moves away from general categorizations, to moral judgements which are 'built upon a full grasp of all the particular circumstances of the situation, including the motives and intentions of the agent'.[33] It seems that Aristotle may have accepted extenuating circumstances in such a case, as he says: 'It is possible for the person struck to be the agent's father, although the agent is only aware that he is a human being, or one of the company, and not that he is his father.'[34]

Oedipus – for the purposes of this discussion we should set aside the question of whether he is to blame for killing another human being – did perform an act which resulted in the death of his father, but is not responsible for patricide since his ignorance of the fact that the man he killed was his father is excusable. Thus, Aristotle seems to be drawing a distinction between what was done and why it was done, such that the 'why' question has an effect on the evaluation of what was done and may be more crucial in deciding whether to apportion blame.[35] Oedipus is an involuntary agent, since he acted in ignorance of the thing (including person) that is affected by his act, like Merope in Aristotle's example.[36]

This Aristotelian emphasis on knowledge of particulars and its crucial role in characterizing acts as voluntary is not shared by all commentators in the area. For example, Nagel argues that 'there is a morally significant difference between reckless driving and manslaughter',[37] but I think that this conclusion arises from a confusion between legal punishment and moral blame. When discussing these cases, Nagel introduces legal considerations, for example reckless drivers 'would probably be *prosecuted* for manslaughter'[38] and 'the *penalty* for attempted murder is less than that for successful murder'.[39] However, legal questions may be answered differently from questions of moral blame, for example if the justification for legal punishment is deterrence, the two issues may be quite separate. The appropriateness of a particular legal punishment should not lead us to draw any conclusions about moral blame, because of the specific nature of the law. In the interests of justice, because of the epistemic difficulties with establishing a person's intentions, the law can only punish cases where there is an established *actus reus*.[40] It is when this legal requirement is applied to cases of fortunate drunk driving that we end up with a result that differs from the decision about moral blame, since it is crucial for the law that the act was not a *legal* crime, a fact which can be morally irrelevant.[41]

Nagel also presents a distorted picture of negligence. In support of the idea that our moral evaluation of an agent will depend on the lucky or unlucky results of his act, he argues: 'The mens rea which could have existed in the absence of any consequences does not exhaust the grounds of moral judgement. Actual results influence culpability or esteem in a large class of unquestionably ethical cases ranging from negligence through political choice.'[42] In support of this view he asks us to examine our intuitions about the following case:

> If one negligently leaves the bath running with the baby in it, one will realize, as one bounds up the stairs towards the bathroom, that if the baby has drowned one has done something awful, whereas if it has not one has merely been careless.[43]

But again, this only makes sense if we accept a legal conception of negligence. Legal negligence involves a failure to comply with an objective standard of conduct, but does not include proof of intention or a specific state of mind.[44] The law may rely on outcomes to determine the severity of the punishment for different offences, but it is not immediately clear why morality should do so as well.[45] In the Nagel baby-in-the-bath case, both the lucky and the unlucky agents have been careless, regardless of the result. The unlucky result is awful, but our evaluation of the culpability of the agents for their act of leaving the baby unattended should not be affected by the result. What both agents are morally culpable for is putting the baby's life under unnecessary, easily avoidable and reasonably foreseeable danger; whether this danger was averted due to luck or not is not morally relevant for the evaluation of these two agents.[46] This does not mean that actual results never influence our moral judgements, rather that they are not relevant in this case. Since what makes this case an example of moral luck is the argument that the lucky results are part of the moral evaluation, if I am correct in arguing that this is a mistake, then this is not a genuine case of moral luck.[47]

I take it that a similar point about the importance of moral luck is being made by Lewis when he observes the injustice involved in punishing more leniently an offender who maliciously intended and set out to kill but was prevented, due to bad luck, in achieving his aim, than an offender similar to the first in all respects apart from being successful. He observes that:

> The most intelligible cases of moral luck are those in which the lucky and the unlucky alike are disposed to become wicked if tempted, and only the unlucky are tempted. But then, however alike they may have been originally, the lucky and the unlucky do end up different in how they are and in how they act. Not so for the luck of hitting or missing [a murder victim]. It makes no difference to how they act.[48]

This approach makes sense because it takes the act to be an event which is complete once the agent has done his part and evaluates him morally for that act and not for anything extrinsic that may then intervene to change that act. Although Nagel objects to an approach which results in paring down 'each act to its morally essential core, an inner act of pure will assessed by motive and intention',[49] the Aristotelian picture need not lead to such an extreme. Equally, however, we should not accept the other extreme – Nagel's option of allowing factors out of the agent's control to influence moral evaluations. One extreme proposes an unrealistic picture of moral evaluation of the agent distinct from the world in which he operates, whereas the other wants to judge him on account of happenings over which he has no control. The answer is found somewhere in the middle between two extremes and can not be identified without reference to particular cases.

So far, then, I have shown that there are good grounds in Aristotle for responding to the possibility of situational luck and luck in how one's actions turn out. His response to the problem of moral luck centres around the idea of the virtuous agent. The virtuous agent will have the necessary perception and prudence to make the best of a bad situation should he find himself in one as a result of factors out of his control. These faculties will also help him predict how a situation will turn out and the results of his actions.

However, since the acquisition of virtue, through the development of perception and prudence, takes time and effort, most agents faced with moral situations affected by luck will not be fully virtuous, but rather continent. It is a characteristic of continence that it is a weak and fragile state and as a result the continent agent may lapse into incontinence from time to time as his contrary desires drag him in the opposite direction from his reason. Furthermore, the continent agent's ability to deliberate and his clarity of thought will not be as developed as those of the fully virtuous agent, and as a result he will be more prone to mistakes. Moral luck, therefore, will have a more profound effect on the continent (and incontinent) than on the fully virtuous agent.

Furthermore, we have seen that considerations about luck are relevant when elements in the situation the agent is faced with are not under his control, but luck is also instrumental in placing the agent in such a situation in the first place. As we saw in Nagel's example of Germany during the Second World War, some agents are faced with morally difficult tests, whereas others avoid them, simply as a matter of luck.

I have argued previously that the virtuous agent will make the best of a bad situation and as a result it should not matter greatly whether he is tested often and to a great degree, as his virtue is a permanent and strong disposition which will hold under all sorts of pressures. However, this is not the case with the less-than-fully-virtuous agent. For, the continent agent who is lucky enough not to have been faced with the Nazi moral test will find it easier to remain continent, whereas the unlucky continent agent will be severely tested and probably fail. The collaborator's case is so perplexing because we want to hold the German responsible for what he did, even though we recognize that a number of other agents would have done the same thing in his place, but were fortunate enough not to have to face the problem.

What is disquieting about the above case is that any one of a number of other agents would have acted likewise had they been unlucky enough to be faced with this situation. The continent agent faced with the Nazi test failed and became incontinent and perhaps even vicious. The English continent agent remained continent, but only because of his good luck. How can we then praise the English agent for something that was outside his control, and blame the German for succumbing to the test that others would have failed as well? We may accept that the fully virtuous agent would have made the best out of a bad situation had he found himself in Nazi Germany, like Oscar Schindler, but the apprentice craftsman – the merely continent agent – is unable to cope with the bad material and turns into a bad craftsman as a matter of luck. The 'bad craftsman', that is the continent man who is still learning to be moral, will fail the moral test and lapse into incontinence or even vice. He will fail the test of having to deal with an extremely difficult moral situation since he will not be mature enough to respond to such a difficult test. As a result he will not only fail this specific test, but this failure will have negative repercussions for his overall development as a moral agent.

Aristotle seems to be aware of such considerations when he points out that: 'it is possible on the one hand to have such a disposition as to succumb even to those temptations to which most men are superior, or on the other hand to conquer even those to which most men succumb'.[50] However, many moral tests occur *before* we have fully established dispositions. Again from Aristotle: 'every formed disposition of the soul realises its full nature in relation to and in dealing with that class of objects by which it is its nature to be corrupted or improved'.[51] We can assume that if the relevant class of objects is not available or not available at the right time and in the right way, then the corresponding disposition will not be developed. Again, two agents who start from an equal footing in terms of moral strength may progress or fail to progress in their moral development solely because of factors outside their control. If the two moral agents are like two delicate plants, one of which is fortunate in receiving tender care, mild weather conditions, cover and protection, and so on whereas the other is neglected, exposed to the elements, grown in poor soil, and so on, it is easy to see that one plant will flourish whereas the other will perish.

One more idea emerges from this discussion. Aristotle has been accused of being elitist because some of his virtues are only available to those with material goods or a high social position. The position that external goods are necessary for virtue (or for the exercise of certain virtues) has been rejected by other philosophers[52] possibly because of the implication of making morality dependent on external contingencies, but seems to be part of Aristotelian ethics: 'Nevertheless it is evident that eudaimonia stands in need of good things from outside, as we have said: for it is impossible or difficult to do fine things without resources',[53] and 'Most people suppose that the eudaimon life is the fortunate life, or not without good fortune; and no doubt correctly. For without the external goods, which are in the control of luck, it is not possible to be eudaimon.'[54]

Aristotle's choice of virtues seems to be influenced by his picture of the Athenian gentleman, who was well off and led a particular lifestyle. The virtues of liberality – a virtue in the field of giving and receiving money; magnificence – dealing in large amounts of money; and magnanimity – dealing in the field of public honour are directly related with the possession of material goods and with a particular conception of society and what is honourable within a specific culture. Similarly some virtuous activities, namely perfect friendship, are also dependent on contingent factors as they require the availability of appropriate friends. The discussion of such virtues has prompted commentators to argue that Aristotle has a contempt for the morality of artisans or barbarians[55] and to claim that 'Aristotle's social bias is unmistakable.'[56]

This interpretation of Aristotle, which is quite difficult to resist, seems to imply that if one has the bad luck to be born in the wrong country or in the wrong social position, then virtue (or at least full virtue) is beyond his reach. However, given that we accept this as a correct interpretation of Aristotle, it is not immediately clear that this should be an objection to his theory. Aristotle cannot be held accountable for describing how things are and if it is the case that opportunities for moral development are open to the influences of luck, it cannot be the philosopher's fault if he points this out. If Aristotelian virtues are elitist, this may be connected with an unfortunate fact about the human condition, namely, that attaining virtue is not open to everyone and success or failure is not entirely in the hands of the individual agent. Under this interpretation, not only is moral luck an unavoidable part of the human condition, but under some versions of this account this is far from being an *unfortunate* fact about the human condition.[57] As we have seen, Nussbaum sees moral luck as a positive feature of the human condition. She identifies exactly the same features which others find worrying in such a conception of moral luck, but sees them as enriching, empowering and essential features of a fruitful life. So, Aristotle's account may be elitist, but this may be because it is an accurate account of the features of human moral life and this need not even be something we should be afraid of or an influence we try to eliminate from human moral life.

Also, it is important to note, by way of mitigating possible criticisms of Aristotle, that he does not claim that the possession of external goods is synonymous with virtue. On the great-souled man, Aristotle says:

> But in reality only the good man ought to be honoured, although he that has both virtue and fortune (external goods)[58] is esteemed still more worthy of honour, whereas those who possess the goods of

fortune without virtue are not justified in claiming high worth, and cannot correctly be styled great-souled, since true worth and greatness of soul cannot exist without complete virtue.[59]

So, external goods on their own do not necessarily imply virtue, even though they and the actions that result from possessing them (e.g. giving away to charity) may be admired by the general public. True greatness of soul requires virtue as well as possession of external good. The exercise of some virtues then requires external goods, but the possession of external goods is no guarantee of virtue.

Another area in which luck plays a role is the case where an agent has firmly established dispositions, but luck affects the opportunities that he has for displaying them. An agent may never have had the opportunity to display the virtue of courage and thus earn the praise which we bestow on another agent who, due to luck, was faced with a situation demanding a courageous response and responded well. If for the purposes of the example we assume that courage is displaying the appropriate amount of fear in situations of just war, then it is plausible that some agents will never be faced with just wars and will never exhibit their virtue. Whereas some agents are required, due to contingencies, to deal with moral problems which are far too difficult for them, other agents are not given the opportunity to act from their firm dispositions. Again this is a case where situational luck plays a significant role as it affects the opportunities for action.

A small aside is necessary here on the importance of *acting* in Aristotelian theory. I have argued already that a theory of character is also a theory of action. However, I think it is a mistake to argue that an agent can only have a particular virtue if it is displayed in action. It is true that we draw inferences about the character traits possessed by agents from their acts. However, an agent who never finds himself in circumstances which require acting in accordance with a particular virtue and therefore never exhibits this virtue, does not necessarily lack this virtue altogether. Some commentators[60] argue that for Aristotle there cannot be virtue without action, and appeal to passages such as the following: 'Nor anyone would desire life for the pleasure of sleep either; for what is the difference between slumbering without being awakened from the first day till the last of a thousand or any number of years, and living a vegetable existence?',[61] and,

> Now we stated that happiness is not a certain disposition of character; since if it were it might be possessed by a man who passed the whole of

his life asleep, living the life of a vegetable, or by one who was plunged in the deepest misfortune. If then we reject this as unsatisfactory, and feel bound to class happiness rather as some form of activity . . .'[62]

However, such passages deal with extreme conditions where the agent does not act at all. The case before us is less extreme; the agent is not presented with suitable opportunities for acting in accordance with a certain virtue, he can still display his other virtues. So, although it is generally true that to have a character trait is to act in accordance with it, it is not necessarily true that lack of action implies lack of a particular character trait.

Another variation on this theme is the case where the agent possesses the virtue and it is appropriate that he should act in accordance with it, but circumstances prevent him from acting, for example he is physically prevented from acting. In such cases the agent remains virtuous as it was his intention to act, and he did everything within his power to turn his reasoning into action, but since the act was prevented his *eudaimonia*[63] may be disturbed. For how can he be fully *eudaimon* when he sees the demands of virtue go unfulfilled?

One more point needs to be made with respect to the virtuous agent's immunity to luck. I have argued that the fully virtuous agent is afforded a measure of immunity from luck, because of his developed ability to reason and his established and firm dispositions to put the results of his reasoning into action. However, even this qualified immunity from moral luck is not unassailable. Aristotle argues that in extreme cases, even virtuous agents can be excused for being affected by bad luck; 'the happy man can never become miserable – although he cannot be entirely happy if he falls in with fortunes like those of Priam'.[64]

There is some controversy about how this passage ought to be interpreted. Ross argues that Priam's fortunes cannot diminish his *eudaimonia*, but can diminish his *makariotés*, his contentment and enjoyment in being *eudaimon*.[65] However, this account has been challenged by Nussbaum on the grounds that the words *eudaimon* and *makarios* are used interchangeably in the text to refer to the virtuous man and there is nowhere any indication that an agent can possess one without possessing the other.[66] Her interpretation of the example of Priam is that *eudaimonia* needs external goods as it is impossible to do fine things without resources.

Before examining the implications of this exception it is worth pointing out that Priam is not an example of a virtuous agent faced with extreme bad luck as Nussbaum presumes him to be and takes Ross to be accepting.[67] The text should not be translated as 'Priam's luck', but rather as 'the luck of a Priam'. The difference is that the first translation identifies Priam as a person, whereas the second uses him as a by-word for bad luck, which seems to be closer to the meaning of the original.[68]

In any case, this observation does not prevent us from accepting Nussbaum's point about the uses of *eudaimon* and *makarios*. If she is correct, then the virtuous agent is affected by luck in a very fundamental way. The virtuous agent who is affected by extreme bad luck of the type encountered by Priam is less *eudaimon* now, not because he is more 'miserable' as a side effect of his bad luck, but rather because he has lost the external elements necessary for exercising his virtue. According to Nussbaum, Priam lost his city, his sons and finally his life, and thus it was impossible for him to exercise his function in life, which was to govern. Similarly, if the virtuous agent loses the external goods necessary for the exercise of his virtue, then he cannot be fully *eudaimon*. Under such conditions of extreme bad luck, virtue is devastatingly vulnerable to luck, since to be virtuous involves acting virtuously and the bad luck in this case means that action is impossible. Aristotle's recognition that we are creatures who have to operate within the constraints of the world, and who have to be judged according to the actions they perform, coupled with his implicit acceptance of the randomness and uncontrollability of luck highlight the vulnerability of the moral life.

Finally, there is one more type of case in which the influence of luck is apparent – that of moral dilemmas. Williams identifies moral dilemmas as cases where I ought to do each of two things, but I cannot do both.[69] Moral dilemmas create problems because they present a picture of conflicting 'oughts' such that the agent discovers that one of them does not apply. Prior to Williams it was expected that an adequate moral theory would not allow for genuine moral dilemmas because of the logical force of the 'ought'.[70] Williams reverses this line of thought by arguing that there are genuine moral dilemmas, and if a theory does not account for this it is because the theory is inadequate and unrealistic. According to this analysis, then, even virtuous agents are affected by moral dilemmas, since there is no right answer such that the rejected option is not in some sense regrettable. The 'material' that the agent has to work with is such that there is no way out of the problem that does not carry a moral cost.

The case of Agamemnon is a case of a moral dilemma. Agamemnon was faced with a choice between killing his daughter at the command of the gods, or allowing his army to fall into disarray and fail to sail for Troy in order to recover his brother's wife. The king was faced with two conflicting obligations: an obligation to his daughter as her father and an obligation to his soldiers as their leader, in a situation such that satisfying one obligation would mean violating the other. It is difficult to say with certainty what Aristotle would expect the virtuous agent to do here.

Agamemnon finds himself in this situation due to bad luck, so, assuming he is a virtuous agent, he ought to make the best of a bad situation. He is not compelled as in the more straightforward case of physical force, but perhaps we could say that he is forced to kill his daughter through fear of something else. It may be that specific answers are not available and that one has to be vague until faced with particulars.

Such a vague and, it could be objected, uninformative answer is not inconsistent with Aristotle's whole approach to ethics. Since he has warned us that his account will be inadequate because of the very imprecise nature of ethics,[71] we cannot accuse him for not providing a more specific answer. Having said that, there are two more passages in the *Nicomachean Ethics* which may guide us in this decision. The first establishes the importance of the many over the one:

> For even if the good of the community coincides with that of the individual, it is clearly a greater and more perfect thing to achieve and preserve that of a community; for while it is desirable to secure what is good in the case of an individual, to do so in the case of a people or a state is something finer and more sublime.[72]

The other passage can be taken to show Aristotle's support of Agamemnon's choice. It is the only mention of Agamemnon in the *Nicomachean Ethics* and worth quoting at length:

> in each of these types of constitution we find a sort of friendship, to the same extent as there is justice. That of a king for his subjects consists in outstanding beneficence; because he does good to his subjects (assuming that, being good himself, he is concerned to promote their welfare, like a shepherd caring for his flock – which is why Homer called Agamemnon 'shepherd of the people'). A father's affection is also of this nature, but there is a difference in magnitude of the benefits; for the father is responsible for the child's existence, which is considered to be the greatest good of all and for its upbringing and education. These benefits are also attributed to ancestors. Also by nature a father is qualified to rule his children, and ancestors their descendants, and a king his subjects. These friendships involve an excess; which is why parents are honoured as well. So in these relations justice is not the same on both sides, but is in accordance with merit; for this is true of friendship also.[73]

Aristotle's mention of Agamemnon as an example of a ruler who under-stood the outstanding beneficence required by a ruler for his subjects in the same paragraph as the discussion of the special character of friendship between parents and children shows Aristotle's awareness of the difficulty of Agamemnon's dilemma and his approval of the king's final solution.[74]

Interesting though these passages may be, they do not provide conclu-sive evidence for Aristotle's possible answer to moral dilemmas. In general there seem to be several strategies open in dealing with moral dilemmas:

1. One is to deny the existence of moral dilemmas. There is always a right answer, even if it seems very difficult to identify it.
2. Another is to see moral dilemmas as presenting us with undecidable questions. There is no right answer as the alternatives are terrible[75] and presumably agents are simply extremely unlucky to come across such situations.
3. Yet another is to allow for disagreements between two agents faced with the *same* situation. In such cases, both agents are right in their different solutions to the same case.[76]
4. Finally, another solution is to allow for disagreement between two agents as to the right solution, accepting that both solutions are right, but that no two agents are ever faced with the same situation.

One further distinction with regard to moral dilemmas is whether by 'the right choice' one understands a choice that is the best, given the situation, but which unavoidably has a great cost in the alternative forsaken, or whether by 'the right choice' makes the loss of the alternative forsaken negligible simply by being right.

From the limited evidence of the discussion of Agamemnon, it seems that Aristotle's view on moral dilemmas may have been that there is a correct answer to moral dilemmas, but that it varies according to the particulars of the situation and that it is very difficult to find. Ultimately, Aristotle's answer to the problem of moral dilemmas, following his general approach to ethics, can only be given if we have knowledge of the particulars of each case.

> Sometimes indeed men are actually praised for deeds of this 'mixed' class, namely when they submit to some disgrace or pain as the price of some great and noble object; though if they do so without any such motive they are blamed, since it is contemptible to submit to a great disgrace with no advantage or only a trifling one in view. In some cases again, such submission though not praised is condoned,

when a man does something wrong through fear of penalties that impose too great a strain on human nature, and that no one could endure. Yet there seem to be some acts which a man cannot be compelled to do, and rather than do them he ought to submit to the most terrible death: for instance, we think it ridiculous that Alcmaeon in Euripides' play is compelled by certain threats to murder his mother! But it is sometimes difficult to decide how far we ought to go in choosing to do a given act rather than suffer a given penalty, or in enduring a given penalty rather than commit a given action; and it is still more difficult to abide by our decision when made, since in most of such dilemmas the penalty threatened is painful and the deed forced upon us dishonourable, which is why praise and blame are bestowed according as we do or do not yield to such compulsion.[77]

In short, the influence of moral luck in cases of dilemmas cannot be known in advance of knowing the particulars of the case. Furthermore, it may well be that when faced with a moral dilemma, it is impossible for the virtuous agent to emerge with his *eudaimonia* intact.[78] As with the case of Priam's bad luck, some extreme circumstances are such as to affect even the *eudaimonia* of the virtuous. Some strains are too great for human nature to endure and some disgraces too unbearable, even if the alternative is even worse. Bearing such disgraces and enduring such strains may mean that the agent cannot emerge unscathed.

3.4   Conclusion

The influence of luck is evident and pervasive in Aristotle. Constitutive luck affects the raw material an agent has to work with. Even at this early stage some agents may be entirely doomed in that their natural constitution is overwhelmingly and unavoidably evil. Even if most of us have a mixture of good and bad natural tendencies to work with, early childhood influences, habits, teachers and so on guide our development, and the availability and quality of these influences is entirely a matter of luck. We have seen how, due to the gradual nature of Aristotelian moral development, agents on the road to virtue are more vulnerable to luck than perfectly virtuous agents. Situational and developmental luck may have devastating consequences for the future development of continent and incontinent agents, while some agents altogether avoid difficult moral decisions because of their good luck. Difficult and tempting circumstances one comes across, opportunities for displaying virtue, the availability of ingredients necessary for virtue, early influences and so on all play a crucial role in moral development and are all outside the agent's control. Questions of voluntariness, ignorance and negligence also relate to the degree to which agents can be expected to control situations. Fully virtuous agents, as opposed to merely continent or incontinent agents, are afforded a certain immunity from luck, because of the settled and stable state of their character, but even they are subject to luck under extreme circumstances and possibly when faced with moral dilemmas.

Both motives and outcomes are important in the moral evaluation of agents for Aristotle, but there are possible exceptions. We saw how the naturally virtuous agent's actions result in good outcomes even though he has not truly chosen virtue for its own sake. Although the naturally virtuous person is not accorded proper praise as his motives are not true, he is still to be praised for the results of his action. On the other hand, Aristotelian theory is a theory of action, but single attempts to act may be praiseworthy even if the outcome of the act is not what was expected. Thus, bad resultant luck may affect the acts of agents, without necessarily affecting their evaluation. Like many issues in Aristotelian theory, though, again this is a question of degree. Extreme bad resultant luck can be as devastating to the agent's chances for *eudaimonia* as other kinds of luck.

We also saw how, for Aristotle, the influence of resultant luck is limited, as he does not accept some cases as genuine cases of moral luck. The examples of the drunken drivers, the attempted murderers and the baby in the bathtub are re-described so that what we hold the agent responsible for is what was voluntarily chosen at the time at which the act was performed, rather than any accidental outcomes.

It seems, then, that constitutive, developmental, situational and, to a lesser extent, resultant luck can affect the agent's development and his character. What remains to be seen is whether this constitutes a problem for Aristotelian moral theory and how it affects responsibility.[79]

4
Aristotle and Reason

4.1 Introduction

We have seen so far that luck is allowed to play a role in Aristotelian theory. So, for Aristotle, luck is part of the moral life, but it remains to be seen how big a part luck plays in the moral life. One possibility is that luck is all there is to morality and morality is simply a collection of lucky instances. Following Nussbaum,[1] I shall call this the 'luck view'. However, Aristotle wants to resist this possibility. As Nussbaum puts it:

> The luck view is rejected not because it has been found to be at odds with scientific fact about the way things are in the universe, discovered by some value-neutral procedure, but because it strikes a false note, i.e. is too much at odds with our other beliefs, and specifically with our evaluative beliefs about what sort of life would be worth living. For we believe that human life is worth the living only if a good life can be secured by effort, and if the relevant sort of effort lies within the capabilities of most people.[2]

This rejection of the view that all there is to morality comes down to luck appeals to our fundamental worries about the possibility of moral luck. This is perhaps one of the points that Williams wanted to make when he said that the term 'moral luck' is an oxymoron. If morality comes down to luck, then it is not easy to see what meaning our lives have. All our efforts, our striving and our choices are essentially meaningless, as well as all our judgements of others. The idea that luck attacks the way we hold other people responsible is a fundamental problem, but not the only big problem raised by considerations like the 'luck view'. If luck is all-pervasive, then it attacks the idea that human lives have meaning. If anything we do could turn out either way, regardless of our efforts and because of factors outside our control, then why should we try to do anything? Even more fundamentally, what we 'choose' to do, the things we care about and what moves us are not really down to us and therefore we do not have any real choice. With lack of control comes lack of meaning in what we choose and what we do, and ultimately lack of importance or significance in what we do and who we are:

> if it is better to be happy as a result of one's own efforts than by the gift of fortune, it is reasonable to suppose that this is how happiness is won; in as much as in the world of nature things have a natural tendency to be ordered in the best possible way, and the same is true of the products of art, and of causation of any kind, and especially the highest. Whereas that the greatest and noblest of all things should be left to fortune would be too contrary to the fitness of things.[3]

It seems to me that what Aristotle is saying here is that it is simply not fitting that the good life, the best life an agent can have, should be left to contingent factors, so that it can be acquired by people who do not deserve it. The problem here is a conceptual one: How can we make sense of morality if all there is to it is luck? Therefore it must be the case that there is more to morality than just luck.

These are fundamental philosophical problems, to which there are no (easy) answers. However, they motivate the desire to see morality as more than just luck. For those who are happy with the view of morality as reducible to luck, there is no more that can be said. This issue, that morality *must* be, and *has* to be, more than luck, is not really open to discussion, as it is not possible to persuade those who do not see this point to change their minds.[4] The force of this idea, that is that there must be more to morality than just luck, is such that it informs our understanding of what morality, choice and the voluntary are.

We need to be clear, then, that the discussion of Aristotle that has proceeded is only one aspect of his theory. We have focused on ways in which Aristotelian ethics recognizes, accommodates and accepts luck, but this is not the whole story. This acceptance of the influence of luck is not whole-hearted or unqualified. This chapter will try to present the rest of the Aristotelian story when it comes to the relationship between luck and morality.

4.2 Immunity to luck

If then the influence of luck is not comprehensive, there must be some area of human endeavour which is immune to luck; and that is the function of reason and the intellect. The idea that human life is subject to luck is only part of the picture, the other part is a view of human beings as rational beings, capable of voluntary choices, governed by reason, a part of human morality which is not influenced by luck; 'Where there is most insight and reason, there is the least luck; and where there is the most luck there is the least insight.'[5]

Reason is a defence against the contingencies which affect the human life. We have already, in the previous chapters, come across some hints that this must be so. In the previous discussion we saw how the fully virtuous agent can resist some influences of luck which prove insurmountable objects for those less than fully virtuous. The reason why the virtuous agent can do so is because he has developed fully the capacity to perceive the morally salient elements of a situation as well as the ability to exercise his practical wisdom which underlies all the virtues. These two capacities, perception and practical wisdom, which are functions of reason, allow him to 'see' more clearly and to judge more clearly, thus avoiding or overcoming the problems raised by moral luck.

The picture of the moral agent, then, is one of two sides making one whole: on one side human beings are creatures subject to luck, on the other we are rational creatures capable of overcoming the influences of luck. Nussbaum's picture of humans as plants, receptive to external influences outside their control, is now enlarged to include humans as rational agents: 'Neither inert objects nor perfected gods, neither simply pushed around from without or spontaneously self-moving, we all reach out, being incomplete, for things in the world. That is the way our movements are caused.'[6] Humans are an amalgam of reason and elements open to luck. We must resist not only the view that all moral life is completely and comprehensively subject to luck, but also the opposite picture that morality is completely immune to luck.

We have seen why the 'luck view' is unattractive – as it leads to a life devoid of all meaning and importance – but why is the opposite view unattractive? Why should not we aspire to a life as 'perfected gods', fully escaping the influence of luck? For Nussbaum this view is equally unattractive: 'If we imagine the life of a needless and divine being . . . we find that most of the central human ethical values will not be valuable or even comprehensible in such a life',[7] and

What we find valuable depends essentially on what we need and how we are limited. The goodness and beauty of human value cannot be comprehended or seen apart from that context. And the point is not merely epistemological: the persons and actions we now call just and generous simply would not *be* valuable in an animal or divine context.[8]

We should not aspire to a divine perspective as that perspective is not the human perspective and misses out on all the things which make a human life important. The perspective of a needless being, perfectly immune to luck, is a perspective from which it is difficult or even impossible to understand value. The very possibility of luck makes human life rich, interesting and valuable. Luck is a double-edged sword then; on the one hand threatening the very things we value, but on the other hand allowing us to be the kind of beings who *can* value. To eliminate the influence of luck would be to eliminate value from our lives.

4.3   Reason

Appealing as this picture may be, we are still left with at least one really pressing question: Given that we are both plants and rational beings, both subject to luck and expected to be in one sense immune to luck, how do we make decisions about responsibility and the attribution of praise and blame? This is a fundamental question that goes hand in hand with any exploration of human morality and which cannot be easily set aside. How do we attribute responsibility to beings that can be at any time the subject of luck as plants, or the object of reason as rational beings?

So far I have tried not to prejudge the conception of human beings as both plants and rational beings, but now it becomes more pressing to understand what we mean by this. How should we understand this creature which is both a plant and a rational creature? Do we all share in both aspects, one side becoming more dominant while the other loses ground? Or are the two sides more closely intertwined? To come to any conclusion on this question and the wider question of attributing responsibility we have to look in more detail into the role of reason in Aristotelian theory.

One way in which we can understand the role of reason in moral theory is to assume that it is entirely detached from the influences of luck. So that although a large part of the human life is open to influences from luck, reason is not. Reason is then a defence against the contingencies of the world, a mechanism through which one can overcome situational, developmental and constitutive influences. According to such a picture, Raskolnikov and Roy share in this ability to reason equally; and the explanation why one agent overcomes impediments to moral action, while the other does not, must be that the former exercised his reason while the latter did not. What distinguishes the moral agent from the agent who failed in his struggle against contrary contingencies is an act of reason, equally available to all and whose exercise is a matter of choice. As this ability to reason is not affected by luck, presumably it is equally available to all moral agents, at any time of their lives, to countenance or encourage the influence of luck.

This picture of the function of reason as completely immune to luck will be examined in greater detail in Chapters 6 and 7, within a discussion of the Kantian understanding of morality; but whether it succeeds or fails as a plausible picture of the moral life is not a pressing concern here, as this understanding of reason is *not* Aristotle's understanding. Why it is not an Aristotelian picture may become clearer if we look at what is involved in Aristotelian moral reasoning.

Virtue is a settled disposition, lying in a mean relative to the individual and the situation, determined by the right reason and by what the prudent man would use to determine it.[9] As we have briefly seen, Aristotelian ethics does not rely on principles in order to determine moral questions, unlike, it is argued, deontological and consequentialist theories.[10] What it relies on instead of a principle or formula is an ability to 'see' the relevant features of a moral case and an ability to judge the relevance and weight of these features in making moral decisions.[11] Moral decision-making is a complex and unpredictable business, and this method of making decisions tries to capture the essential unpredictability, variety and complexity of the moral world. A particular feature that is not only relevant but also crucial in one's deliberations in one case may be entirely irrelevant in another. For example, the skin colour of an employee who charges his employer with racial discrimination is a relevant feature in deciding this case, but the skin colour of a person drowning is entirely irrelevant in deciding whether to save him or not. Indeed the specifics of each case and their relative importance can be so varied and complex that it is impossible to capture them in a rule or principle. Rules may well operate as 'rules of thumb', and can be relied upon for some tasks in moral education, but they can never capture every aspect of what virtue means or requires.[12]

Moreover, the ability to judge the relative weight and importance of all these features of situations, as well as how different virtues apply to each case and relate to each other, is also something that cannot be captured in finite fixed rules. The ability to perceive the relevant features of a situation and the practical wisdom to see how they relate to each other and come to a decision are part of what it is to be a virtuous man (the other part is having trained and habituated desires that facilitate the smooth flow from reason to action).

Since these abilities, perception and practical wisdom cannot be captured in a principle, they cannot be taught *solely* by imparting principles. Principles or rules can be used to help the young and operate as rules of thumb, since generalizations with respect to the virtues are possible. However, as with all generalizations, the important part is to be able to recognize exceptions and special cases. The expertise to see beyond the rules of thumb to the particulars of the situation is what is required of the mature moral agent.[13]

So, if these abilities are essential for virtue, how are they developed in the student of virtue? An important part of Aristotelian moral development is the availability of the right role model. The virtuous agent can operate as a role model for the student of virtue as he is an illustration of virtue in action. For the student of virtue the road to virtue is not always clear, and the availability of an appropriate guide can be crucial. It is plausible to assume that the problems posed by some moral cases will be easier than those posed by others. With the proper guidance we can ensure that the student of virtue is initially confronted with easy – in the sense of clear-cut – moral problems until his understanding of the virtues and what is required increases and he is better equipped to deal with more complicated and demanding cases. The moral problems the student is faced with are crucial then, as they affect the student's knowledge. 'The known' can be understood in two ways: what is known to us and what is knowable in itself. What is known to us is obviously dependent on the kind of experiences we have had, so the cases one comes across will affect one's knowledge. To find out 'the that' the student must come across cases where this applies and where that this is the case is pointed out to him:

> Perhaps then for us at all events it is proper to start from what is known to us. This is why in order to be a competent student of the right and the just, and in short of the topics of politics in general, the pupil is bound to have been well trained in his habits. For the starting point or first principle is the fact that a thing is so; if this be satisfactorily ascertained, there will be no need to also know the reason why it is so.[14]

But how does all this relate to reason and luck? Well, according to this picture the ability to reason morally is an ability which we develop; an ability which we can develop well or badly according to influences which are not always or not entirely under one's control. Whether the student of virtue will come across a suitable role model is a matter of luck, whether he will encounter easy moral problems is a matter of luck and whether the situations he finds himself in will lead to greater understanding or greater confusion is a matter of luck. So even if we assume that the ability to reason morally is not influenced by constitutive factors (a rather far-fetched assumption), its development is influenced by developmental and situational luck. To digress briefly, I am assuming that the ability to reason morally is not affected by constitutive factors in order to show that accepting this contentious point is not necessary for showing that reason is affected by luck in other respects within Aristotelian theory. I think that since perception and practical wisdom are abilities, the capacity to develop them must be influenced by constitutive factors, but I am willing to set this point aside.

4.4 Choice and the voluntary

This picture of the development of reason and its vulnerability to luck is a correct picture of Aristotelian ethics in that it is derived from established and well-documented ideas from Aristotle's work. It is still not a complete picture, however. There seems to be another side to the function of reason which becomes evident in numerous passages discussing the importance of choice and the voluntary for virtue. I will quote all these passages together even though they are derived from different discussions because they all share a particular perspective:

> But honour after all seems too superficial to be the good for which we are seeking; since it appears to depend on those who confer it more than on him upon whom it is conferred, whereas we intrinsically feel that the good must be something proper to its possessor and not easy to be taken away from him.[15]

> it is absurd to blame external things, instead of blaming ourselves for falling an easy prey to their attractions [pleasures]; or to take the credit of our noble deeds to ourselves, while putting the blame for our disgraceful ones upon the temptations of pleasure.[16]

> We deliberate about things in which our agency operates but does not always produce the same results.[17]

a man is the origin of his actions and that the province of deliberation is to discover actions within one's own power to perform.[18]

But if it is in our power to do and to refrain from doing right and
wrong, and if, as we saw, being good or bad is doing right or wrong,
it consequently depends on us whether we are virtuous or vicious.[19]

By a voluntary action, as has been said before [Book III], I mean any
action within the agent's own control which he performs knowingly,
that is, without being in ignorance of the person affected, the instru-
ment employed, and the result . . . ; and in each of these respects both
accident and compulsion must be excluded.[20]

What these passages have in common is an outlook on moral
decision-making according to which agency, choice and control play
central roles, according to which an agent's actions belong properly to
him, and according to which, praise and blame are merited by the agent
because of what he has chosen to do. And this picture of the moral life
is at odds with the influence of luck.

According to Aristotle, there are two elements to virtue and virtuous
action, namely: 'Hence in as much as moral virtue is a disposition of the
mind in regard to choice, and choice is deliberate desire, it follows that,
if the choice is to be good, both the principle must be true and the desire
right, and the desire must pursue the same things as principle affirms',[21]
and again: 'Now the cause of action . . . is choice, and the cause of choice
is desire and reasoning directed to some end. Hence choice necessarily
involves both intellect or thought and a certain disposition of character.'[22] Of the two elements that make up virtue, we saw in the previous
chapters how desires and dispositions with respect to desires are influenced by luck. The original material agents have to deal with in terms of
constitutive make-up is affected by luck, as well as the development of
the dispositions which is influenced by developmental and situational
luck. At the time it seemed that the difference between what is naturally
available to us and virtue could be found in choice supported by reason.
However, there is now good reason to suppose that the development
of this faculty is also subject to luck. Unless we suppose that we are
all born with a fully developed capacity to reason, an implausible
assumption within the wider context of Aristotelian theory, we must
accept that the way different agents develop their reasoning abilities
will be influenced by luck. So how do we reconcile this picture of the
moral life as comprehensively intertwined with luck, with the above
quotations?

A clue as to how we can understand this perplexing situation, according to which moral development is subject comprehensively to luck, but we can still employ notions such as responsibility and control, may be found in the following quotation: '. . . [the good life] can be attained through some process of study or effort by all persons whose capacity for virtue has not been stunted or maimed'.[23] We can make sense of this passage if we accept that the good life is not available to all. It seems to me that Aristotle is saying that the good life is available only to those who have escaped contrary early influences which could have stunted or maimed their capacity for virtue, who have had all the opportunities to develop in a favourable manner, who have the constitutive make-up necessary to apply themselves and excel at the study of virtue, as well as the opportunities to develop the right dispositions with respect to desires and encouraging influences for the development of their rational powers and so on; if all this is available and favourable then the student of virtue has a chance of sharing the viewpoint of the good. To become virtuous is to share the viewpoint of the good, which must mean to choose and affirm the good for its own sake. This is because to appreciate the good is to appreciate the demands it places on moral beings and the motivational force it exerts on moral beings to act in accordance with it. For those beings, at that stage of sharing the viewpoint of the good, praise, blame, responsibility, control and choice are appropriate notions. And in as much as students of virtue are agents who only have their own point of view at present, but are developing the capacity for coming to see the point of view of the good in the future, they can also be appropriate objects of praise and blame.

However, for those who are subject to extreme bad luck, perhaps this point of view is not available. Unnatural pleasures, or pleasures which become unnatural as a result of arrested development, natural depravity, disease and mental illness, abuse in childhood or habit, are best understood within the sphere of bestiality.[24]

4.5 Conclusion

How should we conclude then on the Aristotelian answer to the problem of moral luck? First, we should recognize that Aristotle never set out to provide an answer to this problem which has been set out in terms of the modern debate. Therefore, we cannot be entirely certain that he would appreciate our understanding of the difficulties raised by moral luck. Having said that, there is good textual evidence that Aristotle perceived at least some of the problems raised by moral luck as issues which he should deal with. For example, the question of whether external goods, the availability of which is subject to luck, are necessary for virtue is directly dealt with by Aristotle. So part of the Aristotelian answer to moral luck can be constructed by direct reference to the text.

Secondly, further answers to moral luck can be constructed from the general approach which Aristotle brings to ethics. As we have often seen, Nussbaum develops the general themes in Aristotelian ethics to answer questions posed more recently. The value of such work is immense and it is certainly possible to discuss issues not directly discussed by Aristotle in an Aristotelian mode or in accordance with the spirit of his theory. However, it is not clear how we should conclude when different parts of Aristotle's work on the same question point in different directions.

Keeping the above in mind, we can come to some tentative conclusions about Aristotle on moral luck. As a general picture, it seems that Aristotle's work is partly characterized by a tension between luck and morality. On the one hand, we have very-well-publicized elements of Aristotelian theory – namely the ideas that the moral life develops in stages; that this development is subject to various influences, for example habituation, training, role models and so on; that the quality of such influences is crucial in terms of the future direction of the agent's character and so on. All these factors are open to influences from various kinds of luck, that is constitutive, developmental, situational and, to a lesser extent, resultant luck. On the other hand, we have a conception of reason that allows agents to have choice over moral decisions and actions – actions which are then described as voluntary and for which the agent is held responsible.

Given that many features which are crucial in terms of character formation are open to luck, it still remains to be seen how we should want to respond to this. One possible response is to try to show why this is a false picture of the human condition. For example, if this picture clashes with our understanding of moral equality, we could charge Aristotle with being elitist (essentially the charge that there is something wrong with the idea that morality is not equally available to all) and turn to some other moral theory for our answers. Or we could accept this picture of moral life as correct, regrettable, but also unavoidable. For example, it may be true that the moral life is vulnerable to luck, and that this goes against our understanding of morality as requiring equality and justice, but as this is a correct picture of how things are we should uphold it and rather reject the understanding of equality and justice as idealistic and inapplicable. A further possibility is to accept the Aristotelian picture as correct, but see this as an advantage rather than a regrettable feature of the human life which might lead us to see equality and justice as unrealistic inspirations. For example, Nussbaum's discussion seems to say: yes, the moral life is subject to luck, but it would not be as rich and valuable if it was not subject to luck, so luck is an essential and non-regrettable feature of the human life.

The Aristotelian answer to how we should respond to this picture of the moral life is not clear, perhaps because Aristotle was not concerned to answer this question that we are forcing upon him. Evidently he believed that the picture of the human life as vulnerable to luck is a plausible one, since he spent so much time developing it, and based much of his theory on it. However, there is a tension evident in Aristotle's work in that he is explicitly rejecting this picture as a complete picture and implicitly putting forward a view of reason and the intellect as, at least, partly independent from luck in order to support his claims on choice and the voluntary. So, control over who we are and what we do is still important for Aristotle. What is not clear is how we are to reconcile these two conflicting pictures of the human life.[25] So the tension between lack of control and morality highlighted in the idea of moral luck is still present in Aristotelian theory and there does not seem to be a way of entirely eliminating this tension.

What is important from this analysis, is to remember that although Aristotle is often cited as the inspiration for the idea that the moral life is subject to luck, this is not a complete picture of his theory. He seems to be very much aware of the need for reason to maintain some independence and control. As we shall see in Chapters 6 and 7, Kant, who is well known for his discussion of reason and morality as immune from luck, is also aware of the possibility of luck affecting the moral life. We will also get another chance to see whether Kant is more successful in resolving the tension between the two approaches to understanding the relationship between morality and luck. However, before we proceed to do this, a brief interlude on the Stoics who have their own unique answer to moral luck.

5
The Stoics

5.1 Introduction

So far we have pieced together Aristotle's response to the problem posed by moral luck. The picture that has emerged is one of the phenomenon of moral luck being accepted and accommodated within moral theory. Moral luck is an unavoidable part of the world human beings live in and of their make-up. Any moral theory, on Aristotle's view, has to recognize this, accept it and try to accommodate it as best it can. We shall now look at a different answer to the question of moral luck: that given by the Stoics.

The reason why this chapter will examine the Stoics is that although there are many similarities between the Stoics and Aristotle,[1] on the question of moral luck the two theories seem to diverge. In fact, as we shall see, the Stoics seem to be much closer to Kant[2] than to Aristotle on this issue. The Stoics' moral theory is often discussed along with that of Aristotle, as the Stoics also have a theory of the virtues and rely on the concept of *eudaimonia*. However, their answer to the problem of moral luck has more in common with Kant than with Aristotle. For Aristotle the road to virtue and the *eudaimon* life is beset by the perils of moral luck and although ultimately the virtuous agent is afforded some protection from luck, this protection is not complete. The Stoics make use of 'virtue' and '*eudaimonia*', but have a conception of the moral life as immune to luck, which prefigures Kant's thoughts on the matter. Although the Stoics follow Aristotle in highlighting the importance and making use of the virtues, they also conceive them as unaffected by luck. In order to understand the Stoics' answer to moral luck, we need to examine their attitude towards the passions and the self-sufficiency of the moral life, as well as their understanding of nature and fatalism. A word of caution though first. A number of different philosophers are classified under the title 'Stoics', but there is no monolithic body of Stoic doctrine. Instead there are a number of different formulations of some basic ideas, some of which are not very compatible with others. Some commentators draw sharp distinctions between the earlier and later Stoics, or between Greek and Roman Stoics. I do not intend to comment on these divisions, but I think it should be noted that any views put forward as representing the Stoics do not fully represent every strand of the theory and might even have been rejected by some particular Stoics. As much as possible I shall try to attribute to particular individuals the ideas discussed here.

5.2   On the passions and the self-sufficiency of the moral life

The Stoics have a completely different attitude to the passions from Aristotle. For Aristotle, the passions are not only an aid to virtue, but a necessary part of the virtuous character. Favourable passions not only help the student of virtue on his way to performing virtuous acts, but are an essential part of these acts themselves. The virtuous agent has not only the right reasoning with respect to virtue, but also the accompanying, appropriate emotions. A virtuous act involves not only the act itself but also requires the agent to have the appropriate emotions towards what he is doing. The idea that the appropriate emotions must accompany the virtuous act is developed in the Aristotelian doctrine of the mean. According to the doctrine of the mean every virtue has two accompanying vices. Although virtue is an extreme with respect to what is excellent, it lies in a mean between two vices, an excessive and a deficient vice. Thus, courage is the virtue, whose accompanying emotion is fear; an excessive amount of fear leads to the vice of cowardice, whereas a deficient amount of fear also leads to the vice of rashness. The virtue of courage requires the appropriate amount of fear being exhibited in each situation, not too much and not too little. Thus, the emotions not only facilitate virtue, since they make its practice flow smoothly from right reason, but are necessary for it, since, for example, to experience no emotion of fear where some fear ought to be displayed would make the agent rash.

This Aristotelian doctrine of *metriopathia* (literally meaning a mean in passions) is to be contrasted with the Stoic *apatheia* (lack of passion). For the Stoics, the passions are a potentially harmful influence that has to be contained before it distorts the moral life.[3] The passions are the result of perversion and the causes of instability:[4] 'Passion, or emotion, is defined by Zeno as an irrational and unnatural movement of the soul, or again as impulse in excess.'[5] The passions cannot be harnessed to do the work of virtue because they are not part of reason nor can they be reliably controlled by reason for they can pull in the opposite direction and distract one from the road to virtue.

> grief or pain they [the Stoics] hold to be an irrational mental contradiction . . . desire or craving is irrational appetency . . . the passion of love is a craving from which good men are free . . . pleasure is an irrational elation at the accruing of what seems to be choiceworthy . . . delight is the mind's propulsion to weakness . . . as there are said to be certain infirmities in the body, as for instance gout and arthritic disorders, so too there is in the soul love of fame, love of pleasure, and the like.[6]

Furthermore, they are 'unnatural' since it is the nature of human beings to be rational and the passions do not share in this rationality.

For the Stoics, then, the passions are not under the agent's control and although recognizing the influence of contingent factors, the Stoics want to limit this influence as much as possible.

> There are certain things whose beginnings are in our power, but which later carry us away by their force and leave us no way of turning back. As when people's bodies are dropped headlong from a height they have no control over themselves and, once thrown down, are unable to hold back or delay, but the irrevocable speed of the fall cuts away all reflection and all second thoughts, and they are not permitted to avoid arriving at a place toward which they would once have been permitted not to go, so the soul – if it hurls itself into anger, love, and the other passions – is not allowed to check its impetus: the very weight and the downward nature of the vices must carry it away and take it to the very bottom.[7]

This is one of the reasons behind their rejection of the passions – a rejection that has many similarities with the later Kantian picture. The Stoics are sceptical of Aristotle's plans to habituate and control the emotions. The passions cannot be harnessed and if they are not fully controlled they will eventually lead to turmoil and disturbance: 'they begin, grow, and run riot'.[8] Habituation, education and reason cannot reliably control the emotions, which once activated cannot easily be diverted from their purpose.[9]

For these reasons the Stoics place little or no emphasis on the motivational role of the passions – in this they prefigure Kant, who was also weary of the emotions – as they might lead to loss of control and the tyranny of passion over reason. The wise Stoic avoids the passions altogether as opposed to the Aristotelian sage who controls and uses them:

> the wise man is passionless, because he is not prone to fall into such infirmity…the wise man is said to be free from vanity; for he is indifferent to good or evil report…all good men are austere or harsh, because they neither have dealings with pleasure themselves nor do they tolerate those who have.[10]

By rejecting the emotions as a part of virtue, the Stoics have already managed to by pass some of the problems that moral luck raised for Aristotelian theory. The habituation and education of the emotions were subject to developmental and situational luck as we saw in the previous chapters. By altogether rejecting the emotions, the Stoics avoid the influence of moral luck in this respect. However, the Stoics can further avoid the influence of moral luck, as the rejection of the passions is only part of a wider picture of the moral life as self-sufficient.

As the moral life is self-sufficient, it cannot rely on unreliable passions; similarly other ingredients considered a necessary part of the moral life by other philosophers are also rejected. Arrington speculates that this conception of a self-sufficient moral life may have arisen from the historical and political background in which the Stoics worked. The Stoics developed their ideas at a time of great unrest and upheaval, a time when everything was uncertain and the future unclear. As a result of this climate of social uncertainty, the Stoics may have been driven to a conception of the moral life which was immune to incidental factors in order to avoid the dangers of their own times.[11]

Whatever the explanation behind the Stoic ideal of a self-sufficient life, this idea shaped their moral theory. Another way of ensuring that the moral life is less vulnerable is to reject the influence of external goods. External goods are not necessary for Stoic *eudaimonia* anymore than the passions that are involved in desiring these goods. Indeed all other goods, apart from virtue, are termed 'indifferents':

> 'Indifferent' is used in two senses: unconditionally, of things which constitute neither to happiness nor unhappiness, as is the case with wealth, reputation, health, strength and the like. For it is possible to

> be happy even without these, though the manner of using them is constitutive of happiness or unhappiness...[12]

> Aristo of Chios [admittedly an extreme Stoic]...said that the end is to live with a disposition of indifference towards what is intermediate between vice and virtue, not retaining any difference at all within that class of things, but being equally disposed towards them all.[13]

The only thing that has real value is virtue:

> And yet what reason is there that he should provide a living? For if it be to support life, life itself is after all a thing indifferent. If it be for pleasure, pleasure too is a thing indifferent. While if it be for virtue, virtue in itself is sufficient to constitute happiness.[14]

This rejection of external goods is quite different from Aristotle's admission that extreme bad luck with respect to the external goods necessary for virtue may result in loss of *eudaimonia* and the conclusion that external goods are necessary for the exercise of some virtues. Von Arnim's collection of Stoic fragments even mentions a quotation which claims that even the sufferings of Priam will not disturb the virtuous Stoic's happiness.[15] This is because the Stoics recognize no value in external goods,[16] such as wealth and honour, or relational goods, such as friends or children. All these goods are collectively classed as 'indifferents'; whether they are available or not, whether they are lost or taken away, should make no difference to the *eudaimonia* of the agent. This is because virtue is the only good and the agent should be indifferent to the possession or loss of everything else.

Although 'indifferents' do not have any real value, distinctions can be made between them:

> So while on the one hand it was sufficiently established that what is moral is alone good, and that what is vicious is alone evil, so on the other these philosophers pronounced that nevertheless distinctions do exist between those things which are without influence upon happiness, so that some of them have positive value, some negative, and some neither. Of those things which deserve to have assigned to them a positive value, they say one class consists of those important enough to be preferred to certain others, health for example, soundness of the senses, freedom from pain, fame, wealth and the like things, while another class is not in the same case; and in the same manner,

of those which can only claim a negative value, some supply us with sufficient reason for rejecting them, pain for example, disease, loss of the senses, poverty, disgrace, and the like, which others do not.[17]

Ultimately, however, in terms of virtue all external goods are rejected. This rejection seems to be based on the fact that they are not under the agent's control and as such cannot form a part of the moral life:

> But how lofty, how splendid, how unwavering the character of the wise man is shown to be! He, in-as-much as true reason has proved to him that what is moral is alone good, must of necessity enjoy perpetual happiness and must in very truth be in possession of all those titles which the ignorant love to deride. He will be styled a king by a fairer right than Tarquin, who was too feeble to govern either himself or his people, and lord of the nation by a fairer claim than Sulla, who was lord of three baneful vices, self-indulgence, greed and barbarity, rich by a fairer title than Crassus, who but for his wants would never have sought to cross the Euphrates, without reason for declaring war. It will be right to say that all things are his, who alone knows how to use all things, right to call him beautiful, since the features of the mind are fairer than those of the body; right to name him the only freeman, for he bows to no tyranny nor yields to any passion; right to declare him invincible, since though his body may be chained no shackles can be case round his mind. Nor would he even wait for any period of his life, that the question whether he has enjoyed happiness may be decided after he has spent in dying the last day of his existence... Now if it is true that no one but the good man is happy and all good men are happy, what is there more deserving of worship than philosophy or more divinely glorious than virtue?[18]

The good man is good in virtue of features that are under his control, that is the beauty of his mind, his knowledge, his freedom from passion, the freedom of his mind rather than his body, his control over his mind and so on. Externals such as wordly wealth, freedom from physical constraint, passions, the admiration of others, control over others and so on play no role in his happiness.

This self-sufficient moral life leads to a distinctive view of *eudaimonia*, different from that of Aristotle. *Eudaimonia* is an all-or-nothing affair, which is complete, perfect and independent of externalities at any moment in the person's life. This contrasts with Aristotle's claim that *eudaimonia* requires both complete goodness and a complete lifetime;[19] the Stoic sage is happy at any moment of his life because he has virtue.

The Stoics also reject a developmental picture of virtue and do not accept that the road to virtue is a gradual one.

> It is a tenet of theirs [the Stoics] that between virtue and vice there is nothing intermediate . . . For, say the Stoics, just as a stick must be either straight or crooked, so a man must be either just or unjust. Nor again are there degrees of justice and injustice; and the same rule applies to the other virtues.[20]

For the Stoics, all virtuous actions are equal as are all failures in virtue:

> It is one of their [the Stoics] tenets that all sins are equal . . . For if one truth is not more true than another, neither is one falsehood more false than another, and in the same way one deceit is not more so than another, nor sin than sin.[21]

There are no greater or lesser degrees of difficulty or temptation when called upon to be virtuous.

Not only is the Stoic picture of the moral life immune from developmental and situational luck, but it also avoids the influence of resultant luck. The virtuous life is unconnected from the results of one's actions and external influences. The Stoics put a particular emphasis on how acts are done rather than what is done – an emphasis that one cannot help but compare to the Kantian emphasis on intentions and motives as opposed to results. Cooper offers a particularly clear account of the Stoic position:

> Just as the artistic acts of navigator or doctor are given direction by the goals of their arts, so too those of dancers and actors are given direction – not however, from some goal lying outside the actions themselves which the performer aims to effect, but from the script and the interpretations of the director, or correspondingly from the choreographer. The goals here are simply to act or dance, so directed, in a fully artistic way. Similarly, 'wise', fully rational agents, according to the Stoics, take their direction in their actions from whatever may be the natural objective to pursue at the moment, but their goal is to act 'artistically' in a thus directed way, not actually to get anything, as the navigator or doctor as such wants to do, by acting on those directions. So there is no room for any regret or for a sense of failure

of any kind in case the objectives acted for do not materialize. And, Cicero concludes, seeing one's actions and oneself as an agent in that way is the essential prior condition of learning to lead a life of consistently and fully virtuous action.[22]

For the Stoics, every action involves a 'mental assent' to the action, and being in this mental state rather than performing the action is what is crucial for moral evaluation. Thus, a person would be said to be walking, for example, were he to *assent* to the thought that normally leads to movement of the feet, rather than *perform* the actual movement. It is also important to note that when the Stoics refer to virtue as a skill, they are not interested in the ordinary understanding of a practical skill, but rather refer to the intellectual part of a skill, that is that of mentally affirming the act.[23] The Stoic sage then is morally evaluated with respect to what is under his control, what is really him, and not with respect to irrelevant externalities:

> What is more foolish than to praise in a person that which is not really him? What is more insane than someone who wonders at items that can the next minute be transferred to someone else?...No person should take pride in anything that is not his own...Suppose he has an attractive group of slaves and a beautiful home, a large farm and a large income. None of these things is in him, but, rather, around him. Praise that in him which cannot be given or taken away, which belongs to the man himself. Do you ask what it is? The soul, and reason fulfilled in the soul. For the human being is a reasoning animal.[24]

Another implication of this understanding of virtue is that once virtue is acquired one cannot fall back into vice, this being a consequence of 'the certainty of our mental apprehension':[25] 'For virtue can never be lost, and the good man is always exercising his mind which is perfect.'[26] This analysis makes it clearer why the life of virtue is an all-or-nothing question for the Stoics. If a life of virtue is judged by the results one brings about, then there is the possibility that things could go wrong at different stages of one's life, thus affecting one's standing with respect to virtue. If, however, a life of virtue is a matter of commitment to virtue, regardless of any results one manages to bring about, then this life does not admit to degrees or reversals.[27]

This view of the moral life as self-sufficient thus insulates it from the uncontrollable influences of the passions, the availability of external goods, the results of actions, developmental factors and so on. However, if the moral life is separate from all these factors, what is it dependent on and what does it consist in? To make sense of the Stoic answer to this question we need to look at the importance of nature in Stoic theory and their understanding of fatalism.

5.3 On nature and fatalism

One of the most peculiar Stoical ideas is the claim that events that we would tend to consider extremely important are indifferent to the *eudaimonia* of the agent. Famously, even the death of a child should not disturb the tranquillity of a Stoic sage.[28] This is because everything that happens, failures as much as successes, is part of the rational plan of nature of which we, as human beings, are a mere component.[29] Virtue for the Stoics is a disposition of reason in accordance with goals laid out by Nature, available to everyone and, as a result, giving everyone an equal start in their effort to become moral:

> But when reason by way of a more perfect leadership [than the leadership of impulse] has been bestowed on the beings we call rational, for them life according to reason rightly becomes the natural life... This is why Zeno was the first to designate as the end 'life in agreement with nature', which is the same as a virtuous life, virtue being the goal towards which nature guides us... for our individual natures are parts of the whole universe.[30]

> the good is... the natural perfection of a rational being qua rational.[31]

The centrality and importance of the role of reason is of major concern to both the Stoics and Kant. Seneca argues that the good does not exist in plants or animals, 'for there is no good except where there is a place for reason'.[32] Reason is available to all human beings,[33] it is within one's power to cultivate one's reason and control it in order to act morally: 'Nature has given us the seeds of knowledge... Nature bids us to amplify praiseworthy things.'[34] Reason allows the student of morality to make sense of appearances and be critical of the way he sees the world. Reason can perceive appropriate acts, which are actions adapted to nature's arrangements.[35] The seeds of reason are found in our nature; from Panaetius: the end is 'living in accordance with the tendencies bestowed on us by nature'.[36] Respect for reason is respect for oneself and respect for humanity as the possessor of reason, which also seems similar to Kantian thoughts; in the words of Marcus Aurelius: 'The good of a rational being is community.'[37]

However, although the appeal to reason and a connection between it and nature is present in both the Stoics and Kant, the two theories make quite different uses of this idea. As we shall see in the next chapter, Kant tries to make morality immune to luck and in order to do this he draws a sharp distinction between the intelligible and the empirical points of view. This distinction does not exist in the Stoics. Importantly, the Stoics' reason is universal reason, to be found in our nature.[38]

For the Stoics the development of reason is part of the natural development of human beings, and leads to the virtuous life. Gaining happiness, living virtuously and living in agreement with the rationality of nature are the same thing for the Stoics. Nature endows us with certain instincts and since nature cannot cause harm to its creatures or be indifferent to their survival, these instincts must be good. In a sense then, there is no possibility for constitutive luck since we all naturally have the right instincts. 'The Stoics see morality and the development in humans of a moral point of view as being something natural, namely, what is natural for rational beings.'[39]

Related to the Stoic view of the rational plan of nature is the Stoic view of fatalism. Moral luck in general raises problems of determinism and the Stoic view as developed so far seems particularly vulnerable to the charge that there is no room for free action. However, the Stoics manage to combine the idea of everything happening according to a plan with a qualified conception of freedom for moral agents.

The Stoic position on the question of determinism is rather complicated and must be approached with caution. The work of Chrysippus gives us an account of the Stoic position on determinism. Chrysippus' position seems to be encapsulated in Cicero's account of the Stoic as attempting to 'both escape necessity and retain fate'.[40] Chrysippus drew a distinction between basic and proximate causes.[41] Basic causes 'are connected with the particular qualities which make any object qua object what it is and not another thing. They describe the "fate" of a given object.'[42] Thus, it is a cylinder's fate to roll because 'rollability' is one of its qualities qua cylinder and is a basic cause of the cylinder's movement when it actually moves. It is then possible for a cylinder to roll, whether it does so or not. The man who pushes the cylinder and *actually* makes it roll provides the 'proximate' cause and turns fate into actuality. In this way fate is not the same as determinism, since if the proximate cause does not operate then 'rollability' will remain a potentiality of the cylinder.

The moral domain is also subject to fate of this kind. For example, death is the fate of human beings and mortality their quality qua human beings. The fate of death can look like necessity if the mortal human being does not accept the situation into which he was born. Man cannot escape death any more than a cylinder can escape its 'rollability', and moral wisdom comes from embracing and accepting the inescapable. Although whether a human will die or not is not within his control, what is under his control is his attitude to the inevitability of death. One's attitude to fate is the domain where humans can still have control over themselves, despite the inevitability of fate.[43]

Thus, accepting fate is not the same as becoming a determinist, and does not go hand in hand with abandoning moral responsibility. Fate and moral responsibility, often assumed to be incompatible notions, were not made to be merely compatible, but pre-suppose each other. The moral life involves coming to see and accepting the inevitability of fate, while choosing to have a positive attitude towards it:

Hippolytus: They too [Zeno and Chrysippus] affirmed that everything is fated, with the following model. When a dog is tied to a cart, if it wants to follow it is pulled and follows, making its spontaneous act coincide with necessity, but if it does not want to follow it will be compelled in any case. So it is with men too: even if they do not want to, they will be compelled in any case to follow what is destined.[44]

The question of where man's fate leads him is a more complicated one. Fate for man is what is in his nature, and the highest form of moral excellence is to live in accordance with nature.[45] The dog will follow the cart whether it likes it or not, and man will be equally forced to follow his nature. If one's attitudes are under one's control and affirming one's nature then we are 'pulled along the cart' willingly. In fact, the virtuous life involves having such an attitude that one affirms this 'pull' to such an extent that it is doubtful whether it is still felt as a pull. One of the moral requirements which we come to see if we observe nature is that we are 'made' for having duties to humanity in the same way that a cylinder is made to be 'rollable'.

The Stoic position avoids then the influence of moral luck, even accepts a version of fatalism, but allows room for choice. The agent can choose his moral attitudes, whether he affirms or not the moral requirements, and these attitudes are free from the influence of contingent factors. The ability to do so is available to all agents in virtue of their rational nature and in virtue of the fact that they are part of the greater rational plan of nature:

> Now the term nature is used by them [the Stoics] to mean sometimes that which holds the world together... Nature is defined as a force moving of itself, producing and preserving in being its offspring in accordance with seminal principles within definite periods, and effecting results homogeneous with their sources.[46]

5.4   A solution to the problem of moral luck?

In the previous three chapters we examined Aristotle's response to the problem posed by moral luck. We saw the tension created by the possibility of moral luck between morality, responsibility and choice on the one hand and lack of control on the other. The Aristotelian response to this tension is not so much a solution to the problem of moral luck, but an attempt to accommodate the phenomenon within moral theory. The Stoic response is quite different, as the Stoics attempt to solve the tension created by moral luck by doing away with the possibility of moral luck altogether. For Aristotle, luck is an integral part of the moral life; for the Stoics morality is immune to luck. Aristotle accommodates contingencies and incorporates their influence within his theory; the Stoics reject anything that might threaten the independence and self-sufficiency of the moral life. Aristotle accepts the possibility of luck and acknowledges its influence on morality; the Stoics reject the possibility of moral luck altogether.

Aristotle's attempt to accommodate cases of moral luck is partly successful. As we have already seen, some types of luck can be accounted for in Aristotelian ethics and the influence of other kinds of luck can be avoided or discounted. However, ultimately the tension created by the possibility of moral luck is still present. Aristotle appears to be torn between recognizing the influence of moral luck and holding on to a conception of responsibility, grounded in his thoughts on choice and the voluntary. Because of this, if we are looking for a solution such that the problem of moral luck can be discounted, we probably will not find it in Aristotle. By contrast, the Stoics do not attempt to solve the problem of moral luck, but try to by pass it entirely. The Stoics do not grapple with particular cases of moral luck because they want to make morality immune to luck from the onset. In this they differ from Aristotle, but share the same ambition with Kant. The Stoic response to moral luck is not so much a solution, but a refusal to acknowledge the problem altogether by removing morality from the sphere of luck. It is possible that the Stoics would have a problem with comprehending the concept of 'moral luck' altogether, as they understand morality as immune from the influences of luck to begin with.

If we are faced then with a choice between the Aristotelian response to moral luck and that of the Stoics, it seems that we should prefer the Stoics who altogether avoid the tension present in Aristotelian ethics. In general, it seems that any theory which discounts moral luck entirely is preferable over a theory which attempts to accommodate it, but is not altogether successful. A theory which discounts the possibility of moral luck has the appeal of appearing egalitarian and allowing everyone an equal chance at virtue, free from contingencies outside the agent's making and control. If we can discount the influence of moral luck, we can avoid the inherent tension in the term, that is the tension between morality, control and responsibility on the one hand and lack of control and the inappropriateness of praise and blame on the other. Morality free from luck is a pure morality, where attributions of responsibility are unproblematic. These are very powerful considerations in favour of viewing morality as immune to luck and as we shall see, similar considerations also lead Kant to attempt to free morality from luck. Had the Stoic project of making morality immune to luck been successful it would have much to recommend it, unfortunately, however, there are serious problems with the Stoic account. The Stoic theory discounts luck, but the price it pays for doing so is too high.

Despite the advantages of a theory which discounts moral luck, this attempt at doing so by the Stoics results in a theory that is simply unrealistic. Given how we have developed the Stoic view of virtue, one would expect to find that most, if not all, people would be successful in becoming virtuous. Given that everyone has natural tendencies to virtue,[47] that there are no differences in peoples' ability to reason, that the influence of contingencies is incidental and so on, we would expect that most people would succeed in becoming virtuous. However, this is clearly not the case. Most people are not virtuous and Stoic theory does not have a good explanation of why this is so.

Given the Stoic picture of ethics, it is unclear why things can and do go wrong. The Stoics do not seem to be able to accommodate the fact that a lot of people are vicious. Galen makes this point about the origins of vice with reference to the work of Chrysippus:

> Chrysippus was understandably puzzled about the origin of vice...
> He was unable to discover how it is that children go wrong...For if

children had an appropriate relationship to rectitude, right from the start, vice would have to be engendered in them not internally nor from themselves but solely from outside. Yet even of they are brought up in good habits and properly educated, they are always seen to do something wrong, and Chrysippus too admits this. But he did not have the nerve to falsify the facts on this point at least; he accepted that even if children were reared by no one but a philosopher and never saw or heard any example of vice, they would still not necessarily become philosophers.[48]

If our natural impulses are part of a cosmic, rational, moral plan of nature, then we are all naturally suited to virtue. However, this does not seem plausible. Also, the Stoic emphasis on our shared rationality seems to indicate that the ability to be moral ought to be equally available to everyone, but this does not seem to correspond to how things are.

One possible way out is to argue that although we all have the same natural tendencies, we develop in different ways, which would explain the differences in moral behaviour. However, the Stoic idea that virtue and failure are an all-or-nothing affair as well as the thought that all virtuous acts are equal seems to cast some doubt on this picture. A developmental picture of morality seems to suggest gradual development, subject to setbacks and insights, and failures in some areas, while there is progress in others and so on and this is not consistent with the Stoic picture of a sudden revolution from non-virtue to virtue. Similarly Annas[49] argues that the Stoics 'have no good theory of error to explain why we all live such unnatural lives'.[50] If the Stoics argue that we are born naturally good but are corrupted by appearances and external influences, then the question arises (in the words of Annas): '[h]ow does it happen that not only do most people fail to develop properly, but they organize society in ways which positively discourage the proper development of human nature? For this further problem the Stoics have no direct explanation.'[51] Galen also asks, if everyone is born naturally good how is it that the very first men became corrupted, those without wicked predecessors to pass on the corruption, and how is it that two children brought up by the same person could develop differently.[52]

The above criticisms reflect an uneasiness with the Stoic picture of morality, an uneasiness which the Stoics *themselves* also seemed to be aware of. Despite their proclaimed rejection of external goods, the passions and an understanding of moral development as subject to contingent factors, the Stoics often seem to contradict these ideas in other passages.

Although the Stoics reject the importance placed by other philosophers on what they call 'indifferents', their account of the wise person's contribution to politics and the public life seems to contradict this attitude. Plutarch makes this point when he writes:

> Chrysippus, again, by writing in his treatise on Rhetoric that the sage will speak in public and participate in government just as if he considered wealth to be a good and reputation and health like-wise admits that the Stoic theories are impracticable and antisocial and their doctrines unfit for use and action.[53]

If wealth,[54] admiration by others, honour and so on, which come to one who deals in the public life, are of no real value for the Stoic, it is not clear why advocating such a life is consistent with the Stoic doctrine. The Stoic discussions on suicide which advocate that suicide is acceptable when one's life has been deprived of all goods and all one can look forward to is pain, seem to be inconsistent with their previous claims: 'They [the Stoics] say that the wise man will commit a well-reasoned suicide both on behalf of his country and on behalf of his friends, and if he falls victim to unduly severe pain or mutilation or incurable illness.'[55] If such goods, including health and the avoidance of pain, are indifferent to the virtuous life, why should their absence make suicide an acceptable option?

We have seen how the Stoics reject a developmental picture of morality; however, at the same time Stoics like Chrysippus have a theory of education. Diogenes Laertius tells us that the fact that virtue 'can be taught is laid out by Chrysippus in the first book of his work *On the End*'[56] (as well as by Cleanthes, Posidonius and Hecato), whereas Plutarch relates Chrysippus' views on the order in which ethics should be taught to the young.[57] The very idea that ethics can be the subject of study and gradual education seems to contradict the contention that there cannot be more or less of virtue, as well as the thought that virtue is natural. The Stoics plausibly admit that 'virtue is teachable ... as is evident from the fact that inferior men become good',[58] but although this is an appealing picture of moral development it contradicts the previous Stoic assertions about the nature of virtue. For how can virtue be both natural and available to all through an act of the mind, but at the same the object of education and gradual development which may not be available to all?

Related to this thought is the idea that the passions have to be extirpated for virtue to be possible. The Aristotelian picture of controlling and habituating the passions is vulnerable to luck, but so is the Stoic idea that they must be extirpated. An attempt to extinguish the passions cannot be a sudden, all-or-nothing affair (such a picture would be psychologically implausible), it must be a gradual process with differing degrees of success with respect to different passions. As such it must also be vulnerable to external temptations that arouse the passions and increase their influence.

Two main objections can be raised then against the Stoic account of morality. On the one hand, according to the Stoics we should all be achieving virtue, as this is part of our nature and this option is available to everyone in virtue of our rationality. However, this, clearly, is not the case. The consequence of Stoic theory is that there is no accounting for the possibility of vice, and as vice is fairly widespread we would expect any moral theory to give some account of why this is so. On the other hand, the Stoics seem to be aware of some of the implausible conclusions of their theory. There are passages that give plausible accounts of education and the importance of external goods, yet these passages are inconsistent with the other claims made by the Stoics. Thus, the Stoics themselves seem to counteract their own theory.

5.5 Conclusion

The Stoic conception of morality allows them to by pass the possibility of moral luck before it can pose a problem. The moral life for the Stoics is entirely self-sufficient and insulated from any contingent factors. The passions are extinguished precisely because their influence cannot be controlled and may escape the command of reason. External goods, whose acquisition and possession is entirely a matter of luck, are entirely indifferent to the student of virtue, again because of their contingent nature. The results of virtuous acts are unimportant, and virtue is simply a measure of one's mental assent to virtuous acts, not a measure of their successful execution. Therefore, no external actions which may impede the execution of virtuous acts can affect the virtue of the agent. Because virtue consists in an attitude, the transformation from vice to virtue is instantaneous and complete, as opposed to the gradual, developmental picture proposed by Aristotle. This way the transformation from vice to virtue is independent of developmental factors and external opportunities and hindrances.

This understanding of morality is supported by the Stoic view of nature as a rational, unifying force. Moral agents and their efforts are part of a universal plan and everything that happens, happens for the best as it is part of the plan. The effects of the world on moral agents, then, should not be regretted, as they only seem regrettable from our human, limited standpoint. Ultimately freedom is the ability to see the truth of the above, the inevitability of fate and the ineffectiveness of resistance. Freedom is the choice to assent to fate.

This complex and intricate understanding of morality and freedom results in a theory which never has to face the tension created by the possibility of moral luck. However, although the Stoic attempt to free morality from the influence of luck has a lot to recommend it in its conception, when the details of the theory are considered, it seems implausible and it fails to correspond to how things are. Ultimately, if the Stoics are correct in their understanding of morality, we should expect to find that almost all, if not all, people are moral. Virtue, not vice, should be the rule in a universe governed by the Stoical conception of morality. However, it is not unduly pessimistic to recognize that this is not the case, and the Stoics do not seem to have an explanation as to why most of us, for most of the time, fail to be virtuous. Therefore, although the Stoic ambition to make morality immune to luck would resolve the tension created by the phenomenon and solve the problem of attributing responsibility, their theory fails because it does not correspond to the way things are.

Furthermore, the Stoics themselves are aware of the implausible consequences of some of their claims and attempt to moderate them with their remarks on education, the education of passions and the importance of external goods. These remarks, however, seem to contradict their earlier contentions. In the previous chapters we saw how Aristotle not only accommodates the influence of moral luck within a compelling account of moral development, but how he also wants to maintain some room for a strong and independent conception of reason. The Stoics seem to make the same journey from a different starting point: they begin with an account of virtue independent of luck but also make reference to a developmental picture influenced by contingent factors. What both theories – Aristotle and the Stoics – share is an awareness of the tension between the requirement for some independence from luck and the requirement for a plausible account of moral development.

This tension between two alternative and possibly incompatible explanations will become clearer in the next chapter as we examine the work of Kant. Kant shares with the Stoics the wish to make morality immune from luck and is also aware of the constraints imposed on his attempt to make morality immune to luck by a plausible account of moral development. The next two chapters will examine whether Kantian theory can resolve the tension created by moral luck.

6
Kant on Luck

6.1 Introduction

There is limited discussion of Kant in the debate on moral luck. This is because the Kantian position is presented as entirely incompatible with the possibility of luck and this is interpreted as a serious problem for Kant (interpreted as such mainly by Aristotelian-inspired theories which claim to have a more plausible account of goodness because they are willing to accept it is vulnerable to luck).

Williams[1] sees Kant as seeking a conception of morality immune to luck, but at the same time expects this Kantian aim to be disappointed, since however far back one goes to motives and intentions, constitutive luck will have an effect. However, Williams does not press this point. Instead he focuses on an even more pressing criticism of the Kantian position. The Kantian position on morality can only be understood in the light of related claims on rationality, justification and value. Williams' Gauguin example challenges the very idea of possibility of an agent's reflective assessment of his own actions. Gauguin is presented as being unable to rationally justify his decision at the time it is made. So his challenge is to rational justification and by extension to morality, a notion so tied up with the attempt to escape luck that if Williams is successful we may have to abandon it altogether.

Williams sets the scene for how the Kantian account of morality and its implications for luck will be discussed in the debate over moral luck. Similarly, Nagel sees Kant as rejecting the influence of qualities of temperament and personality as they are not under the control of the will and morality must be possible for everyone. However, he finds this Kantian conclusion intuitively unacceptable, as we are unable to rid ourselves of moral judgements based on these contingent factors.[2]

Nussbaum is concerned that adopting the Kantian point of view on morality – a point of view which sees moral value as the one important type of value which is also immune to luck – will make it impossible for us to understand the Ancient Greek account of the good life. The Ancient Greek concern with contingency, the acceptance (and regret) of insoluble practical conflict as well as the risks of love and friendship make no sense from this Kantian perspective. They appear to pose problems only because the ancients were unaware of the Kantian position on morality. Nussbaum is concerned that from the Kantian point of view, these questions make no sense and therefore we can never understand the ancients' claims. This is because the Kantian relation between duty and practical necessity, along with the special status of moral value, makes it the case that there are no conflicts of obligation. However, this Kantian aspiration to moral purity is ill-conceived. Nussbaum is concerned with conflict, conflicts of values and conflicts of desires, the importance of fragile, untenable goods, and the possibility of moral dilemmas. If that then is the correct view of goodness, Nussbaum is rightly concerned that Kant's 'demand for consistency among the principles of practical reason led him to defuse what his own view would naturally lead him to see as a deep conflict of practical reasons'.[3] For Kant, conflict is impossible, as the very notions of duty and obligation express practical necessity and two moral laws cannot, by definition, conflict. However, it is Nussbaum's contention that conflict in the practical world is unavoidable because of its inherent contingency and therefore the Kantian demand for inner harmony is bound to fail. Not only that, but approaching all moral theory from the Kantian perspective is bound to present a distorted picture of the good life. By accepting the Kantian picture, we risk giving up something of real importance: the fragility of goodness. Making life immune to luck risks eliminating from the human life all those vulnerable, contingent ingredients which make it valuable.

All these thoughts set the scene for how Kantian theories are understood in relation to the problem of moral luck:

- either Kant cannot truly avoid some types of luck, such as constitutive luck,
- or his attempt to discount them leads to counter-intuitive implications,
- morality is vulnerable to luck in a way which conflicts with Kantian aspirations about the autonomy of morality, and
- perhaps further than this, a failure to have a correct understanding of the moral life is a failure to see its intrinsic vulnerability, contingency, perplexity and ultimate importance in its fragility.

6.2   Kantian immunity from luck

There is good reason to interpret Kant on moral luck as Williams, Nagel and Nussbaum have done, and this is because much of Kantian theory is about immunity from luck. The main source of these kinds of claims is the *Groundwork*, but they are reflected in other works and underpin the Kantian understanding of freedom, autonomy and morality.

The Stoics have been compared to Kant because they both share a view that allows room for immunity from moral luck. However, in many respects the Stoics have a different story about how this is possible from Kant. As we shall see, Kant's conception of freedom differs significantly from that of the Stoics. Where for the Stoics, freedom involves recognizing and accepting the inevitability and rationality of the laws of nature, for Kant the laws of nature are about what *does* happen, whereas the laws of morality are about what *should* happen. Understanding the relation between Kant's conception of nature and his conception of morality is a complex matter; however, Kant certainly does not reduce the moral to the ethical. As we shall see later on, it is a matter of interpretation whether one sees Kant as isolating morality from nature or whether he elevates the natural to the level of the moral, thus achieving some kind of integration between them.

First, however, we need to examine the division between nature and morality. The division is reflected in ethics, one part of which is empirical, the practical anthropology, and the other rational, the morals. The basis of morality in reason, and its 'cleansing' from anything empirical that is appropriate to anthropology, is crucial for Kant, as the moral law must carry absolute necessity, so that:

> consequently the ground of obligation must be looked for, not in the nature of man nor in the circumstances of the world in which he is placed, but solely *a priori* in the concepts of pure reason; and that every other precept based on principles of mere experience – and even a precept that may in a certain sense be considered universal, so far as it rests in its slightest part, perhaps only in its motive, on empirical grounds – can indeed be called a practical rule, but never a moral law.[4]

Again in the *Religion* we are told that the ground of obligation of the moral law cannot be the idea of another being above man forcing the recognition of one's duty or any incentive other than the law itself.[5] Thus, Kant sets the ground for a total rejection of the influence of luck in the sphere of the moral. Before we go on to look at the different types of luck identified previously, it is clear even from these introductory remarks why Kantian theory has been identified with the attempt to eliminate the influence of luck in morality. For Kant it is not just resistance to luck which is built into the concept of morality – the resistance which gives rise to the oxymoron – but complete incompatibility. With this elimination of the influence of luck come two advantages: the first is a sense of justice and fairness in making judgements of moral praise and blame; it is possible to make sense of moral responsibility and to do so in an equitable way. In the first part of the *Groundwork*, Kant explains in detail how the worth of the good will cannot be due to natural inclination, or the results of our actions, or the motives which aim at expected results, because all these could have been brought about by other causes. If we assume that morality is grounded in any of these heteronomous considerations, it is impossible to make moral judgements of praise and blame and to say that agents could have done otherwise.

The second advantage is a shared immunity from luck. As rational beings, as beings who can share in morality, we are also immune from luck. Crucially, for Kant, we cannot make sense of ourselves as rational beings without presupposing the idea of freedom, that is the idea that the agent is the originator of his choices and actions. The causality of freedom is the ability to be moved by reason (and reason alone without reference to the inclinations) and it leaves no room for the influences of luck.

The Kantian view, then, is founded on an understanding of morality that is, as of necessity, immune from luck. If we consider these thoughts in isolation, it is clear why commentators would think that the Kantian picture discounts the influence of luck. There are numerous instances where this indeed seems to be the case.

For Kant constitutive luck is excluded since the nature of man should not be a ground for obligation, and resultant, developmental and situational luck are dealt with when the circumstances of the world are also rejected as grounds for moral obligation. Specific passages provide ample evidence for such an interpretation. In the *Religion*, Kant writes: 'Man himself must make or have made himself into whatever, in a moral sense, whether good or evil, he is or is to become',[6] a passage which is interpreted to mean that there can be no excuse by appeal to constitutive luck.[7] Similarly, in the discussion of the malicious lie in the *Critique of Pure Reason*, Kant points out that even though the act may have been determined by a bad disposition or a way of life, we nonetheless blame the agent.[8] Kant also goes on at length about constitutive bad luck:

> There are cases in which human beings, even with the same education that was profitable to others, yet show from childhood such early wickedness and progress in it so continuously into their adulthood that they are taken to be born villains and quite incapable of improvement as far as their cast of mind is concerned; and nevertheless they are so judged for what they do or leave undone that they are censured as guilty of their crimes; indeed they themselves (the children) find these censures as well founded as if, despite the hopeless natural constitution of mind ascribed to them, they remained as accountable as any other human being, this could not happen if we did not suppose that whatever arises from one's choice (as every action intentionally performed undoubtedly does) has as its basis a free causality, which from early youth expresses its character in its appearances (actions); these actions, on account of the uniformity of conduct, make knowable a natural connection that does not, however, make the vicious constitution of the will necessary but is instead the consequence of evil and unchangeable principles freely adopted, which make it only more culpable and deserving of punishment.[9]

Furthermore, it is not enough that one acts in conformity with the moral law, as this is something that may happen due to luck, but one must affirm the moral law by acting for its sake. It is interesting to pause here and note that even on this picture of strict rejection of moral luck, there are similarities with the Aristotelian picture of virtue. Virtuous acts may be performed accidentally, habitually or unreflectively, but virtue proper requires awareness of what one is doing and conscious choice of the act for its own sake. Acting out of duty may, incidentally, produce similar results to acting from duty, but it is only the latter that has true moral worth as it involves acting out of reverence for the moral law. Acting from duty cannot occur accidentally, or without reason. Not only that, but the source of the action cannot be empirical. The action must be attributed to the agent and must be chosen by him without reference to anything external such as inclinations. The *Groundwork* deals exclusively with the rational part of ethics, the morals; its aim is to: 'investigate the Idea and principles of a possible pure will, and not the activities and conditions of human willing as such, which are drawn for the most part from psychology'.[10]

Kant seems to reject any possibility of constitutive moral luck. All the talents, for example intelligence, wit, temperament; all the qualities of temperament, for example courage, resolution, consistency of temperament; and all the gifts of fortune, for example power, wealth, honour, health, can all be good, but they can also be bad. The good will is unconditionally good, the highest good and the condition for all the rest. This idea is reminiscent of the Stoic idea that the only thing that is good unconditionally is nature, as everything else can be put to good or bad uses.[11] This similarity suggests the possibility that Kant was somehow inspired by the Stoic idea that there is only one unconditionally good thing, and used it in formulating his conception of the good will.

Kant goes to great lengths to establish that the good will is good without qualification, so much so that it remains good regardless of whether it succeeds in bringing about good consequences:

> A good will is not good because of what effects or accomplishes – because of its fitness for attaining some proposed end: it is good through its willing alone – that is, good in itself. Considered in itself it is to be esteemed beyond comparison as far higher than anything it could bring about merely in order to favour some inclination or, if you like, the sum total of inclinations. Even if, by some special disfavour of destiny or by the niggardly endowment of a step-motherly nature, this will is entirely lacking in power to carry out its intentions; if by its utmost effort it still accomplishes nothing, and only good will is left (not, admittedly, as a mere wish, but as the straining of every means so far as they are in our control); even then it would still shine like a jewel for its own sake as something which has its full value in itself.[12]

Moral value must be independent of the vagaries of fate. This rejection of the evaluation of moral worth of the act based on its consequences is also emphasized later on, in the discussion of acting out of duty.[13] The value of an act does not come from the relation of the will to the effects it produces, as these can be obstructed due to misfortune outside the agent's control, but is to be found in the principle of the will. Since the good will is good unconditionally, it is not influenced by inclinations – as inclinations affect the sensible self and the good will is part of the intelligible self – or consequences, and the maxims in accordance with the good will are inferred through reason; the good will seems to be part of the intelligible world.

6.3 The intelligible world

The preceding remarks make it quite clear that luck cannot have any influence on morality. This claim is cashed out with reference to the Kantian understanding of the intelligible/sensible distinction and their relation to nature.[14] Morality conceptually requires immunity from luck, as we saw we cannot make sense of moral responsibility otherwise. Postulating an intelligible self makes it the case that morality is a concept with application.

Kant seems to be distinguishing two influences of nature on man – on his intelligible self and on his sensible self:

> For man is a being who has the power of practical reason and is conscious that his choice is free (a person); and in his consciousness of freedom and in his feeling (which is called moral feeling) that justice or injustice is done to him, or by him, to others, he sees himself as subject to a law of duty, no matter how obscure his idea about it may be. This in itself is the *intelligible* character of humanity as such, and insofar as he has it, man is good in his inborn predispositions (good by nature). But experience also shows that there is in man a tendency to actively desire what is *unlawful* even though he knows that it is unlawful – that is, a tendency to evil – which makes itself felt as inevitably and as soon as he begins to exercise his freedom, and which can therefore be considered innate. And so we must judge that man, according to his *sensible* character is also evil (by nature).[15]

So by nature, man is both free, rational and able to act morally, and at the same time restricted by empirical contingencies. The only sense in which one can be influenced negatively is if one has a predisposition to choose evil maxims because of inclinations that are part of one's sensible self. However, the intelligible self always remains free, and the possibility of acting morally is available to everyone. The idea that rationality, in Kant through the idea of the intelligible self, is available to everyone is also mirrored in the Stoical ideas examined previously. This idea of the availability of morality to everyone is crucial for Kant, as it is a consequence of his understanding of freedom and autonomy. It is exactly because we are free that we must presuppose the ability to act in accordance with the moral law in all agents and therefore the possibility of doing so must be practically open to everyone.[16]

Kant also reserves an important role for reason, which is grounded in his conception of nature; guiding the will in the good. Again the distinction between intelligible and sensible is crucial here. Reason is naturally available to all human beings, in a way similar to the Stoic idea that reason proceeds from nature for everyone:

> All moral concepts have their seat of origin in reason completely *a priori*, and indeed in the most ordinary human reason just as much as in the most highly speculative: they cannot be abstracted from any empirical, and therefore merely contingent, knowledge. In this purity of their origin is to be found their very worthiness to serve as supreme practical principles, and everything empirical added to them is just so much taken away from their genuine influence and from the absolute value of their corresponding actions ... Since moral laws have to hold for every rational being as such, we ought rather to derive our principles from the general concept of a rational being as such, and on this basis to expound the whole of ethics – which requires anthropology for its application to man – at first independently as pure philosophy, that is entirely as metaphysics (which we can very well do in this wholly abstract kind of knowledge).[17]

The very idea of reason is tied up with the necessity of freedom:

> Reason must look upon itself as the author of its own principles independently of alien influences. Therefore, as practical reason, or as the will of a rational being, it must be regarded by itself as free; that is, the will of a rational being can be the will of its own only under the Idea of freedom, and such a will must therefore – from a practical point of view – be attributed to all rational beings.[18]

In this sense Kant is appealing to the nature of the intelligible world which not only can be reached through reason, but through reason that all human beings share by virtue of their humanity. However, the end of nature for the sensible self is the happiness of the particular being. This end of happiness is best served by one's inclination, not by reason. Where for the Stoics virtue, happiness and a life of reason were the same, for Kant the cultivation of reason for the attainment of the unconditional good of a will may restrict the attainment of the conditional good of happiness, that is the intelligible and the sensible self diverge and their goals may conflict. This is another way in which Kant fortifies his theory against assault from moral luck, as happiness is vulnerable to the contingencies of luck, but takes second place in Kantian theory, forming part of the sensible not the intelligible self.[19]

Kant goes as far as to argue that actions are commanded by duty and grasped solely by reason regardless of whether there has been an opportunity to actually act them out:

> actions of which the world has perhaps hitherto given no example – actions whose practicability might well be doubted by those who rest everything on experience – are nevertheless commanded unrelentingly by reason; and that, for instance, although up to now there may have existed no loyal friend, pure loyalty in friendship can be no less required from every man, in as much as this duty, prior to all experience, is contained as duty in general in the Idea of a reason which determines the will by *a priori* grounds.[20]

6.4   Interpreting Kant on the intelligible/sensible distinction

It seems, then, that Kant has a conception of morality as immune to luck and he can make sense of this by relying on a specific understanding of freedom, rationality and morality in the intelligible world. However, the concern is that the Kantian picture is implausible or counter-intuitive. This concern can be formulated in a number of ways. Within the literature on Kant, one expression of this concern is unease with the relationship between the intelligible and the sensible worlds. I will go on to consider this below. Another way of presenting this objection is to rely on an Aristotelian understanding of virtue and character, concepts which have intuitive plausibility, and argue that Kant fails to make room for these concepts. I will consider this charge further on in this chapter. The fundamental question, relating to both interpretations of this objection, is how we should understand the important Kantian claim that the fundamental moral principle must be *a priori* and owe nothing to empirical contingencies, while at the same time accepting a plausible picture of human nature as subject to contingencies. If we fail to find a satisfactory answer to this question, the charge against the Kantian is that he is exclusively preoccupied with a metaphysical account of the good, while ignoring its practical instantiations.[21] We would then have to construct a defence of Kantian metaphysics, knowing that even if we were successful our conclusions would have no application to real human beings. If we are tempted to reject Kantian theory because of its extravagant metaphysics, there are two alternatives: either acknowledge that luck has some influence on morality or accept an error theory. The Aristotelians opt for the former option. It is important then to see if there are any interpretations of Kant on this point that can avoid the difficulties of understanding the intelligible/sensible distinction as a metaphysical claim.

First, then, we have to consider the exact relationship between the intelligible and the sensible worlds. Of course, this is an enormous topic and it is not the aim of this chapter to give an exhaustive account of it. Rather I will hint at some interpretations of this relationship which will help us make sense of the Kantian picture on moral luck. The worry is that these two views, of the intelligible and the sensible, may not be easily reconciled, leading to a problematic picture of judgements of responsibility. Kant himself warns us that natural necessity and freedom are 'mutually repellent concepts' whose unification is unfeasible.[22] Furthermore, it is not just philosophers who are unsympathetic to the Kantian cause who find problems with a unified understanding of the intelligible/sensible distinction. Scruton, for example, in a short but influential analysis of Kant, concludes that the paradox of freedom remains unsolved, and sympathizes with the Kantian claim that we will therefore never understand it.[23] The problem is that, according to some readings, the theory ends up claiming that humans inhabit two worlds, one of determined appearances and one of freedom and the intelligible. In one world, everything is causally determined, whereas the other world, of things-in-themselves, is outside causality and even outside space and time. It is then unclear how these two worlds relate to each other and how we should make sense of these two worlds. Furthermore, since the intelligible world is outside time, it is difficult to see how it could relate to the sensible world; and since free will is outside the realm of experience, it is unclear how we can make judgements about moral responsibility in an ordinary sense (it even looks like one initial, free act of choice in the intelligible world determines a whole series of causal events relating to one's character from then on).

However, there are possible solutions to this problem, in rejecting the metaphysical understanding of the intelligible world in favour of seeing the distinction as a distinction between 'two points of view'. Humans do not reside in two worlds, rather they take on two perspectives, that of spectator and that of agent. Freedom relates to our ability to form judgements, rather than having to do with our actions, and is understood as the freedom to be constrained by the moral law. Attributing this kind of freedom to ourselves is necessary if we are to make sense of the possibility of judgement. We need to be able to regard ourselves as free, in the sense of being able to give ourselves principles guided by the moral law, but at the same time regard ourselves as caused. Kantian theory posits two radically different and wholly incommensurable conceptions of ourselves: that of the 'spectator', from which I must view all human beings (including myself) as causally determined natural automata, and that of the 'agent', from which I view myself as a free but wholly unrecognisable member of a supernatural noumenal realm.[24]

According to this kind of view, our account of ourselves as rational, moral beings is different and opposed to our account as natural beings.

A version of such an account of 'two points of view' is presented by Allison. Henry Allison offers a detailed and sensitive account of Kantian freedom. We need to attribute an intelligible character to ourselves because of our conception of ourselves as rational, free and autonomous beings. If we do not do so, it becomes impossible for us to act, and the concept of 'agency' becomes nonsensical. Thus, Allison argues: '[t]he contrast between empirical and intelligible character is not between two ontologically distinct characters, which are somehow causally related, but between "two points of view", representing two models of agency in terms of which the activity of a rational agent can be construed'.[25] The intelligible self is then understood as practical spontaneity which regulates our conception of ourselves as rational agents with an empirical character. Unlike the previous account of the two points of view above, which sees the individual as spectator and as agent, Allison interprets the distinction as relating to two conceptions of agency. Similarly, Rescher argues that although we cannot know things-in-themselves, our understanding is committed to supposing their existence in an experience-independent realm. We must postulate things-in-themselves because of how our mind operates, otherwise we cannot impute objectivity; '[w]hat is at issue here is a matter of a (practically rational commitment to an indispensable useful conceptual resource'.[26]

How we understand the relationship between intelligible and empirical characters is constrained by Kant's understanding of causality and the noumenal. The empirical character should not be merely a product of causation, but at the same time there cannot be an inference from the noumenal to the phenomenal. Allison concludes that what is needed 'is an account of empirical character that enables us to regard it as in some sense an expression or manifestation (and not simply a result) of an intelligible activity, without requiring us to assume that it yields an insight into the true nature of this activity'.[27] Similarly, Rescher points out that '[w]e do not *know* things-in-themselves and *discover* their causal agency; instead we *think* things-in-themselves and *impute* explanatory efficacy to them'.[28] At the same time it is important to postulate the existence of an intelligible self, as it is the ability to act spontaneously, the capacity to act on imperatives, that defines free agency. So in a sense, it is the Kantian ambition to make morality immune from luck which drives this whole project. To conceive of oneself as a rational agent is to conceive of oneself as a being capable of acting on the basis of an ought, capable of spontaneity. The claim is not as

> to how rational beings must think, but rather as a statement of how rational beings must (ex hypothesi, in virtue of their stipulated rationality) be thought to think... Our commitment to the causality of freedom in rational agents bound by the moral law is inherent in the very conception of a moral agent acting through his (ex hypothesi available) resource of freedom of the will.[29]

Therefore, one has to attribute an intelligible character to oneself. It is important that we keep in mind that:

> the transcendental idea of freedom, which provides the content to the otherwise empty thought of an intelligible character, has a merely regulative, nonexplanatory function. What it regulates is our conception of ourselves as rational agents. It does so by providing the conceptual basis for a model of deliberative rationality, which includes, as an ineliminable component, the thought of practical spontaneity. Once again, the basic idea is simply that it is a condition of the possibility of taking oneself as a rational agent, that is, as a being for whom reason is practical, that one attribute such spontaneity to oneself. Moreover, as the example of the malicious lie is intended to show, it is likewise a condition of the imputation of actions and, therefore, the assignment of responsibility. Finally, since this spontaneity is merely intelligible, its attribution requires the attribution of an intelligible character. Thus, insofar as we take ourselves and others to be rational agents existing in the world of sense, we are constrained to attribute both an empirical and an intelligible character to our agency.[30]

Our first concern then with the Kantian picture had to do with unease over the relationship between the intelligible and the sensible. This conceptual account of the intelligible goes a long way towards easing this concern, especially as it avoids the problematic implications of a metaphysical understanding of the distinction. It also allows us to draw some conclusions regarding the role of luck in Kantian theory, which help to make sense of some Kantian claims. It is indeed correct to see

Kant as rejecting the influence of luck on morality. For Kant, acting morally is always within our power, since we always have the power to reason as part of our intelligible self and this remains so no matter what has influenced our sensible self:

> Every evil action must be considered, whenever we seek its rational origin, as if the human being had fallen into it directly from the state of innocence. For whatever his previous behaviour may have been, whatever the natural causes influencing him, whatever they are inside or outside them, his action is yet free and not determined through any of these causes, hence the action can and must always be judged as an *original* exercise of his power of choice... However evil a human being has been right up to the moment of an impending free action (evil even habitually as a second nature), his duty to better himself was not just in the past: it still is his duty *now*, he must therefore be capable of it and, should he not do it, he is at the moment of action just as accountable, and stands just as condemned, as if, though endowed with natural predisposition to the good (which is inseparable from freedom), he had just stepped out of the state of innocence into evil.[31]

Any appeals to upbringing, temperament, impotence and tempting circumstances are simply excuses and involve being dishonest to ourselves. Neither is there an excuse resulting from an appeal to one's settled character over time, as every single act should proceed from reason which is available to everyone, always and no matter what their past:

> Now even if one believes the action to be determined by these causes, one nevertheless blames the agent, and not on account of his unhappy natural temper, not on account of the circumstances influencing him, not even on account of the life he has led previously; for one presupposes that it can be entirely set aside how that life was constituted, and that the series of conditions that transpired may not have been, but rather that this deed could be regarded as entirely unconditioned in regard to the previous state, as though with that act the agent had started a series of consequences entirely from himself.[32]

Thus, the choice to be moral is equally available to Hitler and Mother Teresa.

This picture contrasts sharply with the Aristotelian emphasis on gradual development, habituation, education and viewing a life over a long period of time as a progression towards morality. When we refer to this kind of virtue, that is virtue acquired little by little, for Kant, we are referring not to a 'change of heart' but to 'a change of mores'.[33] Proper moral virtue is not a matter of gradual reform, but 'a *revolution* in the disposition of the human being (a transition to the maxim of holiness of disposition). And so a "new man" can come only through a kind of rebirth as it were a new creation....'[34] This revolution is possible because what needs to change is one's maxims and this is an act of reason, not a gradual reformation in the mode of sense:

> Education, examples and instruction cannot produce this firmness and steadfastness in our principles gradually, but only, as it were, by an explosion that results from our being sick and tired of the precarious state of our instinct.[35]

All of which brings us to the second formulation of the objection about the intelligible/sensible distinction. The last few decades have seen a return to an Aristotelian approach to moral theory. Central to this approach has been a shift of focus towards the concepts of virtue and character. I will say more on the emergence of virtue ethics in the next chapter, but for our purposes it is important to note that virtue ethics originally defined itself in opposition to deontology and consequentialism. Much of what was claimed to be offered by virtue ethics was what was claimed to be missing from Kantian moral theory. Such claims included the idea that virtue ethics gives a proper and significant role to the emotions, whose role is dismissed by Kant; that it recognizes the importance of concepts such as virtue and character, which are neglected by Kant; that it has a realistic moral psychology, recognizing the gradual nature of moral development and the vulnerability of such a project to contingent factors, which Kant ignores in making morality immune to luck; and so on. Overall, the charge against Kantians has been that they present an implausible or counter-intuitive picture of the moral life, setting aside many aspects of it which we consider important in making practical judgements. In response neo-Kantians have redeveloped these ideas from within deontology and we will look at a couple of these projects later on. However, first we need to consider the role of virtue, character and the emotions in Kant, how they affect questions raised by moral luck and their place in the overall Kantian scheme. As the next chapter follows on from this one, I will conclude both at the end of Chapter 7.

7
Kant on Virtue

7.1 Kantian virtue

Many recent commentators have appealed to *The Doctrine of Virtue* in order to illustrate that Kant should not be criticized for not taking concepts such as virtue and character into account in his moral theory. It is indeed wrong to accuse Kant of ignoring virtue and character, but it is also wrong to assume that when Kant discussed virtue and character, and when Aristotle discussed virtue and character they were necessarily talking about the same thing. The quotes referred to in the previous chapter already hint at a radically different concept of virtue from the Aristotelian picture of gradual development and eventual harmony between the right reason and the right desire. It is important therefore to say a bit more about Kantian virtue. In doing so we will also consider whether Kantian virtue differs from Aristotelian virtue and, in part, whether Kant occasionally misinterprets Aristotle on virtue.

There seem to be two different understandings of virtue in Kant. On the one hand, in passages like those quoted earlier, virtue is an instantaneous revolution in the will. It is an immediate and full commitment to the moral law, an act of choice which is open to all of us, at any time in our lives, regardless of previous acts, influences or circumstances. Kant discusses this kind of virtue in the *Religion*. Rather than acquiring this kind of virtue, we choose to have it restored in us, as it relates to our original predisposition to the good. In a sense, this revolution to virtue involves a re-orientation to the incentive of the good, which was always present in us, as it cannot be lost, but which we can lose sight of. This kind of virtue, *virtus noumenon*, that is virtuous according to the intelligible self, is 'in need of no other incentive to recognize a duty except the representation of duty itself'[1] and comes about through a change of heart, a rebirth.

Although, as we shall see, Kant goes on to talk about gradual development of virtue, this understanding of virtue in the intelligible self is
central to his project. It is this kind of moral change of heart which is
immune to luck, and must be so, as otherwise we would be motivated
by a motive other than that of duty. This change is also necessary for
moral worth, as it lies in the root of one's attitude towards the good. If
this change of heart does not occur, true moral virtue cannot be achieved
merely by a change of habits and reform of conduct. This is because any
such gradual change, without the underlying revolution in orientation,
is bound to conform to the principle of self-love and not the principle
of duty. To borrow Kant's own examples, one converts to moderation
for the sake of health, to truth for the sake of reputation and to justice for
the sake of peace or profit, all of which are heteronomous considerations.

The intelligible/sensible distinction, then, has a corresponding distinction on virtue. Virtue in the intelligible self is central to the Kantian project,
as it involves a re-orientation to the motive of duty, which must underlie
any further development. Of course, no such corresponding notion as
the intelligible world and all its implications exists in Aristotle. And it is
this notion of the intelligible that grounds the Kantian claim of moral
immunity from luck. However, although there are no such corresponding
notions in Aristotle, as we saw in Chapter 4, there is a similar aspiration
to make room for a strong conception of reason. Aristotle shares a broad
aim with Kant, which is the aim of allowing room for reason, choice and
the voluntary. In Kant, this is clearly expressed, elaborated and defended
through the idea of the intelligible world. In Aristotle, one has to look
closer in the text for evidence of the independence of reason and the
importance of choosing virtue and choosing it for its own sake.

The Kantian picture of virtue, so far, is quite different from the
Aristotelian one, although I would like to suggest that there are similarities
in what motivates the two projects. However, Kant also understands virtue
in another sense, virtue in the empirical world, which corresponds more
closely to our usual understanding of Aristotelian virtue.

Virtue in the empirical character is a naturally acquired faculty,
developed through a period of time and through a gradual change in
habits and conduct. This understanding of virtue is very similar to
Aristotelian remarks about virtue. The *Metaphysics of Morals* outlines all
the factors which affect the development of this kind of virtue, such as
education, habituation, role models and so on. It is this understanding
of virtue that neo-Kantians appeal to in order to respond to criticisms
regarding the implausibility of the Kant picture. Kant does not ignore
virtue, neither does he have fewer resources than Aristotle in explaining

the concept (although it may well be that commentators have focused exclusively on other aspects of Kantian theory to the detriment of his thoughts on virtue). Furthermore, this conception of virtue, virtue in the sensible character, is subject to all sorts of contingencies and influences, which make it realistically subject to the influence of luck.

So far, I have focused on the similarities between Aristotelian virtue and Kantian virtue in the empirical character, and although the broad outlines are very similar, it does not mean that the concepts are identical in their detail. In what follows I will examine Kantian empirical virtue in detail and often through Kant's own interpretation of Aristotle, with respect to a number of details such as the role of habituation, the mean and the emotions. In what follows I will be discussing Kantian empirical virtue rather than virtue in the intelligible self, unless otherwise indicated.

7.2   Habit and moral examples

Kant seems to understand the role of habit in virtue in similar terms to Aristotle:

> virtue is not to be defined and valued merely as an aptitude and... a long-standing habit of morally good actions acquired by practice. For unless this aptitude results from considered, firm and continually purified principles, then, like any other mechanism of technically practical reason, it is neither armed for all situations nor adequately secured against the changes that new temptations could bring about.[2]

Kantian habit is an unreflective disposition, acquired through repetition and performed without thought and because of this it cannot be virtue proper, in the same way that Aristotle also differentiates between unreflective habit without choice and knowledge, and virtue. Also, it is interesting to note that in the preceding passage Kant could be interpreted as being against a rigid, inflexible approach to ethics. A mechanical, rigid, inflexible response cannot adequately deal with new and different situations, so a more practically adaptable approach may be required. Some virtue ethicists have made quite an objection out of the claim that Kantian theory is rigid, as opposed to the situation-sensitive Aristotelian account,[3] but perhaps there is less ground for such a claim than previously thought.

In any case, Kant is right in rejecting such a conception of virtue solely as a habit, which is something he does later on as well:

> An *aptitude* (*habitus*) is a facility in acting and a subjective perfection of *choice*. But not every such *faculty* is a *free* aptitude (*habitus*

libertatis); for if it is a *habit* (*assuetudo*), that is, a uniformity in action that has become a *necessity* through frequent repetition, it is not one that proceeds from freedom, and therefore not a moral aptitude.[4]

For if virtue consisted solely in habituation, it would belong to anyone with a natural inclination towards forming and retaining habits. Furthermore, the habits one did acquire would have no necessary connection with the demands of morality, but would depend on the random experiences one was subjected to. For Aristotle, habituation is a tool for the acquisition of virtue, it does not consist in virtue, nor can it function alone. Habituation can only be beneficial if it is guided towards the right direction and is accompanied by education, such that at the right stage of development the student apprehends the point of his habits and reaffirms the habits by an act of reason. Not any habitual act will do, but rather in order to become just one has to habituate himself in just actions. Thus, for Aristotle, a virtuous act performed out of habit does not proceed from a truly virtuous disposition.

Having said that, there is a significant difference in how Aristotle and Kant view the role of habituation. For Aristotle, habituation is a tool in the long road to virtue and may well be a starting point in beginning to shape one's dispositions. Understanding Aristotelian virtue takes a long time and involves developing one's moral perception and practical wisdom in order to perceive the right reason. Cognitive development is as important as development of affective states which support the right reason. For Kant, the starting point must be acceptance of the moral law. Any habitual behaviour must result from firm principles if it is to act as a mechanism for practical reason. Habituation may help shape practices, but the conversion to the moral law is instantaneous and precedes any of this gradual development.

I would want to say that the inspiration behind the Aristotelian and the Kantian projects is the same. They both wish to allow room for rationality, choice and, by implication, independent morality. In this project, habituation is merely a tool and should not be confused with either Aristotelian or Kantian true virtue. However, the Kantian account starts with, and has a central and irreplaceable place for, the revolution in the intelligible self, whereas Aristotelian practical wisdom is the result of years of development. Whereas this change in orientation is available to everyone at any time, for Kant, Aristotelian practical wisdom is a much more fragile good, one which most people will fail to achieve.

Interestingly, both Aristotle and Kant have a role for the good example in moral education, but again this role differs. Whereas for Aristotle the virtuous exemplar can act as a role model for virtue and play a central role in moral development, for Kant he is not a model, but only proof that it is possible to act in conformity with the moral law. This is because Kant resents the idea of comparing oneself with another human being and trying to emulate him. It is not others that we should compare ourselves with, but rather the idea of humanity and a direct comparison with how we should be with reference to the moral law.[5] Not only that, but Kant is suspicious of the feeling of admiration towards virtue in others:

> To teach only admiration for virtuous actions, however great a sacrifice these may have cost, falls short of the right spirit that ought to support the apprentice's feeling for the moral good. For, however virtuous someone is, all the good that he can ever perform still is merely duty; to do one's duty, however, is no more than to do what lies in the common moral order and is not, therefore, deserving of wonder. This admiration is, on the contrary, a dulling of our feeling for duty, as if to give obedience to it were something extraordinary and meritorious.[6]

In a sense then, the Kantian standard is much stricter than the Aristotelian one. An implication of Kant's thoughts on the availability of the motive of duty to everyone is that there is less understanding of failure to incorporate the maxim of duty and less admiration for success. In contrast, the Aristotelian project is more understanding of contingent factors which may impede one's final goal, and as a result may allow for some moral merit to attach to partial success.

Thus, a more complicated picture is emerging; various factors such as habituation, education and so on may influence the Kantian moral agent, but they are all secondary to the exercise of reason which leads to the affirmation of the moral law. By comparison, the Aristotelian picture is gradual both with respect to the development of the right reason and the right desire. Both Aristotle and Kant require that the agent stand in a certain relation towards virtue, although for Aristotle it has to be chosen and chosen for its own sake, whereas Kant speaks of reverence for the moral law and the motive of duty.

7.3   The doctrine of the mean

Kant is highly critical of Aristotle's doctrine of the mean: 'The distinction between virtue and vice can never be sought in the degree to which one follows certain maxims; it must rather be sought only in the specific quality of the maxims (their relation to the law).'[7] In a footnote to the above passage, Kant continues:

> what distinguished avarice (as a vice) from thrift (as a virtue) is not that avarice carries thrift too far but that avarice has an entirely different principle (maxim): that of economizing, not for the sake of enjoying one's wealth, but merely for the sake of possessing it, while denying oneself any enjoyment from it.[8]

Whatever the merits of the doctrine of the mean, this criticism is not one of its disadvantages. According to the doctrine of the mean, to every virtue correspond two vices; whereas the question of degree of feeling, which distinguishes the virtue from the vices, is a question of quality, the quality of appropriateness. Vice is here understood as an excess or deficiency deviating from what is appropriate. The degree of feeling appropriate to a virtue reflects the right amount that is required for that reaction to be a virtue. To err by excess or deficiency is not merely a mistake in degree, but a mistake in quality, in inappropriate feeling.[9] Underlying the vices of excess and deficiency is the wrong principle, for example in the case of cowardice, the judgement that my life is more precious than achieving the ends which threaten it, coupled with an excess of fear and concern with my own well-being. It is therefore, not the case that the doctrine of the mean assumes the agent has the right principle but overstates or understates its application.

7.4   Virtue, vice and weakness of will

As we have seen, in one sense, Kantian virtue is part of the intelligible world, it is accessible through reason, it results in an instant transformation of man, it is immune to luck and it is in this sense of 'virtue' that moral worth resides. In the other sense, virtue is part of the sensible world, it is the object of the senses, can be acquired gradually, it is subject to luck and is not the real object of moral worth. It seems to me that the focus of Kant's criticism of Aristotle and the real and significant difference between the two philosophers is that Kant takes Aristotle's references to virtue to refer to virtue as part of the sensible world. For Kant then, Aristotle has missed out altogether on why virtue has any moral worth, for it is only virtue as part of the intelligible self that has moral worth. Furthermore, it is Kant's understanding of virtue in the intelligible world which shapes the concept and distinguishes it from Aristotelian virtue.

Aristotelian virtue is characterized by harmony between the right reason and the right desire. Virtue should flow smoothly into action, the agent's desires in harmony, complimenting and supporting the dictates of his reason. Related to this is the concept of *eudaimonia* as a part of virtue;[10] a feeling of contentment, fulfilment and flourishing. Kantian virtue incorporates both elements of harmony and elements of struggle. Kantian virtue involves struggle because of our nature as finite, rational beings. We are always constrained by the moral ought, since if the moral ought were absent we would have a holy will. So we always feel the force and pressure of obligation upon us. Struggle is also involved in the will being independent from desires. The effect of the moral law is to suppress all inclinations based on feeling and this may produce a feeling of pain.[11] So there are at least two negative conceptions of virtue involving struggle. At the same time, however, there is harmony in virtue as there is a positive conception of freedom as lawgiving of its own. Virtue is not just a self-constraint, but a self-constraint in accordance with a principle of inner freedom, so that virtue is its own end and its own reward.[12] In addition to that, virtue can produce an appropriate feeling of satisfaction:

> For the rest, as the human will is by virtue of its freedom immediately determinable by the moral law, I certainly do not deny that frequent practice in conformity with this determining ground can finally produce subjectively a feeling of satisfaction with oneself; on the contrary, to establish and cultivate this feeling, which alone deserves to be called moral feeling strictly speaking, itself belongs to duty; but the concept of duty cannot be derived from it...[13]

At the same time, we also feel respect for the moral law, which is an ambiguous feeling. It is not a feeling of pleasure, as we give into it reluctantly, feel its burden and feel humiliated when we have to pay tribute to the merit of others. It is important to note that this feeling of respect is not an incentive to morality, instead it is morality itself in the same way that practical reason supplies authority to the law.[14] So some, generally construed positive, feelings are associated with Kantian virtue, but they differ from Aristotelian desire. Aristotelian desire is cultivated and developed over time to support reason. Kantian virtue involves affective states peculiar to it: a feeling of reverence for the moral law, which has some negative connotations, and a moral feeling of satisfaction.[15] Crucially, neither feeling should be interpreted as a motive for acting morally; rather the former is part of recognizing the moral law and the latter, part of seeing humanity's relation to reason, morality and freedom. So far I have considered feelings as part of Kantian virtue as such; I will discuss the role of inclinations in relation to virtue in more detail later on in this chapter.

Kantian vice bears some similarities to Aristotelian vice. The former involves a commitment to immoral principles as the latter involves choosing vice knowingly and for its own sake. The Kantian conception of weakness of will is open to interpretation, but, on at least some accounts,[16] could be seen as similar to Aristotelian weakness. The Kantian weak-willed agent is characterized by a lament, a feeling of regret, which is not present in the vicious agent. It is because of this that we can suppose that the weak-willed has a genuine commitment to morality, although it cannot be fully genuine as it falls short of virtue. Where the Aristotelian incontinent is aware of the struggle between the right principle and the right desire and is aware of losing this struggle, the Kantian is characterized by self-deception. He is susceptible to temptation, but fails to hold himself responsible for this susceptibility. The source of his regret is this susceptibility to what he wrongly interprets as natural weakness. Kantian incontinence is not so much about succumbing to desires contrary to one's better judgement, but is based on a fundamental mistrust of the emotions in general, which in this case have lead to self-deception and avoiding to recognize one's duty. This should also explain why the Kantian picture has no corresponding notion of continence. Struggling and overcoming the emotions *is* virtue for Kant. This is a different conception of virtue from Aristotle, who would interpret Kantian virtue as continence.

7.5 The role of inclinations

Kant's insistence on excluding natural sentiments and inclinations from the domain of the moral for which we are responsible is well documented and one passage in particular is frequently appealed to and criticized. It is worth quoting the passage at length:

> To help others where one can is a duty, and besides this there are many spirits of so sympathetic a temper that, without any further motive of vanity or self-interest they find an inner pleasure in spreading happiness around them and can take delight in the contentment of others as their own work. Yet I maintain that in such a case an action of this kind, however right and however amiable it may be, has still no genuine moral worth. It stands on the same footing as other

inclinations – for example, the inclination for honour, which if fortunate enough to hit on something beneficial and right and consequently honourable, deserves praise and encouragement, but not esteem; for its maxim lacks moral content, namely, the performance of such actions, not from inclination, but *from duty*. Suppose then that the mind of this friend of man were overclouded by sorrows of his own which extinguished all sympathy with the fate of others, but that he still had the power to help those in distress though no longer stirred by the need of others because sufficiently occupied with his own; and suppose that, when no longer moved by any inclination, he tears himself out of this deadly insensibility and does the action without any inclination for the sake of duty alone; then for the first time his action has genuine moral worth. Still further: if nature had implanted little sympathy in this or that man's heart; if (being in other respects an honest fellow) he were cold in temperament and indifferent to the sufferings of others – perhaps because, being endowed with the special gift of patience and robust endurance in his own sufferings, he assumed the like in others or even demanded it; if such a man (who would in truth not be the worst product of nature) were not exactly fashioned by her to be a philanthropist, would he not still find in himself a source from which he might draw a worth far higher than any that a good-natured temperament can have? Assuredly he would. It is precisely in this that the worth of character begins to show – a moral worth and beyond all comparison the highest – namely, that he does good, not from inclination, but from duty.[17]

Kant has been greatly criticized for this passage, for creating an implausible and unrealistic picture: the man who easily, naturally and from great sympathy and emotion acts kindly is not morally worthy, whereas the man who acts kindly from a cold conception of his duty and feels no sympathy and kindness is the true object of moral worth. Therefore, acts that we enjoy cannot have any moral worth.[18] Not only that, but adopting such an impartial standpoint may require us to abandon our commitments to the ideals and principles which make up our character and lead to loss of integrity.[19]

Recently, neo-Kantians have tried to provide a more acceptable analysis of this passage, one which may avoid these objections. Baron makes two points against these criticisms of Kant. She believes that the example is purposefully exaggerated because it is easier to discern that the agent is acting from duty if he also lacks any inclination to perform the act in question. Furthermore, she thinks that the relevant contrast is not between two people one of whom lacks inclination but possesses duty, and the other possessing inclination but lacking duty; rather it is between two people both of whom have the right desires but only one of whom also has a conception of the demands of duty.[20] However, such an interpretation does not seem to me to be true to the spirit of the passage. It is not the case that both agents have the right inclinations and one of them also possesses something additional, that is duty. Acting from duty cannot be an 'extra point in favour'. Kant is clear that the motive of duty is an unconditional good that cannot be compared with others. It alone gives moral worth to acts since it proceeds from a good will and as such it can also stand alone without any need for externals such as inclinations. If the question is whether one who acts from duty may also have good inclinations, we need to distinguish between acting *from* inclination and acting from duty *with* inclination. The first instance is the result of contingent facts about one's constitutive nature, that is the agent was lucky enough to have naturally kind inclinations. The second instance is the source of proper moral worth, and it is in this case that Kant sees a role for cultivating one's inclinations. Any precept proceeding from empirical grounds can only be a practical rule, not a moral law. This interpretation is also re-enforced by other passages, such as the following from *The Critique of Practical Reason*:

> Freedom, and the consciousness of freedom as an ability to follow the moral law as an unyielding disposition, is *independence from inclinations*, at least as motives determining our desire.... Inclination is blind and servile, whether it is kindly or not; and when morality is in question, reason must not play the part of mere guardian to inclination but, disregarding it altogether, must attend solely to its own interest as pure practical reason.[21]

Such passages reinforce the interpretation of Kant as attempting to make morality immune from luck. Natural inclinations and tendencies, such as sympathetic feelings of kindness, are not something we can choose to have or not. By their definition they are given to us by our natural constitution and as such belong to the domain of the sensible character which is open to the influences of constitutive luck. Kant cannot accept that something that is the product of external, uncontrollable and fickle contingencies, could be the basis for attributing moral worth to a person. It is a matter of fortune whether a naturally sympathetic man will act kindly: fortune in that he was originally endowed with a sympathetic disposition (note that Kant refers to patience as a gift) and fortune in that this disposition came to light at that particular moment and was not overshadowed by something else, such as personal sorrows. The truly moral man who acts from duty can be relied upon to do so regardless of the vagaries of moral luck. Even if it is the case that most people acting out of duty may also possess favourable natural inclinations, Kant's example of the man acting solely from duty with no inclination is purposefully extreme, to illustrate that a morality based exclusively on *a priori* reasoning cannot be affected by natural dispositions and the opportunities for their exercise. Further on[22] he points out that were morality to be a matter for our inclinations we would not be able to command anyone to be moral as we cannot command inclination.

An important point of interpretation here is whether such passages seem to recommend that the inclinations should be entirely extirpated, or suppressed by reason, or that such a degree of independence from the inclinations is required that they are silenced.[23] An implication of such an interpretation is the idea that Kantian virtue is more like Aristotelian continence, involving constant struggle against unruly inclinations. However, not everyone agrees with this interpretation of Kant on the inclinations and the subsequent charge that Kantian virtue amounts to no more than Aristotelian continence.[24]

There are two possible responses to this kind of charge. One is to argue that the motivation behind finding a role for the inclinations in Kantian theory may have more to do with an Aristotelian understanding of the moral life and its alleged advantage over Kant, than it has to do with Kantian theory as such. It may be that Kantians need to resist the objection at its inception, that is a Kantian need not accept the Aristotelian account of the importance of the emotions in the first place. If there is a role for the emotions, then it should be a Kantian role, rather than an attempt to allow Kantian theory to accommodate the insights of Aristotle. As such Kant does have an account of the feeling appropriate to virtue, but this is a decidedly Kantian approach.[25] There is a specific aesthetic capacity of feeling, a certain spiritedness, associated with doing one's duty, which is 'neither an instinctual drive that harmonized with reason, nor a morally well habituated inclination operative in conjunction of right reason and right desire'.[26] This is a technical term accompanying virtue (above identified as satisfaction with doing one's duty) and certainly different from an Aristotelian understanding of the desires. Its source is consciousness of our rational nature, in the same way that the feeling of respect is associated with the moral law, rather than any empirical inclinations. There is nothing commensurate to this feeling in Aristotle, and perhaps Kantians ought to resist the temptation to talk of inclinations in Aristotelian terms.

The second type of response is more willing to take the criticism on board in that it accepts that the emotions do have an important role to play in constructing a plausible account of morality, while it then goes on to find such a role for the emotions within Kantian theory. Baxley tries to find such an accommodating role for inclinations in Kantian theory. She points out that the Kantian's objection to inclinations is not against inclinations as such, but rather their adoption as grounds for action. The problem is our tendency – our tendency to evil – to give priority to inclinations when they are opposed to the claims of morality. She can then allow some room for inclinations which have been cultivated in accordance with reason, and can use this idea to make sense of remarks in works such as the *Metaphysics of Morals* which call for us to cultivate our emotions if we are to act morally. Thus, pathological passions, those which conflict with our moral duty, should be met with moral strength, whereas practical feelings, those which are responsive to the authority of reason, can be helpful in the moral sphere: '... general feelings of love and respect, as well as more specific person-directed feelings, like sympathy and gratitude, are allies of duty in the sense of facilitating our ability to carry out our various duties of virtue'.[27] Sympathetic feelings can, it is claimed, facilitate virtue by helping with the move from general requirements of imperfect duties, prompt beneficent actions and allow us to express our morally required actions in a humanely engaging way.[28]

Of course, such attempts to give a role for the emotions within Kantian theory are appealing, especially since they make the theory more plausible and explain some of the apparently perplexing remarks in some of Kant's works. However, a fine line has to be drawn, as such inclinations should not be seen as motivating or in any way supplementing or supporting the motive of duty. Baxley sees their role as being to 'prompt' or engage the agent, but does that mean that an agent without the appropriate inclinations fails to be motivated by duty as he fails to be prompted or engaged in the first place? This will not do, as it seems to give the inclinations a more central role than a Kantian would like. Crucially, the inclinations cannot be the ground for action, but may prompt or engage the agent to act, and therefore this account will be successful only if we can make sense of this distinction. This role of 'prompting' or 'engaging' cannot be fundamental, as it should not take over from the motive of duty, but then it is unclear whether this role is necessary in the first place.

More worryingly, this engaging role for the inclinations may threaten the role of duty as obligation and rational constraint. Human beings are finite and have to strive against their sensual natures, and any Kantian account has to be careful not to eliminate this feature of the theory as this would threaten the foundation of human freedom.[29] Kant himself makes the point:

> For, a command that one should do something gladly is in itself contradictory because if we already know of ourselves what it is incumbent upon us to do and, moreover, were conscious of liking to do it, a command about it would be quite unnecessary...That is to say, if a rational creature could ever reach the stage of thoroughly *liking* to fulfil all moral laws, this would mean that there would not be in him even the possibility of a desire that would provoke him to deviate from them; for, to overcome such a desire always costs the subject some sacrifice and therefore requires self-constraint, that is, inner necessitation to what one does not altogether like to do. But no creature can ever reach this stage of moral disposition.[30]

If this 'prompting' or 'engaging' role of the inclinations is successful, it may negate the idea of obligation, duty and struggle in Kantian morality. Fully engaged inclinations prompting us to act in accordance with the dictates of reason would negate the possibility of deviation from the dictates of reason.

Finally, inclinations are likely to deceive us; we misrepresent the demands of morality so that we are more likely to fulfil them; full of self-conceit we misjudge ourselves to be morally better than what we are; full of jealousy we misjudge others to be morally worse than what they are. We must constantly guard against the motive of self-love. These kinds of thoughts explain some of Kant's more perplexing remarks. He is mistrustful of others benefiting us, since gratitude involves a feeling of obligation generated by the receipt of benefits. The agent now stands in an inferior position to his benefactor, which is difficult to acknowledge and may lead to feelings of ingratitude. This is the propensity to evil in all of us coming to the fore here, manifested as resentment towards those who have benefited us, illustrating that natural feelings ought to be approached with mistrust. Given our propensity at self-deception, can we really trust ourselves to make good use of our inclinations? Underlying this concern is the Kantian idea that fundamentally virtue is not about harmony, but rather strength; the strength to subordinate the motive of self-love to that of morality where they should conflict. And crucially the emotions cannot be guaranteed not to conflict with the dictates of morality. It is this background which leads us to adopt a weary stance towards the emotions, which is entirely missing in Aristotle and allows him to accept a fully engaged role for the emotions. The gradual picture of moral development in Aristotle allows him to adopt a more trusting attitude towards emotions which have been guided and shaped from their very inception.

Any Kantian who wishes to make use of the inclinations must have this sub-context in mind, or risk presenting a rather Aristotelian theory of emotions which can be trained to follow, engage and help reason. It seems to me that mistrust of the emotions is fundamental to Kantian moral theory in more than one way. It may be that the ambition to reconcile the inclinations with reason is generated by Aristotelian criticisms of Kant, and in meeting these criticisms Kantians take on board the Aristotelian's understanding of the role of the inclinations. As a result, Kantians engage in a decidedly un-Kantian aim, on decidedly un-Kantian grounds.

7.6 Kantian character

The Kantian understanding of character is multifaceted. Munzel elaborates on more than one understanding of character:

> Morally speaking, character is the steadfast commitment to virtue that is realized through a resolute conduct of thought (Denkungsart) that is morally good in its form and that, in exercise, entails both causal and reflective elements. Anthropologically speaking, it is the formative task of the specific rational being we are, that is, of the rational human being in relation to loving nature. Aesthetically speaking, it is the task of producing, on the ground of freedom, the work of art proper to us qua humanity. Ontologically speaking, it is the achievement of the unity of the natural and moral orders in the individual, a unity that results in the concrete actualisation of the moral law in the world.[31]

On the one hand, a person *has* character when he has moral character. This character has intrinsic worth and is about what the agent is prepared to make of himself; '[t]he man of principles, from whom we know for sure what to expect, not from his instinct, for example, but from his will, has character'.[32] This sense of character is the sense in which we spoke of the intelligible character of virtue, or virtue in the noumenal, above. The term *Denkungsart*, used in all these cases, is difficult to translate, especially when we already have in mind Aristotelian understandings of virtue and character. Previously I translated it as intelligible virtue, but this has to be understood as a technical Kantian term. It is a 'cast of mind' or 'mode of thought' which can be re-orientation of thought towards the good, and refer to the agent's overall commitment to the moral law.

On the other hand we have the concept of *Sinnesart*. A person can have this or that physical character and be subject to certain natural tendencies and temperament. This is what can be made of a man[33] and seems to correspond to the sensible character. Although comparisons are difficult to draw, it is this sense of character which is closest to the Aristotelian understanding. In this sense, character develops gradually, is affected by habits, education and so on. Kant recognizes the diversity of natural talents different people may have and accepts that different people may develop themselves differently. He points out the necessity for cultivating one's talents in accordance with duty rather than following from natural inclinations, since this affirms man's freedom. Furthermore, certain states, for example poverty, are to be avoided not because they diminish one's happiness but because they may make one more vulnerable to the temptations of vice.[34] Although the capacity for moral feeling is present in every human being, there is an obligation to cultivate and strengthen it. The practice of virtue, in this sense, is similar to the practice of Aristotelian virtue in that they are both vulnerable to contingencies. However, *Sinnesart* refers to inclinations, emotions and mental and emotional attributes, and does not have a cognitive component as Aristotelian virtue does. Not only that, but crucially, empirical impulses cannot act directly on the will as causes of actions. They can serve as incentives to action, but they can only determine the will insofar as they are taken up as a maxim.[35] So although one's sensible nature may well be subject to contingencies outside one's control, an agent, by virtue of his rationality, can always stand outside one's desires and inclinations and judge them as *possible* grounds for action. To take the thought a step further, not only do inclinations bear no direct relation to evil, but they act as opportunities for demonstrating the robustness of moral power, that is virtue.[36]

To be a good human being, then, one has to start with a revolution in the *Denkungsart*; thought being central to the Kantian conception of character. This is followed by a gradual reform of the mode of the senses, the *Sinnesart*. Furthermore, the two are related, as the intelligible character has a formative or cultivating influence on the sensible character. Character, in a general sense, then, is the ordering of one's life in accordance with reason. Reason allows us to respond in a fitting way to the moral law, that is accept its necessitation; and under reason's guidance we can order our way of living, that is direct our aptitudes and sensibilities. It involves not only steadfast commitment to the good, but also good sensibilities; '... pure practical reason thereby succeeds in becoming subjectively practical; having procured an empirical character for itself in and through the capacity for choice, it imparts its rule as a regularity manifest in choice making and in the phenomenal appearances that result'.[37]

Finally, we have the concept of *Gesinnung*. This is the notion of virtue as strength, identified above, but it can also have a wider application. It is best understood as self-control over not just the inclinations, as in the case of controlling opposing forces, but a wider self-control over the processes of thought, 'specifically of choice making or the subjectively practical use of reason in human moral life. It is self-control that makes us fit as thinking beings to fulfil our human vocation and as such remains definitive of what it means to have good character.'[38] It should be understood as steadfastness or fortitude in the ordering of one's senses under moral principles.

> For while the capacity (*facultas*) to overcome all opposing sensible impulses can and must be *presupposed* in man on account of his freedom, yet this capacity as *strength* (*robur*) is something he must acquire; and the way to acquire it is to enhance the moral *incentive* (the thought of law), both by contemplating the dignity of the pure rational law in us (*contemplatione*) and by *practising* virtue (*exercitio*).[39]

In this sense, the Kantian *Gesinnung* has similarities with Aristotelian proper virtue, as they both are steadfast, settled dispositions, offering continuity of personality.[40] As such it may share in some of the advantages of Aristotelian character, in terms of giving an explanation of agency over time, as consistent and unified.

The Kantian picture of character and virtue is quite complicated and there are numerous interpretations of the main terms. The question now is how would such a picture of morality respond to the problem of moral luck. In a sense, the problem of moral luck is a practical problem about the attribution of responsibility, so an objection could be raised with respect to how practical attributions of responsibility are made under the Kantian picture. We have seen how Kant attempts to present a picture of morality as immune from luck, and we can even grant that he succeeds in this project, while still asking about judgements of responsibility in a practical sense.

There are a number of ways of looking at this problem. For one thing, true moral worth is attributed to the intelligible self,[41] but we have no access to an agent's intelligible self so as to judge his true moral worth. One's empirical character can be judged to be good or evil only in a limited sense as true moral worth comes from the motive of duty, but at least we can base such a limited judgement on evidence from the agent's nature. The concern is that one's empirical character may differ from one's intelligible self. When one's maxims conform to the moral law only coincidentally and originate from incentives other than the moral law, man's 'empirical character is then good but the intelligible character still evil'.[42] The opposite is also possible, that is one's intelligible self is good, but one is prevented from acting or perhaps there has not been enough time to affect a change in the mode of sensibility, and the sensible self seems evil. Not only that, but our own motives are opaque to us. It is not that our own motives are opaque to us because of the metaphysical status of the intelligible self, but even under conceptual understandings of the intelligible, we ourselves can never truly know the quality of the motives from which we choose to act:

> For a human being cannot see into the depths of his own heart so as to be quite certain, in even a single action, of the purity of his moral intention and the sincerity of his disposition, even when he has no doubt about the legality of his action. Very often he mistakes his own weakness, which counsels him against the venture of a misdeed, for virtue (which is the concept of strength); and how many people who have lived long and guiltless lives may not be merely fortunate in having escaped so many temptations? In the case of any deed it remains hidden from the agent himself how much pure moral content there has been in his disposition.[43]

How a Kantian might want to answer this objection depends on how he construes the relationship between the intelligible and the sensible. If these two accounts are understood as two standpoints in the agent, that of spectator or that of agent, then there are two standpoints from which actions can be considered. Actions may be causally conditioned or free, but we cannot say of an action that it is neither or both. Allison's account of two modes of agency gives a different answer. The intelligible self is a morally practically regulative idea of reason, which provides direction for the whole of the agent's moral life and thus brings a maxim as a general determination of the will to bear on decisions about particular actions. Thus agents are held responsible for genuine expressions of agency, as these involve an act of spontaneity (which may even include accepting inclinations as the appropriate ground for action).

Finally, it is the striving to make the incentive of every action conform to the motive of duty that is what the moral law prescribes, rather than the actual pure moral content of his mind. So crucially, the notion of responsibility found in Kant is such that it is incompatible with the influence of luck. What I mean by this is that in-as-much as moral luck poses a problem with ascriptions of responsibility and in-as-much as these ascriptions are practical, the Kantian answer to the practical examples may be incomplete. Where actions fail to conform with duty, it is clear that agents have no moral worth. However, 'we will also be faced with great ambiguities in trying to judge others' action or our own past action. Patterns of action will always be compatible with the ascription of various maxims, and if maxims cannot be known directly or with certainty, we may often be unsure which if several maxims should be ascribed to an agent.'[44]

7.7 Conclusion

The Kantian concepts of virtue and character are extremely complex and it is a mistake to assume that they easily correspond to their Aristotelian counterparts. Both theories make certain assumptions in their understandings of character and virtue, such that it is difficult to then straightforwardly compare like with like.

As we saw previously, the Aristotelian answer to the problem of moral luck is twofold. On the one hand, Aristotle accepts and embraces the vulnerability of the good life. On the other, there is an aspiration to make room for a conception of reason, choice and the voluntary. Similarly, the Kantian picture is multifaceted. On the one hand, commentators are right to interpret Kant as giving an account of morality as immune to luck. This immunity from luck is central to the Kantian project and is indeed possible through the notion of the intelligible, whether this is applied to virtue or character. At the same time, the Kantian can offer a plausible picture of the good life as vulnerable to contingencies. This is achieved through the ideas of empirical virtue and character. Of course, to accept such a picture, one has to give a convincing account of how the two conceptions of the intelligible and the empirical interact and influence each other. Giving such a complete account is beyond the scope of this work, although I have tried to hint at possible solutions.

It seems to me that, fundamentally, Kant elevates the natural through his understanding of reason, will and choice. Rather than dismissing natural impulses, he allows them a role within his understanding of freedom and agency. The choice to be moral is available to all of us, all of the time, since we must see ourselves as agents who have choice if we are to make sense of ourselves. In its shape, this claim has something in common with the Aristotelian claim that the natural is not to be feared and avoided, but rather embraced. For Kant, nature is more often contained and resisted, whereas for Aristotle it can be shaped and can assist in the project of reason, but both have an account of reason such that it can include a plausible understanding of the natural. Of course, the details of the position and their fundamental claims vary greatly, but it is not the case that Aristotle can respond to the possibility of moral luck, whereas Kant's theory is devastated by it. Ultimately, the project for Kantians may well be to find a way to both hold on to a commitment to freedom and give a plausible interpretation of moral anthropology (a project which has indeed merited a lot of attention in recent interpretations of Kant).

What we can say is that it is a mistake to represent Kant as being solely pre-occupied with making morality immune to luck. However, at the same time, it is a mistake to assume that Kant is merely elaborating on Aristotelian notions of virtue and character. Kantian virtue and character may share some common characteristics with the Aristotelian concepts, but fundamentally these are quite different terms used in radically different ways. If the Kantian is to respond to modern objections about the plausibility of his theory, he should do so on Kantian grounds, rather than allowing the theory to be manipulated to accommodate an Aristotelian understanding of character and virtue. That is, Kantians should not be held hostage to not having an *Aristotelian* understanding of character and virtue.

Finally, a big part of this discussion has been an implicit comparison between the two theoretical accounts of character and virtue. Clearly, the distinction between the intelligible and the sensible, whether understood as a metaphysical or conceptual account, occurs solely in Kant and there is no corresponding account in Aristotle. However, the noumenal is postulated because of our nature as rational inquirers, and we have seen how Aristotle also has a special role for reason, choice and the voluntary. In a sense, both theories have a central role for reason and its place in understanding virtue. Virtue proper cannot be accidental, brought about by mistake or unknowingly, and it cannot be purely the result of unreflective, natural inclinations, but must stand in a special relationship to reason. In this respect, Aristotle shares some of the Kantian ambition for immunity from luck.

The details of their understanding of virtue and character though differ. Fundamentally, Kant sees at the start of his project a radical conversion in one's mode of thought towards virtue. For Aristotle, the acquisition of knowledge and the ability to choose virtue and choose it for its own sake are gradual. Where Kant starts with the revolution on the mode of thought and then allows room for a gradual and time-consuming change in the mode of mores, the Aristotelian project is a life-long development towards the final (but by no means available to everyone) acquisition of practical wisdom and a firm and stable disposition to virtue. The role of inclinations here is different. In the Kantian project their role is open to interpretation and although they clearly cannot be the ground for action, they may have some role to play in engaging reason. For Aristotle, the role of the right desire is more central. Not only is virtue understood as the right reason complimented by the right desire, but a great deal of effort goes into shaping one's emotions during moral development. Aristotelian situational appreciation seems to have a large affective element, having to do with being 'moved' in the right way, by the right circumstances and in the right time.

Furthermore, crucially, Kantian virtue as a revolution in the intelligible self is available to everyone, at any time, in virtue of our rationality as human beings. Aristotelian virtue is 'reserved' for the lucky few who have had the right influences, nurturing environment, favourable opportunities and so on. For most of us, the moral life is one of gradual development and shift from continence to incontinence depending on situational factors. As a consequence of the above, for Kant, moral praise or blame is an all-or-nothing affair, as an agent either has moral worth or he does not (although there are problems with knowing even one's own moral worth). For Aristotle, there is some merit to be attributed for partial success and we should even welcome in a sense those who possess natural virtue as opposed to virtue proper. Finally, Aristotelian virtue is a state of harmony, whereas Kantian virtue is a state of struggle. This is because the moral law is always perceived as a constraint and this notion of duty as constraint is present only in Kant. However, both concepts of character give an enduring and unified account of agency over time.

What can we conclude then with respect to the initial dissatisfaction expressed by writers such as Williams, Nagel and Nussbaum with the Kantian position on moral luck? Initially, it is important to recognize that the Kantian position is more complicated than is sometimes given credit for. Also, in a very basic sense, both Aristotle and Kant share an understanding of the tension between the requirement for rationality and responsibility, and the need to offer a plausible conception of human nature and the contingencies which affect it. Having said that, the Kantian project relies on the intelligible/sensible distinction and one could object to it on the grounds that this distinction does not work. Or one could argue that some of the implications of the distinction itself, or the wider Kantian picture, are unacceptable. For example, even allowing for a Kantian role for the inclinations may not be sufficient. An Aristotelian could argue that the very conversion to virtue, choosing virtue for its own sake, involves an affective element. The suggestion here would be that our very grasp of virtue requires emotional elements in conjunction with cognitive abilities. So it is not just the application of virtue which requires favourable inclinations, but its very understanding.

Related to this point is the further idea that immunity from luck requires us to reject the influence of factors such as natural temperament on our moral judgements. This observation is at the heart of some of the moral luck examples. It is not that we would like the examples to be resolved by giving an account of morality as immune to luck, but rather that we want to hold on to our problematic judgements in respect to some of these examples, *despite* acknowledging that they are problematic. This is exactly why the Williams and Nagel examples are so perplexing and interesting. In a sense, we do want to continue saying that agents are responsible for actions, when clearly, significant elements of the case are outside their control. Similarly, there are some goods, arguably essential to the good life, which can only be understood as fragile and subject to luck, such as friendship. Perhaps we would not want to give up on such goods as part of virtue, or on their conception as vulnerable to luck.

Finally, one brief point on the role of nature. Aristotelians seem to allow for our natural impulses to be shaped and to compliment the rule of reason. For Kant, nature is either divorced from morality or elevated to the moral through the proper exercise of reason (depending on how one interprets Kant). Perhaps this is one final point that one could object to in the Kantian picture, and perhaps it is this Kantian distrust with our contingent natures which leads to some commentators objecting to the Kantian picture of virtue as being clinical and cold.

8
Virtue Ethics and Neo-Kantians: Slote, Hursthouse and Herman

8.1 Introduction

In 1958 Elizabeth Anscombe published a paper that was to change the focus of interest in moral philosophy.[1] In 'Modern Moral Philosophy' she argued that moral philosophy should re-divert its attention to the work of Aristotle, embrace the Aristotelian emphasis on moral psychology and abandon the Kantian preoccupation with duty and obligation. She drew a picture of modern moral philosophy from Sidgwick onwards as sharply contrasted with the Aristotelian use of 'moral'. She saw the dominance of the ideas of 'duty' and 'obligation' as arising from what she called a 'law conception of ethics', where: 'To have a *law* conception of ethics is to hold that what is needed for conformity with the virtues failure in which is the mark of being bad *qua* man (and not merely, say, *qua* craftsman or logician) – that what is needed for *this*, is required by divine law.'[2]

Anscombe's paper provoked renewed interest in the ethical work of Aristotle and his emphasis on the virtues, flourishing and character.[3] The result is a substantial and still growing literature on 'virtue ethics', which is, more often than not, presented as an alternative to Kantian and Consequentialist ethics.[4] Many recent moral philosophers are sympathetic to Anscombe's views about the need for a return to the Aristotelian way of understanding philosophy and they all agree that she has uncovered a serious deficiency in the way moral philosophy was being discussed. It is interesting to note, however, that as soon as they attempted to flesh out exactly how to correct this problem by re-focusing on character, the virtues and so on there is serious confusion and dis-agreement about the content of any such revival theory. The general agreement that an analysis of terms such as 'virtue' and 'character' should play a major part in any theory did not necessarily explain what this part should be and how it should be understood. Thus, much of the ensuing literature is concerned with exactly this question: the virtues and character are important, but exactly what role should they play and how does this give virtue ethical theories greater explanatory power than rival theories?

As a result of trying to answer this question, a number of theories now claim the title of 'virtue ethics'. The term 'virtue ethics' is now so broad and ill-defined that opponents of the theory (group of theories?) severely criticize it for this.[5] So one of the questions which should occupy anyone wishing to either criticize or promote virtue ethics is exactly what the theory is supposed to be about, as there have been a number of different versions of the theory put forward by different writers.[6]

However, to return to Anscombe's work, her paper was right in at least one respect, but at the same time wrong in at least one other respect. She was right in that modern moral philosophy had indeed neglected the questions she raised and the specific ways of answering them which are characteristic of Aristotelian ethics. There was no emphasis on moral psychology[7] (and this still remains more or less the case), the virtues, conceptions of flourishing, the importance of character and education and so on. However, at the same time, she was wrong in placing the blame for this on the work of philosophers such as Kant.[8] Recent commentaries on Kant's lesser known works (lesser known at least in the English-speaking world), such as *The Doctrine of Virtue*, have argued that Kant's work was not as restricted in its scope as Anscombe makes it out to be.

The discussion of Aristotle has indicated that, for Aristotle, moral luck is a possibility which has to be accommodated within his theory. The features of human, moral life are such so as to be vulnerable to luck, for example some people are more fortunate than others in their constitutive make-up, others have an abundance of good fortune in the shape of external goods, whereas others are only called upon to act in favourable circumstances and so on; and the differences based on luck are allowed by Aristotle to affect the overall ethical appraisal of a human life. By contrast, the Stoics (at the same time prefiguring Kant) rejected many of the ideas central to Aristotle, which make moral life vulnerable to contingency. They rejected a picture of virtue reliant on external goods, fickle passions, degrees of difficulty or gradual development. Similarly, one of the driving forces behind Kant's moral philosophy has been that his picture of the moral world should be one where the opportunity to act morally is available to all equally and free from contingencies.

Thus, in a sense, Aristotelian moral theory is not egalitarian; although reason, choice and voluntary action are still central to Aristotle, there are many opportunities for bad luck to divert the moral project. On the other hand, Kant's moral picture is strictly egalitarian; the moral life is open to all, equally, at any time of their lives and under any circumstances. The role of reason is central for Kant, virtue in the noumenal involving a sudden revolution in the mode of thought. Although there is room in the Kantian picture for a sensible character, potentially vulnerable to contingencies, this room is strictly limited.

This chapter looks at the work of modern philosophers working in the Aristotelian and Kantian traditions, that is virtue ethicists and a neo-Kantian, as they have emerged in the wake of Anscombe's criticisms. Modern philosophers are well aware of the work carried out by their colleagues working in rival traditions. Works such as Anscombe's paper, contrasting different traditions, are plentiful.[9] The result is that many commentators are aware of the conventional weaknesses of the traditions within which they work and try to show why their modern versions can compensate for established objections. The increase of interest in virtue ethics has also had the side effect that many neo-Kantians have re-focused their interest in those aspects of Kant's theory that deal with virtue. This is in recognition of the importance of moral concepts such as 'virtue' and 'character' and in an attempt to counter objections that Kantian ethics cannot deal with such concepts. Virtue ethicists, on the other hand, have found one of their greatest problems to be finding a distinctive grounding for their theory.

While retaining the basic background of the problem of moral luck, this chapter attempts to look at how virtue ethicists have tried to deal with the problem of moral luck and what connections they retain with Aristotle. The next chapter will consider how neo-Kantians have responded to the challenges set down by virtue ethics and whether they have maintained the Kantian ambition to keep morality immune from luck.

8.2   Virtue ethics

As already indicated above, there is no one theory of virtue ethics. Anscombe's paper gave rise to a number of different theories which try to address her concerns and go under the umbrella term of 'virtue ethics'. Perhaps what holds these theories together is a reliance, to a greater of lesser degree, on the notions of 'virtue' and 'character', which are traditionally associated with the work of Aristotle. By extension then, most of these theories will claim some connection with Aristotelian moral theory.[10] Commenting on or even identifying and cataloguing all these new theories and the relations between them would be a worthy task in itself, but one well beyond the scope of this book. Instead, I will focus on two representatives of virtue ethics, Michael Slote and Rosalind Hursthouse.

One way of attempting to distinguish between all these different versions of virtue ethics is by looking at how they answer a common question: What is the grounding of virtue ethics? Whatever the disadvantages of deontological and consequentialist theories, one of the advantages they share, which it is claimed is as yet missing from virtue ethics, is that each rests on a strong groundwork of theoretical discussions. These philosophical discussions, whether they are supportive or critical of deontology and consequentialism, at least serve to define the boundaries of these theories. Even though there is still great scope for disagreement within these traditions, there are well-defined, commonly accepted ideas as to what constitutes a deontological or a consequentialist theory and what its aims are. Without wanting to exaggerate the degree of conformity of thought within these traditions, it is safe to say that deontology and consequentialism are well defined in a way which is lacking in virtue ethics. This is evident in the number of 'survey' articles[11] of virtue ethics which identify a number of different approaches, all of which claim for themselves the title of 'virtue ethics'. Some of these different varieties of virtue ethics have been developed in response to objections and questions from critics of the theory, and one of the pressing questions which has served to guide the development of this work has been 'what is the grounding of virtue ethics?'

This question seems to be asking what is the basis for the justification of the theory's reliance on the concepts of 'virtue' and 'character'. Deontologists and consequentialists may also make use of 'virtue' and 'character', but they do so in a way such that right behaviour is theoretically prior to virtue and character in order of justification. Deontologists may ultimately rely on duty and the moral law, consequentialists on benevolence or utility, but what do virtue ethicists ultimately rely on? One way of phrasing this concern is Alderman's question:

> Nevertheless, however central the appeal to character has been in moral argument or however central I argue it ought to be, a first obligation of any argument such as this is to suggest some prima facie reasons as to why character is a more adequate final court of appeal in moral philosophy than either rights, goals or rules.[12]

This question is subtly related to the problem of moral luck. The Aristotelian discussion on moral luck was not conclusive on the question of the relationship between reason and character. One's character, for example its developments, opportunities for its display and so on, is subject to the influence of moral luck without this being, in itself, an influence that Aristotle would want to avoid. At the same time Aristotle also uses a notion of 'choice' and 'the voluntary' which implies a strong and independent ability to reason. In a sense, then, retaining a conception of responsibility, associated with true choice, implies a conception of reason immune to luck. As we saw previously, Aristotle does not seem to be aware of this tension or to provide any clear answers for its resolution. Another way of putting the same concern is to say that although we have a clear and plausible picture of character formation, we do not know the origins or nature of this ability to reason morally and do so independently of constitutive factors. This concern relates to recent objections raised against virtue ethics because many of these objections question the grounding of virtue ethics:

> What is definitive of virtue ethics, I take it, is that it makes virtues not just important to, but also in some sense basic in, the moral structure: they are so deep in the structure that they can be said to generate or to animate the rest of it…it makes the assessment of agents more basic than the assessment of actions…The criterion for correct choice proposed by virtue ethics, therefore, is not a slate of general principles, but a person: our standard is a person with informed dispositions in wise balance. But this criterion cries out for clarification at two points. If virtues are dispositions of the *right* sort, how do we decide on the *right* sort? And how do we decide on the *right* balance between them?[13]

If what is crucial is having dispositions of the right sort, we are entitled to ask what determines certain dispositions as being those of the right sort. For Aristotle, our dispositions are partly determined by contingent factors and are therefore subject to the influence of moral luck. This aspect of Aristotelian theories has inspired critics to accuse it of relativism.[14] That is, since the right sort of dispositions can be affected by incidental factors that differ from one culture to another or from one person to another, there is no one answer to what are the right dispositions. Thus, the answer to what are the right dispositions to have can differ from one culture to another or from one individual to another depending on factors outside the agent's control. However, this is only part of the Aristotelian picture; the other part consists of the notion of 'reason' that allows us to make judgements about choice, voluntariness and responsibility. It seems to me that what many recent virtue ethicists have been concerned with is to find an answer to what should be the grounding of this conception of 'reason'.[15]

Finding an answer to this question has resulted in the development of different styles of virtue ethics. Some commentators rely on a notion of flourishing and may couple this with a teleological view of nature,[16] others appeal to common-sense intuitions,[17] others try to argue for the conceptual primacy of *aretaic* notions over *deontic* notions,[18] another possible appeal is to the role of an ideally virtuous role model,[19] others have argued for the theoretically dominant position of the virtues because of their explanatory primacy,[20] whereas there are also a wealth of commentaries on what may have been Aristotle's own answer to this question.[21] From these possible answers I will look at the work of Michael Slote and Rosalind Hursthouse.

Slote has written extensively and in detail on virtue ethics. Many of the works in the field of virtue ethics consist of short articles dealing with limited, specific points because developments in this area of moral theory have been quite recent. However, Slote – having published shorter pieces of work – has also published detailed and lengthy accounts, in which he elaborates on his distinctive version of virtue ethics. It should be noted that, in fact, Slote has given us two versions of virtue ethics: his original work on common-sense virtue ethics and a later development, inspired more from Hume than Aristotle, based on moral sentimentalism.[22] I will be concentrating on his original development of virtue ethics, common-sense virtue ethics, partly because he claims that this account avoids the problem of moral luck.

The claim in Slote's words is that:

> a non-moral virtue ethics can avoid the paradox and contradiction that arises in common-sense morality with respect to moral luck, and we have attempted to do this by showing how a virtue ethics that avoids both specifically moral concepts and common-sense or other moral judgements can safely accommodate itself to luck or accident, that is, to their partial role in determining what virtue-ethical attributions apply or fail to apply.[23]

If he is correct, then we will have a theory of the virtues that is immune to moral luck, a satisfactory account of which, neither Aristotle nor Kant have been able to give.

8.3 Slote

Slote's virtue ethics seems to develop around two ideas which are relevant to this discussion: the first is the idea of an agent-based theory and the second a move from morality to ethics. Agent-based theories are contrasted with agent-focused theories. Agent-focused theories are distinguished from other theories because their understanding of the 'moral or ethical life' is based on an understanding of 'what it is to be a virtuous individual or what it is to have one or another particular virtue, conceived as an inner trait or disposition of the individual'.[24] According to Slote, Aristotle's theory is agent-focused. For such theories, being virtuous 'involves being keyed in to facts independent of one's virtuousness about what acts are admirable or called for'.[25]

Agent-based theories, on the other hand, are more radical in that:

> the ethical character of actions is not thus independent of how and why and by whom the actions are done. Rather, what is independent and fundamental is our understanding and evaluation of human motives and habits, and the evaluation of actions is entirely derivative from and dependent on what we have to say ethically about (the inner life of) the agents who perform those actions.[26]

Ultimately Slote's discussion of what we have to say about the inner life of agents seems to come down to intuitions:

> Most ethical theories make some sort of ground-floor ethical assumptions, assumptions used to explain or derive other ethical judgements or facts, but not themselves based on any further ethical assumptions... something exactly analogous also holds for agent-based moral conceptions. As in science, the use of fundamental or ground-floor explanatory assumptions doesn't require us to treat certain ethical assumptions as sacrosanct and is entirely in keeping with intellectual open-mindedness.[27]

Slote argues that '... moral facts and conclusions aren't to be found "out in the world", but, rather, emerge from moral motivation directed toward and relying upon perceived human, social and causal facts'.[28] Slote's theory then, which he calls 'common sense virtue ethics', relies on 'perceived human, social and causal facts' and 'ground-floor ethical assumptions', in other words then, intuitions.[29]

The second idea crucial in Slote's analysis is a move from morality to ethics. Slote argues that *aretaic* notions[30] are wider than moral evaluations as there are some traits of character which we find admirable which are not connected to the moral:

> the virtue ethics I espouse will avoid making use of specifically moral notions. Its fundamental aretaic concepts will be those of a virtue or an admirable trait, action, or individual and ... the latter notions in their common usage and application are not specifically moral.[31]

> Roughly speaking, only what concerns people other than the agent or trait possessor counts intuitively as a moral virtue or as morally good, but by our common lights both other-benefiting and self-benefiting traits and actions can be admirable (instances of) virtues...The virtue ethics I will be developing will discard specifically moral aretaic concepts in favor of 'neutral' aretaic concepts like admirability and (a) virtue.[32]

8.4 Slote on luck

Slote claims that his version of virtue ethics avoids many of the problems that have plagued deontology and consequentialism, amongst which is moral luck. His understanding of the problem is that we tend to think worse of/blame some people rather than others because of things that are outside their control. Common-sense moral thinking[33] makes room for moral luck by allowing differences in moral judgement of cases where the only difference is the result of luck. Slote's version of virtue ethics avoids the problem of moral luck by relying on ethical rather than moral notions of evaluation.

He uses the example of a man looking for work during the Depression to explain why this is so.[34] If we, at least partly, equate the notion of a good father with that of a good provider, then whether the man will be a good father will depend on how lucky he is in finding a job. However, although moral notions are connected with the idea of blameworthiness, ethical notions are not. Instead of using moral notions, we should use ethical notions to make 'intuitively plausible judgements of admirability and deplorability that have no essential connection to blameworthiness'.[35] Thus:

> [j]udgements about how good a provider someone has been can be (seen as) detached from any commitment to moral condemnation and

allowed to function (merely) as forms of *ethical appraisal*, and it is certainly easy enough to see how a failure to be a good provider might in no way be either blameworthy or reprehensible.[36]

Similarly, vicious killers, who cannot help their conditions, and psychotic people can be ethically criticized because 'they are in a terrible way to be', but moral blame is not appropriate:

> in speaking thus of a vicious dog, we don't assume that the dog could have helped becoming vicious or is blameworthy for being so. It may have been made vicious by the cruel treatment of its master, and it is, and of course we know that it is, a matter of luck to some extent whether a given puppy is treated kindly or cruelly by those who raise it. Clearly, in the case of dogs, the judgement of viciousness in no way commits anyone to a judgement of reprehensibility or blameworthiness, and there is absolutely no reason to think human viciousness as described above should be conceived any differently... When we call a dog vicious or claim someone is a vicious killer or psychopath we are clearly evaluating in a non-superficial an important way, but such a negative assessment of what someone or something is deeply like does not commit us to the moral evaluations that land us in such difficulties in connection with luck. The vicious killer may not be able to help being as he is or acting as he does, but in characterizing him as we do, we are expressing a highly negative opinion about him. We are saying that one way he (centrally or deeply) is in a terrible way to be, and the example is a good one, therefore, of the possibility of ethical criticism without moral blame.[37]

Assessments of character then need not rely on moral concepts, but can be made on the basis of admirability or deplorability of traits of character. These assessments in turn will be made on the grounds of what common-sensically and intuitively counts as admirable or deplorable.

If Slote is correct in his analysis, then he has uncovered a moral theory (if his theory can still be called a *moral* theory) that succeeds in solving the problem of moral luck and remains a virtue ethical theory. At the same time, Slote can claim that his move from 'morality' to the wider concept of the 'ethical' brings him closer to the spirit of Aristotle.[38] However, unfortunately his theory seems to be subject to a number of different problems.

8.5 Critique of Slote

One major problem is that it is not clear whether Slote fully appreciates the problem of moral luck. We have seen that in one sense the idea of 'moral luck' implies an oxymoron, as the idea of 'morality' suggests responsibility and praise/blameworthiness, whereas luck suggests loss of control. Slote's examples are all of cases where the agent is not initially responsible for what he has done, that is the father has lost his job through no fault of his own and cannot find another one because of the large numbers of equally well-qualified other applicants, the killer has a medical condition and so on and he concludes that these agents should not be the subjects of *moral* blame but rather *ethical* deplorability. This conclusion is supposed to be supported by his general move from the moral to the ethical. However, there are several difficulties with such a position.

First, it is unclear whether *any* theory would hold a mentally ill person responsible for his actions. Mental competence is a presupposition for the attribution of moral blame, and an agent who is not mentally competent is simply not responsible for his actions. He may be held legally accountable for his actions, but even in such a case the plea of legal insanity recognizes this essential lack of accountability.[39] In saying that this vicious killer is similar to a dog, Slote seems to be drawing our attention to the ways both the dog and the killer are not rational and therefore not responsible for their acts. Slote seems to be altogether avoiding the crucial problem here, which is, that although we know that all dogs lack the ability to reason morally, it is not always easy to say so of all killers. The problem with such extreme murderers is exactly whether they are mad or bad and whether an extreme kind of 'badness' is simply madness.

Secondly, I cannot see why a judgement of ethical appraisal of deplorability is less severe than a judgement of moral condemnation of blameworthiness. For the idea that emerges from Slote's work is that his theory can avoid the problems posed by moral luck because it altogether avoids moral judgements. However, why is not Slote's theory, in his terms, still subject to *ethical luck*? After all, the father in Slote's example may not be morally blameworthy, but he is judged, according to Slote, to be ethically deplorable *for something that was outside his control*. So the tension between morality and lack of control is transformed into a tension between ethics and lack of control. I do not see why the wider concept of the 'ethical' as such is immune to luck; after all a judgement of deplorability for something that was outside the agent's control seems, on the face of it, as a pretty unfair judgement that retains the tension between ethics and luck, if not the tension between morality and luck. Driver recognizes this problem for Slote when she writes:

> For many people it was bad luck on a cosmic scale that they happened to be born in the Pre Civil War south where slavery – an immoral practice – was taken for granted. Because of this bad luck these people lack a quality, perhaps some form of fairness or compassion, that very similar people alive today do not lack, but would have lacked under those circumstances. Thus, they are criticizable for its lack, on Slote's view, whereas those alive today are not criticizable. This seems odd, even if the issue of blame does not arise.[40]

Driver's point here seems to be that even an ethical judgement of deplorability against those agents who are supporters of slavery due to factors outside their control is problematic.

Thirdly, at a more fundamental level, although Slote claims support from Aristotle in his distinction between the moral and the ethical, it is not at all clear that there is Aristotelian support for Slote's interpretation of these examples. Slote's unfortunate father is like Aristotle's unfortunate captain, as they both find themselves in a difficult situation through no fault of their own. The unfortunate captain is judged not to have acted voluntarily in the true sense of having made a choice to jettison his cargo as circumstances forced his actions. Similarly the unfortunate father's actions were non-culpably out of his control and his decision was made for him by circumstances not of his own making. So not only is the unfortunate father not blameworthy, but his actions are not even deplorable. As the father's act was not a voluntary act, it is not an act that should be taken into consideration in assessing his character. Also, Slote's distinction between the ethical and the moral, at one level, seems to be between acts whose concern is the good of others (moral) and acts whose concern is the agent himself and others (ethics). However, there does not seem to be any Aristotelian support for a distinction on these grounds between ethics and morality. One of Slote's examples of a self-regarding virtue is prudence which, according to an Aristotelian understanding of the concept, is not a self-regarding virtue at all. Prudence or better translated as practical wisdom, for Aristotle, is not about looking after one's own concerns, but is the ability to see how the demands of all the different virtues come together and the ability to resolve moral problems.[41] Thus, Slote's examples of moral luck are problematic in themselves as instances of moral luck in the first place, and even his solution to them as problems of moral luck can also be objected to.

Another major problem with Slote's theory is that it is not always clear that we *should* want to abandon a notion of moral blameworthiness. There are many cases where we do want to attribute blame to someone for his voluntary choices and Slote's theory, peculiarly, does not seem to leave room for this. It is not just that we want to say that a grossly negligent builder who kills someone is in a 'terrible way to be', but that we want to blame him for being negligent and irresponsible. In one sense then, Slote's theory is too extreme as he uses the notion of 'ethical appraisal' in cases where its use is unjustified, for example the mental murderer and the unfortunate father, but in another sense it is too weak as it does not make room for judgements of moral blameworthiness in cases where it is required to do so, for example the case of the negligent builder.

Lastly, Slote claims that another reason why his theory is not subject to luck is because the moral quality of an action is determined by the moral quality of its motives:

> For if we judge the actions or ourselves or others simply by their effects in the world, we end up unable to distinguish accidentally or ironically useful actions (or slips on banana peels) from actions that we actually morally admire and that are morally good and praiseworthy.[42]

Slote is partly right and partly wrong and the reason for this is because he does not distinguish between different kinds of moral luck. He is partly right as a theory which evaluates motives certainly avoids the effects of *resultant* luck. However, he is also partly wrong as a theory of motives does not necessarily avoid the influence of constitutive and developmental luck.

Part of the difficulty here is that Slote interprets several examples as examples of resultant luck. He considers the Nagel-type examples of negligent drivers and accepts these as examples of resultant luck. However, as we have seen previously, this need not be the case. In fact, we would expect a theory of virtue to resist this interpretation. Surely what both drivers are to be held accountable for is their character traits which lead to such displays of callousness and disregard for the welfare of others. I take it that Dennett makes a similar point in his reply to Slote when he puts forward the example of Russian roulette. If Jones entices your child to play Russian roulette with a loaded revolver, common sense would be quite comfortable with holding Jones equally blameworthy whether your child dies as a result or not. Of course, if your child does die there is 'more harm to regret',[43] but in both cases we wish to hold Jones equally responsible.[44] In cases such as the drunken drivers and Jones then, we would expect a theory of motives to argue that it is not results which matter in moral evaluations, but motives, and that such motives can be judged praise or blame worthy.

8.6 Hursthouse

Rosalind Hursthouse's account of virtue ethics has much closer ties to Aristotle and starts from many of the important Aristotelian insights. Hursthouse's starting point is a rejection of rigid, codified rules and an emphasis on the uncodifiability of ethics. If her virtue ethics is to be action guiding, it is not because it will give us a set of rules applicable to any case we come across. Rather, and this is an advantage of the theory, when seeking advice on how to act, virtue ethics prescribes that we act virtuously, that is act courageously, kindly, honestly and so on. Central to this claim is the notion of practical wisdom. Practical wisdom underlies all the virtues, and in this way we can make sense of the unity of the virtues, and is exactly the ability to 'see' the demands of virtue and resolve apparent conflicts between different virtues. Again following Aristotle, Hursthouse points out that developing one's practical wisdom is a difficult and lengthy project, and much emphasis is placed on mechanisms for moral education, such as the role of the virtuous model as an example of virtue.

A large part of Hursthouse's project is taken up with a comparison of her Aristotelian ideas with Kant. She urges us to consider the similarities between the two accounts rather than adopting a confrontational stance. Thus, she argues that Kant and Aristotle have more in common in their treatment of the emotions than previously thought. The Kantian mistrust of the emotions *on their own* is mirrored in Aristotle, who only sees a role for the emotions if they are properly guided by reason. Acting from inclination is not sufficient for Aristotle any more than for Kant, since acting for the sake of virtue and choosing virtue knowingly is what is important. The significant difference between Aristotle and Kant on this issue is that although for Aristotle virtue is harmony between reason and the right desire, for Kant virtue is always strength in doing one's duty and resisting desire.

Furthermore, Hursthouse controversially argues that if we examine the Aristotelian notion of 'choice' we can make sense of moral motivation and in particular of the idea of acting from duty as part of Aristotelian theory. This is because the Aristotelian idea of acting from virtue involves the agent's acting because she thought she was right, a claim which is also about 'what sort of person the agent is – a claim that goes "all the way down" '.[45] Hursthouse explains that the reason why we should look to the virtuous agent to find out what we should do is because she acts knowingly, for the right reason and with the appropriate feeling, and the more we approximate the moral motivation of the virtuous agent the more we act well. From outside the viewpoint of virtue it is difficult, if not impossible, to grasp what it means to act through understanding the demands of virtue, since:

> one's detailed grasp of what is involved in acting virtuously, in acting for the *right* reasons, is not separable from one's grasp of what each of the virtues involves, and one's grasp of that is not separable from possession of the virtues themselves.[46]

This account is not so much an explanation of the reason for action, but a rejection of several other reasons as appropriate grounds for action, for example acting from inclination, by accident, under compulsion and so on. To act from virtue then is the capacity to 'see' and be motivated by the right reason; and this understanding of moral motivation is quite similar to the Kantian understanding of acting from duty. For Kant the action that has moral worth is similarly not motivated by inclination, or performed accidentally or under the orders of a higher being, but it is chosen out of a sense of reverence for the moral law, an understanding of the demands of morality and why they are binding. Similarly Aristotelian moral motivation can be traced back to an understanding of virtue as demanding what is morally right. Interestingly, Hursthouse, like Kant, also argues that self-knowledge about our own character states and virtue may well be obscure and fallible.[47]

Central to this theory is an account of human flourishing. Actions and agents are evaluated in terms of human flourishing. Particular traits are identified as virtues because they make their possessor a good human being. This, in turn, is understood in terms of 'human nature, on what is involved in being good *qua* human being'.[48] All living things can be evaluated qua speciments of their natural kind. Since human beings are part of the natural world the criteria for evaluating them must resemble those used to evaluate other animals, with the addition of the idea that human beings act 'from reason' rather than 'from inclination'. The characteristic way of human beings is the rational way: by their very nature human beings act rationally, a characteristic which allows us to make decisions and effect change in our character and allows others to hold us responsible for those decisions. So humans are virtuous if they have reasoned dispositions to act so as to promote four ends: individual survival; the survival of the human species; characteristic freedom from pain and enjoyment; and the good functioning of the social group.

8.7   Hursthouse on luck

Hursthouse's thoughts on luck mirror our earlier conclusions with regard to Aristotle on luck. Her account of virtue ethics accepts and embraces the role of constitutive and developmental factors, while maintaining a role for reason, choice and the voluntary.

As one would expect from a modern Aristotelian, Hursthouse dismisses the influence of resultant luck. Faced with a man who acts wrongly, but evades the bad consequences of his actions due to good luck, she concludes that 'although he can congratulate himself on his good luck, he cannot congratulate. himself on having done what is right'.[49] Acting viciously is then more than simply producing bad consequences, and should these consequences be avoided due to a stroke of luck, our evaluation of the agent as vicious still stands. Rather than be apologetic about this feature of her theory, or accept it as a counter-intuitive implication of moral luck, Hursthouse finds this to be an attractive feature of her account. In a sense, then she rejects the influence of resultant luck and sees this move as unproblematic, as it is a feature of the theory that ' "[g]ood action" is so called advisedly, and although it is conceptually linked to morally correct (right) decision and to "action of the virtuous agent", it is *also* conceptually linked to "good life" and *eudaimonia*'.[50] Based on these thoughts, she also concludes that virtuous agents who are unlucky enough to face rare tragic dilemmas, such that require one to do terrible things, cannot emerge unscathed. Such catastrophic bad luck results in a life ruined. So already then, the effects of luck are limited, as we do not evaluate agents based on the results of their actions, but overwhelming bad luck cannot be avoided.

Hursthouse's discussion of issues relating to constitutive and developmental luck reveals her solution to the tension of moral luck. She recognizes the immense impact of natural and environmental factors in one's moral development, but always retains a role for reason. Reason can achieve much in questioning one's emotional reactions, scrutinizing one's thoughts and consciously reflecting on one's decisions. This means that we are responsible for our temperaments, even when naturally contrary, as we can choose to accept our defects or choose to strive to reform them. Of course, change must be gradual and is itself vulnerable and difficult. Total retraining of all our natural tendencies by reason may not be possible, but the moral project for most of us will involve long-term striving and development.

Hursthouse's interpretation of the role of reason, especially evident in her remarks about the similarities between Kantian duty and Aristotle on reason and choice, allows her to find room for evaluations of responsibility, while retaining a plausible picture of moral development. Her account of reason is based on her naturalistic claim that humans have the peculiar capacity to act on reasons, the 'characteristic way' of humans is 'any way that we can rightly see as good, as something that we have reason to do'.[51]

8.8   Hursthouse on reason

Whether Hursthouse succeeds in her response to the problem of moral luck will depend on how convincing her account of reason is. As we saw previously, the strength of the Aristotelian account was a plausible conception of moral development subject to contingencies. At the same time there is also a conception of reason, choice and the voluntary which can ground ascriptions of responsibility. A neo-Aristotelian may then want to take up the challenge of elaborating on this role of reason within a theory vulnerable to luck. One could interpret Hursthouse as attempting to do just that.

Her understanding of the role of reason is certainly not Kantian. She explicitly rejects the Kantian account of moral objectivity which is generated by our conceptions of ourselves as rational beings;[52] for Hursthouse we are neither creatures with immortal souls nor 'beings' who are persons or rational agents. The attraction of naturalism is that we should 'evaluate ourselves as a natural kind, a species which is part of the natural biological order of things'.[53] Therefore, we need to consider what she means when she argues that the 'characteristic way' of humans is the rational way.

By this, Hursthouse does not mean a statistical notion, that is the idea that most humans will behave in such a way, such that if we want to know what is the rational thing to do we should look at how the majority of specimens of the species behave; 'the notion is avowedly normative, and is clearly going to yield judgements to the effect that many human beings are *not* going on "in the way characteristic of the species" and are thereby defective human beings'.[54] However, this may result in a problem. Thoughts of the naturally characteristic way for humans to behave bring to mind at least a partly descriptive concept. Hursthouse's interpretation takes out almost all this descriptive content in favour of a normative understanding of the term. Not only are there things humans character-istically do, but we can reflect on what we do, assess it and change it; '[t]his is a major part of the genuinely transforming effect the fact of our rationality has on the basic naturalistic structure'.[55] Hursthouse wants to introduce this strong normative element, which allows her to say that the characteristic way of humans is reason and this is a unified and common aim, while maintaining the structure of naturalism in that good humans foster the four ends appropriate to our species.

These thoughts open up Hursthouse to two criticisms. First, some 'characteristic ways' that humans behave are bad, despite the fact that they give us enjoyment, for example eating meat, so the theory allows too much. At the same time, some practices do not fulfil the four ends, for example, homosexuality which fails to promote the survival of the species, which leads to the objection that the theory allows too little. Secondly, the reason why we want to say vegetarianism, for example, is good has nothing to do with the four ends; rather it is based on thoughts about the welfare of animals.[56] Hursthouse responds to this by discussing the role of temperance and licentiousness, but this, as Hooker points out, is to shift the focus. A separate account has to be given now of the value of temperance in the light of the four aims, and even then it still remains the case that homosexuality does not promote the survival of the species. So whether a temperate homosexual is morally better than a licentious homosexual is really beside the point. This leads Hooker to conclude that '[t]he criterion of virtue should refer to the promotion of *well-being*, rather than to *survival*'.[57]

Hursthouse does respond to these objections. On the example of homosexuality she points out that this is a practice and not a character trait. Homosexuality *per se* is neither morally good nor morally bad, which does explain why one would want to focus on temperance and licentiousness, presumably regardless of whether they are traits exhi-bited by homosexuals, heterosexuals or any one else. I find this answer very plausible and I would be more than happy to accept such a view of the value of sexual practices, that is, in itself sex is neither morally good nor bad, it is the character traits displayed through it, which can also be displayed through other activities, which are morally good or bad (character traits such as temperance, fidelity, loyalty or untrustworthiness, abuse, lack of concern for others). However, I do not see how Hursthouse can hold on to this claim as well as her four characteristic ends for humans. At least three of the ends, individual survival, continuation of the species and enjoyment, seem to me to be associated with practices rather than character traits. Whether these practices are then carried out in a virtuous way is the same question as asking whether someone engages in sexual activity in a way compatible with virtue. I think Hursthouse is right in saying that having a virtue 'includes certain motivations or reasons for one's actions',[58] I think she is right in pin-pointing what these are with respect to specific virtues and their relation to practices, and I also think she is right in distinguishing practices from virtues. What she has not provided us with sufficient reasons for accepting though is that this project is grounded in the four characteristic ends, and I think this is evident in her own accounts of specific virtues which stray quite a bit from the narrow four ends. Hursthouse claims that what the four ends do is to fit 'our concepts of *virtue* and *good human being* and *excellence* and *defect in living things* (and a number of other concepts) together in the way which I hope yields us the best abstract understanding of the first two',[59] but although it may be the case that this job needs to be done, it is not clear that the four ends succeed in doing it.

It is interesting to also note that Hursthouse appeals to Annas' discussion of the Stoics on nature and rationality as being similar to her own project. However, as we have seen, the Stoics have no answer to why most people fail to develop in the natural, rational way, to 'why we are all living such unnatural lives',[60] and neither does Hursthouse. If rationality is a natural characteristic of human beings, how come so many human beings fail to display it? If rationality is the 'characteristic way' of humans why are so many humans defective? If, however, rationality is a purely normative concept which need not necessarily reflect the way people are actually like, in what sense is Hursthouse's account a naturalistic one that differs from other accounts which see humans as rational agents?

Hursthouse expects this conclusion, that is that most of us will be deficient speciments, but it is not clear why we should accept it. In the words of a recent commentator:

> If it were to turn out that by our standards of a good wolf, the vast majority of wolves failed to meet it, we should probably conclude that our standards are wrong. If the standards for human beings drawn from naturalism imply that throughout history, most human beings have been bad human beings, we should likewise reconsider those standards.[61]

8.9 Modern Kantian ethics: Herman

The next section will examine whether there is a possible answer to the Kantian dilemma about moral luck in the work of a recent neo-Kantian,

Barbara Herman. Recent work by neo-Kantians has done much to bring attention to otherwise neglected works by Kant, such as the *Doctrine of Virtue*, the *Anthropology* and the *Religion*. Partly, this has been as a response to the emergence of virtue ethics. One of the advantages of virtue ethics has been its focus on the concepts of 'virtue' and 'character'. In response, many neo-Kantians have taken up the challenge of showing how such concepts also have a role to play in Kantian theory.

Barbara Herman, by her own admission, tries to develop a 'middle theory', one which 'articulate[s] the contingent structure of rational agency'.[62] Although the moral law is the object of reason alone, its application requires empirical knowledge, which, as such, is subject to contingencies. She is concerned that a successful moral theory needs to accommodate a plausible account of human nature and in particular she thinks that a plausible account of character needs to take inclinations into account. A central difficulty for Kantian theory comes from 'the identification of the aspect of character that makes moral judgment possible with a capacity that involves, or requires for its development, the nonrational faculties'.[63] Part of her project is to resolve this difficulty, within a Kantian framework, however, while liberating 'Kantian ethics from its noumenal baggage'.[64] From the start then, this is a Kantian account with a difference.

Herman focuses attention on the need for self-knowledge and a more subtle understanding of Kantian agency. Self-knowledge is important because of the inevitability of faults of character. Given that people have faults of character, there are two options. We can argue that they are not real faults as they are not true expressions of agency and willing. However, Herman rejects this as hard to accept. It would be hard to accept such an option because it would mean that we could not hold people responsible for their faults of character, as these faults are not true expressions of their agency. As true agency is the only thing that we can hold people responsible for, such an account would result in a very restricted scope for true responsibility, especially for Herman who wants to make room for character in Kantian theory. Alternatively we can:

> widen the scope of the agent's accountability to include matters of character, on the grounds that, given our dependence on desires and beliefs, we must ensure as best we can that the sources of our beliefs are reliable and our desires reasonable.[65]

This is Herman's option, according to which self-knowledge is crucial as it is needed to prevent self-deception and help the agent 'attend to areas of personal susceptibility, temptation, or weakness...'.[66] Thus, temptations, difficulties and so on, that is all factors susceptible to luck, play a role in the agent's development, but self-knowledge counter-balances this influence by making the agent aware of it and allowing him to guard against it. It is interesting here to note that there are echoes of this discussion on the importance of self-knowledge in the work of Hursthouse, who similarly stresses the importance of scrutinizing one's inner states.

In her account of Kantian character, Herman finds a significant role for desires. She argues that in Kant the focus is on the distinction between autonomous and heteronomous willing, a concern with not allowing desires to ground the will, but this leads him to ignore the fact that the relation between reason and desire can be quite complex. It is this complexity that Herman would like to capture and in the process give a qualified role to desires. Her understanding of practical rationality is that '...we are by nature disposed to develop and modify desires in accordance with the requirements of practical reason. Normal human development is reason-responsive.'[67] Desires then can become reason-responsive, although this is a long and difficult process, with no guarantee of success. In developing this account she has remained true to the Kantian prohibition against making desire the determining ground of the will, while allowing reason-responsive desires a role in one's effective motive of action; in her terms, desires can be humbled to reason. Character then is conceived of as desires which have been brought within the scope of reason.

Herman also re-describes Kantian agency:

> Autonomy is the condition of the will that makes agency possible. If we were not rational beings, we would not have wills that could be interfered with. But agency is not completely described by identifying a will as rational. As human agents we are not distinct from our contingent ends, our culture, our history or our actual and possible relations to others. Agency is situated. The empirical and contingent conditions of effective agency set the terms of permissibility because it is through effective agency that autonomy is expressed (made real). Here is a place where consequences matter.[68]

Because agency is situated, morality requires that we attend to differences and recognize cultural and institutional causes of inequalities. Herman's conception of autonomy is wider than the Kantian idea of acting on principles. It also has to do with critical reflection and the recognition that not all the desires and interests that move us are our own. Herman's conception of agency then is, in Kantian terms, impure. Impure because, as we saw, pure Kantian agency is independent of empirical contingencies.

8.10 Critique of Herman

Herman's position has many merits, but what is interesting about it for our discussion is its similarities to Aristotle rather than Kant. Some of these similarities are openly accepted by Herman as a positive feature of her theory. Her account of character is underpinned by an account of gradual development. Making one's desires reason-responsive is a project one may or may not succeed in, or one in which an agent can have partial success:

> Some features of morality may be separated off, as when a person is sensitive and motivationally responsive to actions and situations that introduce risk of physical harm to others, but indifferent to psychological risk or injury, or concerned about immediate injury but not about injustice.[69]

She can then, unlike Kant, account for 'this moral form of aspect blindness' and allow for the possibility of character defects affecting moral judgement. In terms of the discussion of moral luck, all these features of Herman's theory make the moral life vulnerable to the influences of luck. She even qualifies the possibility of developing reason-responsive desires by cautioning that it is only available to those agents 'whose life has proceeded in a roughly normal – that is, noncatastrophic – way'.[70] Her account offers a plausible account of moral motivation, an account of character as realistically influenced by empirical factors and an account of an agent's sensitivity to the particulars of different cases.

On the other hand, Herman has to give up on some central Kantian themes. She clearly wants to distance herself from Kant's reliance on the noumenal, and seems to express worries about how such a view commits one to an implausible account of the motive of the worthy agent as 'extramaterial', 'a miracle every time'.[71] Also, she argues that the purity of the moral motive is conditional, it is purely grounded in the moral law and legitimately regulates our will, but in its effect it can be affected by empirical factors. This allows her to make room for the inclinations, although some of the implications of doing so seem decidedly un-Kantian. For example, her account of an agent's reflective self-understanding and the central role of this concept in her theory seem to contradict the Kantian claims about the opacity of our motives. The Kantian insistence that our motives are opaque to us seems to clash with Herman's reliance of the idea of self-examination. Kant writes that we 'can never, even by the most strenuous self-examination, get to the bottom of our secret impulsions';[72] and that:

> [t]he depths of the human heart are unfathomable. Who knows himself well enough to say, when he feels the incentive to fulfill his duty, whether it proceeds entirely from the representation of the law or whether there are not many other sensible impulses contributing to it that look to one's advantage (or to avoiding what is detrimental) and that, in other circumstances could just as well serve vice?[73]

So it is difficult to make sense of Herman's injunction that we examine the reliability of our beliefs and the reasonableness of our desires, given that Kantian self-knowledge is so limited.

In a sense, Herman is more of an Aristotelian than a Kantian. This is not only the case for elements of her theory which she explicitly accepts are inspired by an Aristotelian critique of Kant – such as the role of inclinations and sensitivity to particulars – but also for the perceived advantages of her theory. She argues that 'the task of moral judgment often requires the resolution of practical perplexity in circumstances where part of getting it right requires being able to recognize and evaluate unfamiliar moral phenomena'[74] and further than it is *Kantian* features of her theory that allow her to make sense of this moral perplexity and its resolution. But in this, I think, she is mistaken. Her concern is that in Aristotelian theory there is no way to criticize one's sensitivity to morally salient particulars, whereas the role of reason in her account, especially in transforming desires into motives, avoids this problem. However, Herman seems to have disregarded the Aristotelian notion of practical wisdom and the relation between virtue and *orthos logos*. Although the details of the account may differ from Herman's, Aristotelian theory has a similarly inspired role for reason. Aristotelian desires are similarly transformed through reason and a recognition of the value of virtue. Not only that, but the process by which this is done may well be similar to Herman's account. She writes: 'As one comes to see the deeper difficulties in devising fair procedures, one's understanding of what the value of fairness amounts to changes',[75] but this is very reminiscent of Aristotle. Developing an understanding of a particular virtue takes time, and involves precisely seeing how difficult it is to appreciate the demands of that virtue and how it relates to obligations raised by various considerations. This is the task of practical wisdom, to see the relevance of virtue and how the virtues should be ordered. And this is why one must start one's moral development with easier tests and progress to a deeper and more sensitive understanding of virtue with time. So in many of these ways Herman's theory resembles Aristotle more than Kant and carried with it a vulnerability to luck.

8.11   Conclusion

One of common-sense virtue ethics' claimed advantages is that it claims to do away altogether with the possibility of moral luck, a project more reminiscent, in its inspiration, of Kantian ethics than Aristotelian. Slote's aim is to sort out the 'untidy mess' luck makes of morality and since judgements of responsibility which are down to luck conflict with our common-sense intuitions, we should jettison these judgements. Slote is drawn to the possibility of luck-free moral judgement, but is explicitly critical of Kant's reliance on a noumenal metaphysics in order to establish morality's immunity from luck.[76] His strategy for resolving the paradoxes of our ordinary thinking differs radically from the Kantian one. However, although the strategies are different, the aim is the same: how to avoid rather than accept moral luck. This ambition, to free morality from luck, is not exclusively Slote's, but is shared by other virtue ethicists:

> Intent on treating every individual as equally bound by morality and equally capable of it, many contemporary virtue theorists tend to detach themselves from some of the distinctive features of classical virtue theory, which was – as the meaning of *arete* makes clear – concerned with stellar *excellence* rather than with basic competence or decency. Because egalitarians take virtue to be an aim, and perhaps an obligation for virtually everyone, and everyone equally, they have tended to follow a deflationary leveling policy about the virtues, identifying the character virtues with basic decency and the cognitive virtues with minimal good sense. The vexed question of whether the active abilities, the habits and skills, required for civic participation, for constructive discussion and deliberation, are equally distributed is assigned to sober and elevating reflections on moral luck.[77]

As I have argued, Slote's project fails on a number of counts. First, it is unclear whether Slote fully appreciates the force of the problem of moral luck, as some of his examples are of agents we would not want to hold responsible in the first place. Secondly, even if we accept the distinction between the moral and the ethical, I am not entirely convinced that judgements of ethical deplorability are immune from luck unlike judgements of moral blame. And in any case, the distinction between the moral and the ethical itself is not entirely convincing. Thirdly, in a sense Slote does too much when he judges the mentally ill to be ethically deplorable, and in another too little, when he does not leave room for judgements which we want to make, for example the negligent builder. Lastly, most of Slote's discussion focuses on the problems raised by resultant luck, and, oddly enough, for a theory of motives, many of the examples he considers are construed as cases of resultant luck.

Slote may or may not see a way out of these problems, but what is most interesting to note is that Slote's ambition with respect to eliminating the influence of luck shares more with Kant than with the Aristotelian attempt to accommodate the influence of luck. In a sense then, we have a virtue ethicist who is more of a Kantian in his starting point with respect to luck than an Aristotelian.

In Hursthouse, on the other hand, we have a more 'genuine' Aristotelian. In her rejection of the influence of resultant luck and her partial acceptance of constitutive and situational luck as part of the good life, she echoes many of our earlier conclusions on Aristotle. Luck is then embraced as part of the moral life, while at the same time Hursthouse works hard to articulate the role of reason. However, it is not clear how Hursthouse's four ends play the role she requires them to play and furthermore, given her account, it is difficult to explain why most of us are not characteristically virtuous. This may well mean that although reason has a central role in her theory, this element of her account is also open to objections and the tension generated by moral luck remains unresolved.

Finally, Herman's account is perhaps too driven by Aristotelian considerations. In her attempt to respond to criticism against Kant with respect to his understanding of virtue and character, Herman may have taken on board more elements from Aristotle than she may have wanted to. She rejects not only the implications of a metaphysical conception of the noumenal, but some of her conclusions appear to be incompatible with other elements in Kantian theory, such as the purity of the moral motive and the opacity of our motives. At the same time other aspects of her theory, such as the resolution of moral perplexity, have more in common with Aristotle than she recognizes.

Of course, it is impossible to give due consideration to the complexity and detail of the three theories examined here in one chapter. Neither has it been my task to provide an exhaustive account of the many, different developments in virtue ethics and Kantianism in recent years. Rather, I have concentrated on three writers whose work exemplifies the tension generated by moral luck and tried to show that perhaps they have more in common in their approach than previously thought. There are many details to disagree over, but I think it is a mistake to polarize the debate between the Kantians and the Aristotelians. There are elements from both 'sides of the camp' present in these theories and perhaps it is counter-productive to insist on maintaining sharp and, supposedly, immediately apparent distinctions.

9
Conclusion

The customary role of conclusions is to summarize the discussions preceding them. This conclusion will fulfil this role, but at the same time will also serve to pull together the threads of all the arguments produced so far. The previous discussion of the question of moral luck has so far raised problems and shown different approaches to the tension of moral luck, none of which are entirely successful in resolving the problem. I will use this conclusion to highlight what lessons should be learnt from this discussion.

9.1 Moral luck

In Chapter 1 we saw why the idea of 'moral luck' is problematic, as we could not find a clear and detailed definition that would meet with general approval. The term was introduced to moral philosophy through the use of examples, but this method was unsatisfactory. As we saw, some of the examples were misidentified as cases of moral luck, either because they were cases of bad luck rather than moral luck, or because the examples were re-described so that the elements whose influence was down to luck were not relevant in the moral evaluation of the agent and therefore the examples were not genuine cases of moral luck. The use of examples to identify moral luck has given rise to a number of works on the issue because the interpretation of the proposed examples has been so controversial and disputed. Following the discussion of Aristotle and Kant, I can now speculate on why the examples of moral luck have provoked such radical disagreement amongst philosophers.

In Williams' terms, Aristotle's and Kant's answers to moral luck come from within specific systems of morality, that is morality used in the restricted sense. Different moral systems exemplify different degrees of resistance to the possibility of moral luck. Different practical examples of moral luck are developed from within particular systems of morality and can be criticized from other systems of morality which do not share the same outlook with respect to moral luck. In short, the disagreements about the classification of a particular example as a case of moral luck may often stem from a difference in perspective. As a result of the fact that some moral systems show a greater degree of resistance to moral luck than others, the interpretation of these examples can be disputed and these disputes are often very difficult to resolve as the systems of morality which lead to different answers are viewed as incompatible with each other.

The answer, then, to the problem of identifying the nature of moral luck cannot be any more detailed than the idea of a conceptual tension between 'morality' and 'luck', unless one is prepared to take on board a particular system of morality. Both Williams and Nagel point out that in some particular systems of morality, namely Kantian morality, there is immunity to luck, and Williams briefly mentions how this approach is to be contrasted with 'certain doctrines of classical antiquity' according to which some aspects of the moral life are subject to luck.[1] However, when both Williams and Nagel go on to discuss their examples of moral luck they do not specify under which particular system of morality or under which understanding of morality these cases are indeed cases of moral luck. Thus, they leave the road open for other commentators to repudiate their examples from within specific understandings of morality. For example, Andre shows why the Gauguin example has been mis-described as an example of moral luck by analyzing it from an Aristotelian perspective.[2] Surprisingly, Williams also writes with reference to the Gauguin example 'I can entirely agree with Andre that an Aristotelian emphasis in ethics, for instance, would not run into the same difficulties.'[3] Part of the confusion, then, resulting from the use of examples to illuminate the problem of moral luck may arise from the fact that different writers write from different – or what they interpret as different – systems of morality.

A related point needs to be made here; some particular systems of morality may show localized resistance to certain types of luck, whereas they are more susceptible to other kinds of luck. For example, Slote's version of virtue ethics is resistant to resultant luck, but vulnerable to the influences of developmental luck. Therefore, Nagel's distinction between different types of luck (with the substitution of developmental luck as a wider idea encompassing situational luck) is a crucial aid in understanding a particular moral system's resistance to luck.

It seems then that we are not any further in providing a definition of moral luck outside a particular system of morality, other than the general thought that there is a conceptual tension between 'morality' and 'luck'. However, Williams' and Nagel's initial discussions can serve as inspiration for a further thought. Both original articles as well as the commentators which followed them perceive a difference in the approach to moral luck exemplified in the writings of Kant and Aristotle. The two philosophers are represented as writing from rival camps when it comes to their answer to the problem of moral luck, but I am not sure this interpretation is correct.

9.2   From Aristotle *or* Kant to Aristotle *and* Kant

The shape of modern moral philosophy is fairly antagonistic. This spirit of 'rivalry', for want of a better word, is exemplified in Anscombe's article 'Modern Moral Philosophy' and the discussions it generated. Anscombe saw Aristotle as providing us with a distinctive method of doing ethics, a way of doing ethics in many ways opposed to the Kantian tradition of ethics. Perhaps due to the great influence of Anscombe's article, perhaps due to other factors, this view of seeing different systems of ethics as opposing each other has prevailed in modern philosophy.[4] Perhaps due to the need to make virtue ethics 'heard' over what used to be the dominant ways of understanding morality – deontology and consequentialism – theorists worked hard to identify the differences between the theories and explain why one had the advantage over the other. Thus, until recently, for moral philosophy the choice was either Aristotle or Kant. Clearly, a third, dominant and well-discussed alternative is consequentialism, but for the purposes of this discussion I have concentrated on the other two.

However, this picture, a choice between Kant and Aristotle, is beginning to change. Partly in response to the virtue-ethical camp, neo-Kantians have worked hard to show how Kantianism can incorporate what have, so far, been the claimed advantages of virtue ethics, thus bringing the two theories closer together. The discussion of moral luck has had the unexpected result of showing why, at least in one respect, our understanding of the search for an adequate moral theory should change from Aristotle *or* Kant to Aristotle *and* Kant.

9.3   Two pictures of the human life

The possibility of moral luck has revealed an understanding of the human life as having two aspects: on the one hand human beings are vulnerable to contingencies, subject to luck and hostages to factors outside their control; on the other hand human beings are autonomous agents, capable of making true choices, the objects of moral responsibility for their voluntary acts and immune to luck. One understanding of Aristotle is that his ethics exemplifies the view of human agents as vulnerable to luck, whereas Kant's morality is interpreted as seeing agents qua agents as immune to luck. However, this interpretation of Kant and Aristotle as focusing on rival understandings of human morality is incorrect. It is a misrepresentation of both Kant and Aristotle.

Both Aristotle's and Kant's understanding of morality is driven by the same two forces: on the one hand the recognition that morality must make sense of and allow room for a conception of responsibility, and on the other hand the appreciation that any conception of morality must result in a plausible picture of the human condition as subject to luck. I would claim that it is a mistake to see either philosopher as exclusively dealing with only one of these requirements.

These two requirements, that of responsibility and that of a plausible picture of the human condition, are interrelated with the understanding of human beings as having two sides. The side of humans which is vulnerable to luck generates the idea that a plausible account of morality needs to accommodate the influence of contingent factors, whereas the view of humans as independent, rational beings allows us to make judgements about responsibility. The preceding discussion of moral luck has shown how both Aristotle and Kant are aware of both these two sides to the human condition, both these forces that operate on our understanding of morality.

The familiar picture of Aristotle is of the philosopher who more than anyone else recognized the influence of moral luck, and this picture is correct. Aristotelian ethics functions in a way that allows for vulnerability to considerations of constitutive, developmental, situational and, to a smaller extent, resultant luck, especially in extreme conditions. Aristotle's recognition of the possibility of moral luck is based on a very plausible picture of how things are and does its best to accommodate the possibility of luck. Constitutive luck can be partly accommodated as its positive influences, those that lead to virtue, are innocuous, that is at least their results have the merit of being indistinguishable from virtue even though they are not, qualitatively, the same as true virtue. The negative influences of constitutive luck, those that lead to vice, are more problematic as the end result, vicious acts, is a problem. However, agents so unfortunate as to have been the objects of bad constitutive luck are described by Aristotle as being in a bestial state of character, a state of character almost outside the normal human range. Their extreme bad luck removes them from the normal sphere of human morality.

Developmental and situational luck are more crucial for Aristotelian character formation and are the kinds of luck more frequently associated with Aristotelian ethics. We have seen how for Aristotle moral development is gradual and dependent on a number of contingent factors. The development of virtue, the habituation in virtuous action, the opportunities for display of virtue, the external goods necessary for some virtues and so on are all subject to luck. However, unlike the continent and the incontinent agents who are fully at the mercy of luck, the virtuous agent is afforded some degree of immunity from luck. The virtuous agent can best accommodate the influences of bad luck as long as these are not extreme.

Lastly, resultant luck is, to an extent, accommodated. Action, in general, is important for Aristotelian ethics, since having the right character means acting in accordance with it and as soon as actions are performed it becomes more important that they have the intended results. However, unless an agent is subjected to extremely bad resultant luck, the fact that some of the results of some of his actions are outside his control does not unduly affect the evaluation of the Aristotelian agent. Furthermore, many of the contemporary examples of moral luck can be re-described to show how what the agent should be held responsible for is something other than the results of his acts which were outside his control, for example Chamberlain and Anna. Thus, many of the ways in which resultant luck is claimed to have an effect on morality can be accounted for in Aristotelian theory.

This understanding of Aristotle is correct and prevalent amongst commentators, but it is not the entire picture. As we have seen, the other half of Aristotelian ethics concerns itself with choice, the voluntary and a notion of independent reason. Virtue is not simply the end result of favourable circumstances and factors, but must involve a conscious understanding of the right reason and a definite choice of virtue for its own sake. This 'choice' seems to involve a notion of reason which is immune to the influence of luck. This is the kind of reason which is usually picked out as characteristic of the work of Kant.

For Kant, a central tenet of his moral theory is to hold that we are noumenally free, which results in the thought that morality is immune to luck. This is a project driven by a conception of 'morality' as equally available to everyone, at any time of their lives, regardless of past experiences, circumstances or even previous choices. This idea of morality is exemplified in an understanding of pure rationality possessed by the intelligible self. Morality is immune to luck, as the very idea of 'moral luck' is almost nonsensical. Morality is simply not the kind of thing that can be the subject of luck. This is the aspect of Kant which has, until recently, characterized discussions of his moral theory. However, as we have seen there is another aspect to Kant. This aspect of Kant's theory makes use of the 'virtues' and 'character'. Indeed Kant's discussion of the sensible character is reminiscent of the Aristotelian thoughts on character formation. Kant's sensible character is established over a long period of time and is difficult to change, is influenced by constitutive and developmental factors, requires good teachers and role models as well as appropriate habits and opportunities for action. Thus, it is unfair to accuse Kant of ignoring all these interesting and plausible accounts of moral character.

It seems then that Aristotle is aware of the need for a conception of responsibility generated by an understanding of reason as independent from luck as much as Kant is aware of the need to give a plausible account of how luck affects the everyday circumstances of our moral lives. Both philosophers are concerned with accounting for both sides of human morality, even though at times they seem to be more occupied with one side of the picture than the other.

This idea is being recognized, even if this recognition is implicit, by modern writers. As we saw, neo-Kantians have been focusing on previously little-known aspects of Kant's theory on virtue and as a result their work resembles what has been seen as the exclusive domain of Aristotelians. Virtue ethicists, on the other hand, seem driven by the concern to justify their theory outside contingent factors, Slote explicitly claiming moral immunity from luck for his theory, while Hursthouse openly claims many similarities between her account of Aristotle and Kant.

The mistaken view of Aristotle and Kant as having developed radically opposed theories comes from failing to see that both writers are concerned with both considerations, that is immunity to luck and a plausible account of the human condition as subject to luck. It is true that Aristotle is more well known for espousing a view of morality as subject to luck and that some of Kant's works concentrate exclusively on building a picture of moral immunity to luck, but it is a mistake to represent either philosopher as being one sided. Thus, a strict distinction between Kant and Aristotle on the grounds that one theory is concerned with immunity from luck whereas the other is not is a misrepresentation of their ethical projects.

9.4 A further distinction

We have come across, in the preceding discussion, a further way of distinguishing between Aristotelian and Kantian ethics: the distinction between character-based and agent-based theories.[5] So far I have tacitly accepted this distinction, but it is now time to question its viability and its usefulness.

In a sense, claiming that Aristotle's theory is a theory of character whereas Kant's is not is incorrect. Aristotle does elaborate on the moral concept of 'character' within his ethics, but so does Kant. Indeed the Kantian conception of the sensible character has much in common with the Aristotelian use of character. Both refer to character in the sense of strong and fixed dispositions, developed over a long period of time and resistant to change, open to external influences and habituation and so on. Thus, in these terms, Kant has a similar understanding of character to that of Aristotle. However, proponents of the distinction between character-based and agent-based theories could argue that although both theories make use of the concept of 'character', only Aristotle makes it *basic* in his understanding of ethics. In this sense the distinction claims that Aristotle and Kant differ in that character plays a basic or foundational role for Aristotle, from which other concepts are derived and justified, a role which is not present in Kant. Is *this* distinction then viable and useful?

It is difficult to give an answer to this question as it is not immediately clear what is meant by describing a theory as being 'based on character'. It is true that Aristotle's understanding of 'character', which corresponds to the Kantian sensible character, plays a fundamental role in Aristotelian ethics, which the sensible character does not have in Kantian ethics. In Kantian ethics true moral worth can only be attributed to the good will and not to the sensible character. However, the Aristotelian understanding of 'character' incorporates a notion of voluntary, moral choice which is not present in the Kantian sensible character as such. Virtue, for Aristotle, is not just the result of habituation, education, favourable influences and so on – all of which are incorporated in the Kantian understanding of the sensible character – but requires a rational choice of virtue done knowingly and for its own sake. The confusion arises because in Kant the two aspects of the self – the intelligible and the sensible – are examined and understood separately. It is only the intelligible self that is the object of morality, it is only the sensible character that is subject to luck. In Aristotle this distinction does not occur; Aristotelian 'character' not only is shaped by luck but also includes an ability to reason that is somehow immune to luck.

How should we conclude, then, with respect to the distinction between character-based and agent-based theories? The distinction relies on a mis-interpretation of Kant and Aristotle. It can only make sense if we assume that the notion of character operates in Aristotle in a different way than it does in Kant. This, however, is not true. The way Aristotelian character has been traditionally understood corresponds to the sensible character and thus Kant should not be accused of ignoring the concept of 'character'. At the same time this understanding of Aristotelian 'character' is mistaken, as the Aristotelian concept has as much to do with immunity from luck (associated with the intelligible self) as it has to do with vulnerability to luck (associated with the sensible self). Both writers, again, are concerned with both ideas. If we still want to claim that one concern is more central to one philosopher than to the other, we have to be very careful exactly how we phrase the distinction and what we imply by it.

9.5 Responsibility

The problem raised by moral luck is essentially a problem of responsibility: given that there are two sides to the human condition, one immune to luck and one that is vulnerable, how do we reconcile the two in order to make judgements of responsibility? This question remains unanswered.

Slote, like the Stoics, attempted to give a picture of a theory of virtue that is immune to luck. The Stoic project was criticized for simply failing to explain the way things are. If the Stoic theory were correct, we would expect to see most agents reach and maintain a state of virtue, and this simply does not seem to be the case. At the same time we saw how the Stoics are aware of the implausibility of some of their claims and how they try to incorporate more plausible accounts of morality in their thesis. However, this results in a theory with two conflicting aspects which are not reconciled.

Slote's move from the moral to the ethical is problematic as a strategy for avoiding moral luck and even if we were to grant him this move, although his system of morality avoids resultant luck, his reliance on intuitions makes it vulnerable to constitutive and developmental luck.

Herman's position is now closer to that of Aristotle, but perhaps the cost here is having to abandon some Kantian elements or leaving it unclear how all elements of the theory are reconciled. Similarly Aristotle wants to incorporate a picture of character as subject to luck while maintaining an understanding of reason as independent whose operation can generate judgements about responsibility, but it is not clear how the two can be integrated. In part, this concern is part of Hursthouse's attempt to give a naturalistic account of reason, which, as we saw, remains problematic.

Should we accept that part of our selves is subject to luck whereas part is immune and the two can operate together, while in some mysterious way maintaining immunity from luck, it is still not clear how we should decide questions of responsibility. What extremes of constitutive, developmental and situational luck can be overcome by an agent's ability to reason and make choices? If we accept that agents have an independent ability to reason morally, we still know nothing about the power of reason to overcome contrary obstacles. How much is too much for reason to overcome?

For Aristotle the decision, because of the nature of ethics, lies in perception of the particular situation. A decision cannot be made on such questions prior to knowing the particular details of each case. Thus, such a question cannot have a general answer in advance of looking at each case. Of course any such judgements of particular cases have to be performed by those who can perceive correctly, that is the virtuous agent. So judgements about responsibility can only be made by those who are skilled in doing so and only when they are faced with particular situations. For Kant the revolution in the mode of thought can take place in any agent at any time and is tied to his understanding of humans as noumenally free. However, our motives are opaque even to us, and it may be impossible to know our own selves in this respect.

9.6   Conclusion

The possibility of moral luck raises fundamental questions about what it is to be human and what it is to be a moral being, questions about freedom, responsibility, choice and control. To find answers to these questions is not the work of one philosopher or one theory, but the underlying project of both moral theory and practice, so it is not surprising that despite detailed discussions neither Aristotle, nor the Stoics, nor Kant, nor the neo-Kantians nor the virtue ethicists can come up with a complete and satisfactory answer.

However, sometimes looking at the problem without arriving at an answer can be illuminating in itself. The discussion of moral luck highlights a tension between morality and lack of control which underpins all the moral theories we have examined. It is a mistake to assume that Aristotelian theory accepts the possibility of moral luck as opposed to Kantian theory which rejects it. Both philosophers, and to an extent all the theories examined, are aware of the two forces that pull in opposite directions: the demand for control and the attribution of responsibility placed on us by our understanding of morality, and the need to accommodate the influences of luck within a plausible explanation of the human condition.

Notes

Introduction

1. Williams, in Statman (1993), p. 251.

1 Moral luck

1. Dennett (1984). Dennett includes a very interesting discussion of the different senses in which we use the term 'luck' and its relationship with determinism, which was the inspiration for many of my thoughts in the preceding paragraph.
2. Williams, in Statman (1993), p. 43.
3. For more on this, see Rescher, in Statman (1993), pp. 145–146.
4. There are extremely interesting connections between responsibility, blameworthiness and the extent to which what took place could have happened to anyone. For example, the driver who causes an accident because he is drunk is more blameworthy than the driver who causes an accident because he momentarily takes his eyes off the road. Some degree of inattention is shared by all drivers and is to be expected from all of them. However, the questions raised here are beyond the scope of this chapter, although they will be touched upon in the following discussion of negligence.
5. Circumstantial or situational luck is luck relating to the circumstances one finds oneself in, for example finding oneself born in Nazi Germany rather than democratic Britain of the same time. What is involved in this kind of moral luck will be explored in detail later on in this chapter and in Chapter 2.
6. Nagel, in Statman (1993), pp. 70–71.
7. There is good evidence that this is at least one of Williams' goals in his paper. He clearly states that his concern is with ideas about rational justification (Williams, in Statman, 1993, pp. 36–37) and he takes Kant as representative of the ideas he wants to challenge. For Williams, Kant argues that '[b]oth the disposition to correct moral judgement, and the objects of such judgement, are on this view free from external contingency, for both are, in their related ways, the product of an unconditioned will' (Williams, in Statman, 1993, p. 35). If for Kant reason is the last vestige against moral luck and Williams is attacking this position, then it is not an exaggeration to say that Williams' attack is on the all-powerful conception of reason, even though he does not use these specific words himself. Further evidence that this is one of Williams' aims can be found in the 'Postscript' (Williams, in Statman, 1993), where he explains that the concerns raised by retrospective justification apply not only to the ethical but to any application of practical rationality (Williams, in Statman, 1993, p. 256). This view of Williams' aim is shared by others as well. For example, Levi sees the Gauguin example as 'a challenge to Reason itself' (Levi, in Statman, 1993, p. 112).
8. Williams, in Statman (1993), p. 38.

9. There is a third possible misunderstanding, which is to assume that Williams was referring to the actual, historical Gauguin and to use information from his actual life to interpret the example. This is Levi's project (Levi, in Statman, 1993), but Williams clearly states in the 'Postscript' (Williams, in Statman, 1993) that he is not interested in the real Gauguin. All that is needed for the example is a Gauguin-like painter who leaves his family in order to paint, creates masterpieces, but could have failed in his project.

10. Williams, in Statman (1993), p. 40.

11. Ibid., p. 256.

12. The idea that moral reasons do not always and necessarily trump non-moral reasons seems to be one of the many arguments that Williams is trying to put forward in this example. This, fairly controversial, suggestion is further developed in Williams (1993, Chapter 10). Williams' arguments against morality's immunity from luck are connected to his arguments against the supreme value of morality. See also note 27.

13. For example, a character-based theory (e.g. virtue ethics) could argue that the grounds for this obligation can be found in a general injunctive to develop one's character, or a deontological theory may call upon agents to develop their talents as a maxim which conforms with the categorical imperative.

14. Andre provides such an Aristotelian analysis of the Gauguin case in Statman (1993). For Andre an Aristotelian response to moral luck involves having 'to admit that we do justify actions partially on the basis of luck, accept the conclusion that we are not consistent Kantians, but reject the implication that our moral scheme is therefore incoherent' (Andre, in Statman, 1993, p. 124). She accounts for Gauguin on the Aristotelian grounds that '[t]he person who can correctly assess his or her chances of success is better-formed than the person who cannot' (Andre, in Statman, 1993, p. 128). This answer still leaves open the question of the influence of luck on developmental factors and character formation, but Andre's aim in this paper is limited. Thus, she can conclude that moral luck plays a smaller role than that suggested by Williams and Nagel. Whether she can retain this conclusion after examining other types of moral luck excluded from this particular paper remains to be seen.

15. The preceding discussion on Williams has drawn heavily on discussions with Kim Thomson. I am grateful to Kim Thomson for her help with this section. A similar solution to some aspects of moral luck is suggested by Peter Vallentyne, who argues that blameworthiness should be allocated on the basis of probability estimates rather than actual outcomes. This view is attributed to Vallentyne, in Slote (1994b).

16. Slote (1994b).

17. Ibid., p. 406.

18. There are other possible grounds for criticizing the Gauguin example. Rescher (Rescher, in Statman, 1993) argues from a Kantian perspective that Gauguin is guilty of a moral impropriety, that of abandoning his family, and that this is the case regardless of the success or failure of any future projects. He also directly opposes Williams by claiming that extramoral objectives should not override moral considerations (Rescher, in Statman, 1993, p. 161).

Nagel, in a footnote, disagrees with Williams about whether the Gauguin example is one of moral luck;

> [m]y disagreement with Williams is that his account fails to explain why such retrospective attitudes can be called moral. If success does not permit Gauguin to justify himself to others, but still determines his most basic feelings, that shows only that his most basic feelings need not be moral. It does not show that morality is subject to luck. (Nagel, in Statman, 1993, pp. 70–71)

19. There are other such attacks on the all-powerful conception of reason; for example, recently John Cottingham has urged philosophers to take the insights of psychoanalysis into account when discussing the power of reason, insights which attack the picture of an all-powerful ability to reason, see Cottingham (1998).

20. All this holds provided that we think that Chamberlain acted to the best of his knowledge and had gone to great lengths to be informed and make a good decision, in the same way that the lorry driver serviced the brakes in his lorry, drove within the speed limit, was alert and so on. In Chamberlain's case this may be historically disputed, but is assumed to be true for the purposes of this example.

21. Nagel, in Statman (1993), pp. 62–63.

22. For example, one is legally responsible in offences of strict liability without necessarily being morally responsible. Or the parents of a serial murderer may feel emotionally responsible for the actions of their child without being in the least morally responsible.

23. Nagel argues that '[i]f Hitler had not overrun Europe and exterminated millions, but instead had died of a heart attack after occupying the Sudetenland, Chamberlain's action at Munich would still have utterly betrayed the Czechs, but it would not be the great moral disaster that has made his name a household word' (Nagel, in Statman, 1993, p. 62). However, Chamberlain can only be held responsible for the betrayal of the Czechs, regardless of what Hitler decided to do afterwards. The betrayal of the Czechs opened the way for Hitler, who turned out to be a genocidal maniac, but this does not make Chamberlain responsible for Hitler's actions. If we are going to hold Chamberlain responsible for Hitler's actions, why do not we also blame Chamberlain's political colleagues for electing him prime minister, and the electorate for voting for them and so on (while holding that none of them were culpable)? If Hitler's intentions were not reasonably foreseeable at the time of the betrayal of the Czechs, it is not clear why Chamberlain was responsible for 'unleashing Hitler'.

24. Hardy (1896), 1994, pp. 388–389.

25. The decision for which we hold Chamberlain responsible being the betrayal of the Czechs and not the unleashing of Hitler.

26. Williams, in Statman (1993), p. 251.

27. This is not the only distinction which Williams seems to be drawing and sometimes it is not clear which distinction he is appealing to. There seem to be at least three different distinctions in the papers on moral luck, which are also mirrored in his other works. The first is the distinction highlighted in this passage between morality in the restricted sense; for example, Kantian as opposed to Aristotelian morality, and the ethical in the wider sense. A second

distinction is the idea that the modern understanding of 'morality' differs from the wider Ancient Greek understanding of 'ethics' (see for example Williams, in Finley, 1981; Williams, 1993). This distinction has been challenged by some authors, for example Annas (1993), whereas it seems to be upheld by others, for example Nussbaum (in Statman, 1993, p. 104 n. 11). Another idea that we have touched upon earlier in this chapter (see note 12) is Williams' claim that moral reasons do not always or necessarily trump non-moral reasons. He therefore, seems to have a wide conception of rationality and a narrower conception of moral reasoning. Finally, another related thought is the idea of a conceptual tension between the terms 'morality' and 'luck', which is what leads him to think of 'moral luck' as an oxymoron. All these distinctions and ideas come up in Williams' papers on moral luck and they all merit serious attention in their own right. Although they are interconnected they do make different points, but it is sometimes unclear which distinction is being appealed to in particular arguments and what role it has to play.

28. Williams (1993), p. 177. For an in-depth analysis of these ideas, see, in particular, Chapter 10 of Williams (1993).
29. Nussbaum (1986), pp. 3–4.
30. Ibid., p. 5.
31. Williams recognizes that 'an Aristotelian emphasis on ethics... would not run into the same difficulties' (Williams, in Statman, 1993, p. 252) because it would not attempt to resist the influences of luck.
32. Nagel, in Statman (1993), p. 59.
33. Nagel actually distinguished a fourth kind of luck, luck regarding antecedent circumstances. This kind of luck seems to be most closely connected with concerns about determinism and freedom of the will. It is not directly discussed by Nagel and I have followed him in this, although Kant comes closest to raising such considerations in his discussion of freedom.
34. Nagel, in Statman (1993), pp. 58–59.
35. I have coined the term 'developmental luck' to encompass all the factors which influence an agent's moral development and which are subject to luck. This term is wider than situational luck, as factors that influence one's development may also include the circumstances one comes across (why this is so will become clearer in Chapter 3). I have continued to refer to situational luck as a phenomenon meriting special attention, because it is widely discussed in the literature and provides some interesting variations on the general theme of the influences of developmental luck.
36. This Aristotelian insight (to be found for example at NE 1094b 11ff.) is considered an advantage of Aristotelian ethics and a point of contrast between Aristotelian theory and other moral theories. The difference is claimed to be in the use of rules or principles in moral deliberation. Theories like deontology and utilitarianism make use of one (or set of) universal, overriding principle which can be applied to all moral problems and provides the agent with the correct answer. By contrast, Aristotelian ethics does not rely on any such one principle, but emphasizes the diversity and unpredictability of ethical cases. As a result, the answer can only be found if one is a virtuous agent, that is a person with a developed and sensitive character who can 'see' the morally relevant features of a situation and their relative weight in each case. Therefore, moral perception and moral prudence (in the Aristotelian sense of practical judgement) are crucial

to moral decision-making. This approach is sometimes called anti-theoretical (e.g. Baier, 1985; Williams, 1993) and it does not necessarily exclude the use of rules for the teaching or application of the virtues; however, it must be understood that these rules are rules of thumb and cannot be relied upon entirely (see Nussbaum, 1990; Roberts, 1991; Wallace, 1991). Thus, Aristotelian theory is flexible and adaptable, where rival theories are rigid and inflexible. Much has been made of this difference between Aristotelian moral theory and rival theories, with some commentators also claiming that such an interpretation of principle-based theories is distorting their use of principles (see Herman, 1993; Baron *et al.*, 1997). The claimed difference between principle-based and character-based theories has been used in recent years to sharply distinguish between different approaches to ethics and argue for their incompatibility, whereas other commentators are at pains to show that irreconcilable differences between different perspectives have been exaggerated (see Baron *et al.*, 1997). An interesting by-product of this discussion is the development of particularism, a theory which highlights the importance of moral particulars in decision-making rather than generalized rules (see Dancy, 1983, 1993).

37. Others, as we have seen, include Williams and Nagel, whereas the recent work of McGinn (1999) in moral philosophy is also an excellent illustration of how philosophy can make use of literature to make points.

38. Plato, *Republic*, Book I, 331a.

39. NE 1095b 10–14 (Loeb).

40. NE 1094b 11.

41. NE 1104a 3ff.

2 Aristotle on constitutive luck

1. See the 'Conclusion', which discusses whether this distinction applies to Kant (and Kantianism) and Aristotle (and virtue ethics). The question of whether the description of outcome-based can be rightly and exclusively applied to consequentialism is not discussed.

2. The distinction implied here is best illustrated by the differences between deontology and consequentialism. Consequentialism is primarily interested in evaluating the outcomes of actions rather than the intentions, motives and so on of the agent who performed these actions. Thus, the agent's state is not relevant to the moral evaluation. By contrast, deontologists are more concerned with the internal state of the agent, that is whether his motive accords with the moral law, than with whether this motive successfully translates into action (for more on whether this is a correct interpretation see Chapters 6 and 7). Aristotelian theory does not seem to go to either of these two extremes, but rather offers an account according to which both outcomes and internal states are, to different degrees, of importance in moral evaluation (see note 4).

3. NE 1098b 30ff., my italics (Loeb).

4. The importance placed on internal states and their manifestation in terms of moral evaluation is not unconditional. In extreme circumstances there can be exceptions to the idea that both motives and outcomes are important in moral evaluation. More on this, though, is discussed later on in this chapter and in Chapter 3.

5. In such cases we are still left with the epistemological problem of knowing whether a person has a specific character trait he never has the opportunity to display, but that is a different problem. We are also left to wonder how this person developed this trait without any opportunities for practising its exercise, but this question will also be set aside.

6. See, for example, Crisp, in Crisp (1996).

7. The seeds of these ideas on the difficulties and temptations facing moral agents on the road to virtue can be found in Foot's seminal work on the virtues (Foot, 1978). Foot sees the virtues as correctives and as the virtues are about overcoming difficulties, it follows that some difficulties will prove overwhelming for those who do not possess complete virtue: '[t]he fact is that some kinds of difficulties do indeed provide an occasion for much virtue, but that others rather show that virtue is incomplete' (p. 11), '. . . the fact that [a man] is poor is something that makes the occasion [for stealing] more *tempting*, and difficulties of this kind make honest actions all the more virtuous' (p. 11). Hursthouse has also recently written along similar lines of thought (Hursthouse, 1999).

8. Perfect or true virtue is distinguished from the appearance of virtue. See discussion of natural tendencies and cultivated dispositions in this chapter.

9. Although true vice seems to be quite rare, like the corresponding true virtue.

10. See, for example, NE 1145a 35–36.

11. NE 1147a 34ff.

12. For more on these thoughts, see McDowell, in Lovibond and Williams (1996).

13. Platts (1979), p. 249.

14. One possible interpretation of the Aristotelian passages on weakness of will is to argue that the virtuous, continent and incontinent agents all share in the right reasoning to the same extent, but the difference between them is the strength of their contrary desires and their ability to resist these desires. So the incontinent and the continent agent understand what is the right thing to do *as well as* the virtuous agent, but they still have contrary desires which they cannot overcome. Moral progress then is the development of the strength of will to resist contrary desires and the weakening of such desires through habituation, education and so on until they are entirely extinguished. This analysis rejects the idea that there is any cognitive difference between the different character states. I think that this analysis is correct in pointing out the different roles desires play at the different stages of moral development, but wrong in rejecting the idea that there are differences in reasoning. Suppose for a moment that in accordance with this analysis the reasoning of the incontinent and the continent agents is as correct as that of the virtuous agent. Correct moral reasoning also involves a motivational element (to entirely deny this would mean that the idea that reason speaks in favour of an action would lose its intelligibility, as McDowell points out, in Lovibond and Williams, 1996, p. 96). It is plausible to assume that once an agent grasps what is the kind thing to do (for example) and why kindness is what is demanded, that this moral demand also exerts a motivational force upon this agent to act in accordance with the demands of kindness. The incontinent agent, according to this picture, fully comprehends the demands of morality and feels the motivational pull of these demands, but is

swayed by contrary desires to do otherwise. For this to be the case, we would have to assume that either the motivational pull of morality is rather weak, in which case why should we be swayed by it at all, or that the contrary desires are extremely strong, which is, it seems to me, an implausible picture since it makes it difficult to understand how these contrary desires can *ever* be overcome. For example, faced with an act of charity or spending the money in a self-indulgent way, we can best understand the incontinent person's decision as a combination of being pulled by strong contrary desires while having an incomplete understanding of morality. For if this agent truly understood why morality demands of him that he should give his money to charity, he would not be tempted to indulge himself in the first place. If he truly understood the value of saving human lives, he would never be tempted to compare it to the value of a new car, for example. It seems to me that truly understanding the demands of morality would exert such a strong motivational pull to act in accordance with them that all contrary desires pale by comparison. Thus, the idea that some people understand moral demands but still do otherwise can only be comprehensible if we assume that this understanding is incomplete. The phenomenon of weakness of will, then, can be best understood as incorporating a cognitive deficiency as well as the existence of contrary desires and the inability to resist them.

15. Burnyeat, in Rorty (1980), pp. 70–71. Commentators often draw attention to Aristotle's discussion of the importance of emotional development and contrast it with other philosophers who concentrate solely on cognitive development, but one must also remember that cognitive development plays a large role in the Aristotelian picture (see note 14).

16. I am grateful to Rosalind Hursthouse for feedback which gave rise to these thoughts. Of course any misconceptions remain my own.

17. NE 1150b 32–34 (Loeb).

18. McDowell, in Lovibond and Williams (1996), pp. 102–103.

19. For example, see Louden, in Statman (1997), who argues that the possibility of acting out of character fuels the thought that it is actions rather than characters, as suggested by virtue ethics, that we should be evaluating when making moral judgements.

20. For a more detailed discussion of such issues, see Athanassoulis (2000).

21. These thoughts are derived from Athanassoulis (2000).

22. Rescher, in Statman (1993), p. 154.

23. Hursthouse (1999), pp. 157–158.

24. Ibid., p. 78.

25. Melville (1924), 1998.

26. Ibid., p. 255.

27. Ibid.

28. Ibid.

29. See NE 1144a 24ff.

30. Melville (1924), 1998, p. 257.

31. In one of the few philosophical discussions of Claggart, Daniel Haybron sees him as an individual who has no capacity for sympathy, has an evil nature and who is not culpable for being this way. However, he concludes that as such characters are not volitionally impaired, they can be blamed for their

actions. This conclusion seems rather harsh given the assumptions that precede it (Haybron, 1999).
32. Mellville (1924), 1998, pp. 236–237.
33. NE 1109a 15–21 (my italics).
34. NE 1106b 35 to 1107a 2.
35. NE Book II iv.
36. NE 1103a 23–25.
37. Although most commentators agree that Aristotle supposed the unity of the virtues, not everyone sees this idea as unproblematic (e.g. see Foot, 1983 or Walker, 1993).
38. NE 1144b 32ff. (Loeb).
39. NE 1144b 1–9 (Loeb).
40. A fully developed virtuous disposition also requires the situational appreciation necessary in order to perceive the morally relevant particulars of each case, as well as the practical wisdom required in order to weigh up different considerations.
41. Burnyeat's discussion (in Rorty, 1980) is an excellent discussion and a necessary read for anyone who wants to make sense of Aristotle's developmental picture of morality.
42. Burnyeat, in Rorty (1980), p. 70.
43. NE 1103a 33ff.
44. See, for example, NE 1095b 2–13.
45. EE 1247b 23–29.
46. EE 1248a 30–34.
47. Both types of character can be distinguished from those who accidentally act virtuously, as such accidents are one-off occurrences, whereas both natural and real virtues persist over time.
48. NE 1148b 19ff.
49. In NE Book VII, Aristotle points out that the possible states of character are superhuman virtue, virtue, continence, incontinence, vice and bestiality. He seems to present them in descending order of goodness.
50. NE 1148b 29–33 (Loeb). Of course, the comparison with female inactivity during intercourse is rather unfortunate, but it relates to a social perception of women as receptacles of sexual attention and therefore not initiators or actors in the sexual act. However, despite the rather dated assumptions of the example, the passage does make its general point successfully.

3 Aristotle on developmental, situational and resultant luck

1. See Chapter 1. Nagel refers only to situational luck and does not seem to be aware of (or possibly interested in) the possibility of developmental luck. Developmental luck seems to be a wider concept, involving all the factors which influence an agent's moral development, one of which is the situations one comes across. I will, therefore, discuss situational luck as a specific instance of developmental luck.
2. Statman, in Statman (1993), p. 13.
3. Dostoyevsky, F. (1865–6), 1991.
4. Ibid., p. 33.

5. Ibid., p. 44.
6. Ibid., p. 77.
7. Ibid., p. 102.
8. Ibid., p. 622.
9. Ibid., p. 630.
10. Welsh (1995).
11. This quote is by Bundy; he is referring to himself in the third person. I am grateful to Michael Bavidge for bringing this quotation to my attention.
12. NE 1103a 23.
13. NE 1103b 23–25.
14. NE 1095a 1ff. (Loeb).
15. NE 1095b 4–6 (Loeb).
16. NE 1100b 35–1101a 7.
17. Issues concerning situational luck are often closely related to issues regarding resultant luck, for example see the discussion of negligence later on.
18. The details of the actions and motives of the historical Schindler may be disputable, but we assume the best motives for 'Schindler' for the purposes of the example.
19. NE 1135b 17–18 (Loeb).
20. NE 1110a 14–19.
21. It seems that the captain, like the craftsman, has also produced a good outcome since it is the best possible one under the circumstances. Also see discussion of dilemmas below.
22. NE 1111a 16–19.
23. NE 1113b 23.
24. NE 1113b 28ff.
25. NE 1113b 30–34 (Loeb).
26. Of course such a conclusion presupposes a degree of control which it is unrealistic to expect from those who are physically or psychologically addicted to substance abuse. More plausible is the position that we should avoid placing ourselves in a position where we are likely to become addicted in the first place, which may include the requirement for self-knowledge in recognizing ourselves as the kind of person who has a tendency to become reliant on drugs and stimulants in the first place and the potential to become addicted.
27. NE 1114a 10ff.
28. See Nagel, in Statman (1993); Lewis (1989); or Statman, in Statman (1993).
29. It may make a difference when considering questions of punishment, but the relationship between moral blame and legal punishment is too vast a topic to be touched upon here, save to point out that legal responsibility and moral responsibility may diverge. See note 30.
30. Such an analysis goes against Nagel's interpretation of the example, but is not without support amongst other contemporary writers. For example, Rescher writes:

> People who drive their cars home from an office party in a thoroughly intoxicated condition, indifferent to the danger to themselves and heedless of the risks they are creating for others, are equally guilty in the eyes of *morality* (as opposed to *legality*) whether they kill someone along the way or not. Their transgression lies in the very fact of their playing

Russian roulette with the lives of others. Whether they actually kill someone is simply a matter of luck, of accident and sheer statistical haphazard. But the moral negativity is much the same one way or the other – even as the moral positivity is much the same way or the other for the person who bravely plunges into the water in an attempt to save a drowning child. Regardless of outcome, the fact remains that, in the ordinary course of things, careless driving puts people's lives at risk unnecessarily and rescue attempts improve their chances of survival. What matters for morality is the ordinary tendency of actions rather than their actual results under unforseeable circumstances in particular cases. (Rescher, in Statman, 1993, p. 158)

31. I am assuming here that success is no indication of wholeheartedness on the part of one agent which is lacking on the part of the other and may be the reason why the attempt failed. This is part of the setting up of this case as an example of moral luck, as success or failure must be the result of something entirely outside the agents' control and cannot be related to their intentions or motivation.
32. Nussbaum (1993), p. 90.
33. Ibid., p. 98.
34. NE 1135a 29–30.
35. This point is also made by Ackrill in his discussion of Aristotle on action when he says: 'Aristotle thus draws a strong contrast between *what* is done – which might have been done from various motives or inadvertently – and *why* it is done. If inferences to the character of the agent are to be made from the character of the thing done, it must have been done "for itself" ' (Rorty, 1980, p. 94).
36. NE 1111a 12, as an example of ignorance of the thing done 'a person might mistake his son for an enemy, as Merope does'.
37. Nagel, in Statman (1993), p. 58.
38. Ibid., p. 61 (my italics).
39. Ibid.
40. The *mens rea* may exist without an *actus reus*, but if the *actus reus* of a particular crime does not occur, then there is no crime.
41. Of course both drunken drivers are guilty of the legal offence relating to drunken driving. The difference between the moral judgement and the legal culpability is that, according to this analysis, both drivers are equally morally guilty of endangering the lives of others even though only one of them kills someone, whereas legally, only one of them is guilty of manslaughter. The lucky driver, although morally as guilty as the unlucky one, cannot be prosecuted for manslaughter as the *actus reus* relating to killing someone while driving under the influence is not present, as he simply did not kill anyone. So the *actus reus* relating to reckless driving is present in both cases, but the legal charge of manslaughter can only be held against one driver.
42. Nagel, in Statman (1993), p. 62.
43. Ibid., p. 63.
44. For example, relating to traffic offences, it is an offence to drive a vehicle without due care and attention or without reasonable consideration for others, Road Traffic Act 1988, s. 3.
45. Offences of strict liability are another example where legal and moral decisions may diverge. Strict liability offences are 'of absolute prohibition' and,

at its extreme, means that an accused whose conduct has caused an *actus reus* will be convicted without any requirement for *mens rea*.

46. It is interesting to note Nagel's choice of words to describe what has gone on: one agent 'has been careless', which seems to focus moral censure on him, whereas the other 'has done something awful', which seems to derive the moral blame portioned to the agent from the outcome of the act.

47. This is not to say that most of us do not take such risks or are so careless a lot of the time, but what this reveals about human characters is a question for psychology or sociology.

48. Lewis (1989), p. 56.

49. Nagel, in Statman (1993), p. 63.

50. NE 1150a 12–15 (Loeb).

51. NE 1104b 19–20 (Loeb).

52. See Chapter 5 on the Stoics and Chapters 6, 7 on Kant.

53. NE 1099a 31–33.

54. MM 1206b 30–35.

55. MacIntyre (1967), p. 67.

56. Ibid., p. 68.

57. For more on this see Chapter 4. Briefly, there are two main responses to the possibility of moral luck: one is to deny the existence of moral luck and attempt to make morality immune to luck (Kant), the other is to accept moral luck as an unavoidable part of the human condition (Aristotle). If one is to accept the unavoidability of moral luck, this could be seen as an unfortunate fact about the human condition, or as a positive feature of moral life (Nussbaum).

58. This is a very unfortunate translation, but I have used the Loeb edition here purposefully to draw attention to this point. The Loeb edition translates at times both *tyche* (luck) and *agatha* (external goods) as fortune, and this could lead to misunderstandings.

59. NE 1124b 25–30.

60. See Nussbaum (1986), for example.

61. EE 1216a 3–5.

62. NE 1176a 34–35 (Loeb).

63. The Ancient Greek term *eudaimonia* is often translated as 'happiness', but its original meaning is thought to be much wider. The Greek *eudaimon* means a favourable demon (or god), so *eudaimonia* seems to be about leading a blessed, prosperous (in a general, wide sense) life, having a good destiny, being content. Achieving this state of *eudaimonia* is a life-long project, but once achieved this is a relatively stable state of being. 'Happiness', on the other hand, is a strong but possibly fleeting emotion, that is often directed at a specific object and is quite fragile. Since 'happiness' is then an inadequate translation for *eudaimonia*, many commentators have taken to using the original Greek word (see for example the work of Nussbaum), and I will follow this practice throughout this work. Similarly for *makariotés*.

64. NE 1101a 6. The Loeb edition translates this passage more accurately with repect to Priam: '... though it is true he will not be supremely blessed if he encounters the misfortunes of a Priam'.

65. Nussbaum cites Ross, W.D., *The Works of Aristotle* (London, 1923), p. 192, as well as Joachim, H.H., *The Nicomachean Ethics* (Oxford, 1951), ad loc.

66. Nussbaum (1986), pp. 329–334.
67. Ibid., pp. 327–330.
68. I am grateful to David Walker and Kim Thomson for discussions on this point.
69. Williams, in Raz (1978), p. 95. Williams also identifies as moral dilemma cases, cases where something I ought to do in respect of certain of its features also has other features in respect of which I ought not to do it, but this possibility will not be discussed here.
70. McConnell calls this the traditional approach and assesses the impact of Williams' writings on the topic, see McConnell (1978).
71. NE 1094b 12–14, see also several passages above.
72. NE 1094b 7–10.
73. NE 1161a 10ff.
74. NE 1161a 8–20. It has been put to me that Aristotle's mention of Agamemnon here may be an attempt at irony. Short of asking Aristotle what he meant it would be very difficult to counter such an objection.
75. This seems to be Wiggins' position in Wiggins (1976).
76. See, for example, Hursthouse, in Crisp (1996), although Hursthouse also seems to be accepting some version of option 4 in Hursthouse *et al.* (1998).
77. NE 1110a 20ff. (Loeb).
78. Recent virtue ethicists have responded to the criticism that virtue ethics cannot deal with the problem of dirty hands. As Hursthouse puts it:

> Given that these situations are those in which, *ex hypothesi*, there is no virtuous *choice* to be made, no action which is partially constitutive of living well, virtue ethics is logically debarred from saying 'In such situations, the virtuous agent *chooses* to do such and such'. But it is not debarred from describing what the virtuous agent 'does' without choosing to do so; perhaps she suffers for the rest of her life. (Hursthouse in Hursthouse *et al.*, 1998, p. 66)

79. There have been some indications as to the possible answer to this problem in the previous two chapters, but the next chapter will present a more systematic and critical account of this issue.

4   Aristotle and reason

1. Sections 4.1 and 4.2 draw frequently from the work of Nussbaum, to whom we owe many of the recent discussions on Aristotle and luck.
2. Nussbaum (1986), p. 320.
3. NE 1099b 20–25.
4. Having said this, I also think that the possibility of such a discussion is purely hypothetical, as I have never come across anyone who truly thinks that all morality is reducible to luck. Indeed it would be difficult to understand how a person could hold such a position and continue to function as a human being.
5. EE 1207a 4–6.
6. Nussbaum, 1986, p. 289.
7. Ibid., p. 341.

8. Ibid., p. 342.
9. Incidentally, this definition of virtue has been particularly important in developing some strands of modern virtue ethics. Some commentators take this as evidence that Aristotle recommends (or that a modern virtue ethics should recommend) that we look to the virtuous man as a guide or standard or ideal for action. However, this seems to me to be based on a misrepresentation of that passage. The passage focuses our attention on the role of the right reason in ethical thinking. Virtue is determined by the right reason and as the virtuous man would determine it, that is by the use of the right reason (NE 1106b 35ff.). Thus, the virtuous man can operate as an example of the recognition and application of the right reason, but it is not clear that he can be accorded as important a role as some virtue ethicists want him to play. What should be highlighted in this passage is the use of right reason (although this may mean that the passage is of no help when asking whether Aristotle's theory is action-guiding) and we should be careful if we appeal to this passage to answer the question 'what should *I* do?'.
10. I think that this idea, if used as a charge against deontological theories, is a bit unmerited (and perhaps the sophisticated consequentialist could also find a way around it), but it still captures an important point about Aristotelian ethics, even if this is not a point of *contrast* with other theories.
11. This account of Aristotelian perception clearly owes much to McDowell, see for example McDowell (1979).
12. For more on the relationship between virtues and rules, see Roberts (1991).
13. The ability to see beyond the rules that normally govern activities and break them in emergency situations or see unpredictable, new connections not captured by existing rules seems to be a feature of expertise in many areas as well as moral expertise.
14. NE 1095b 4–8 (Loeb).
15. NE 1095b 24–26 (Loeb).
16. NE 1110b 12–16 (Loeb).
17. NE 1112b 2.
18. NE 1112b 31–33 (Loeb).
19. NE 1113b 10–14.
20. NE 1135a 24–26 (Loeb).
21. NE 1139a 22–26 (Loeb).
22. NE 1139a 30–34 (Loeb).
23. NE 1099b 19 (Loeb).
24. NE Book VII section v.
25. Indeed it is not clear whether we should be talking about two pictures of the human life, or two sides of the same coin, or an amalgam of different ideas, or different elements in the same person.

5   The Stoics

1. On the general question of Aristotle's influence on the Stoics, see Long (1968) for the position that there was substantial influence or Sandbach (1985), against this position.
2. See Sherman (1997). Sherman has been able to identify only one other study of the connection between Kant and the Stoics in Seidler's works (1981a,b, 1983). I have also come across Reich (1939). Reich provides a detailed study

of the possible influence of the Stoics on Kant and concludes that Kant followed the lead of the Wolffians who were themselves influenced by the Stoics, but refined the theory from lessons learnt from Plato. Annas (1993) also addresses the question in a detailed discussion.

3. Cicero says that the Greek 'passions' ought to be called 'diseases' by a literal translation of the word, DFin, III, 35.
4. DL, VII, 110.
5. Ibid.
6. Ibid., VII, 110–115.
7. DI, 1.7.4.
8. Ibid.
9. For detailed discussions of the Stoics' attitude to the passions, see Sherman (1997) and Nussbaum (1994).
10. DL, VII, 117.
11. See Arrington (1998). This may have also been the reason behind the Epicurean attempt to avoid moral luck. The Epicureans saw the importance of pleasure in human lives, but they also recognized the vulnerability of pleasure to factors outside one's control. Their answer was for the moral agent to limit his desires and needs to a bare minimum, as very modest requirements are more likely to be fulfilled (e.g. if you require caviar for sustenance you are more likely to be disappointed; however, if you desire stale bread, your desires will be easily satisfied and you are more likely to be a happy man). Also from Arrington (1998).
12. SVF, vol. III, 104.
13. Ibid., vol. I, 351.
14. Chrysippus reported in DL, VII, 189.
15. SVF, vol. III, 585.
16. It must be pointed out, however, that the Stoics recognize that some external goods, although they do not have moral value, may be chosen over others. This seems to be one of the first instances when 'moral value' is distinguished from other types of value.
17. DFin, III, 50–51.
18. Ibid., III, 75–76. Commentators come to similar conclusions about the importance of internal states about the whole of Stoic theory; for example,

> It [the Stoic system] recognizes as legitimate objects of endeavour much to which man automatically attaches value, but in the last resort things which they cannot control are of no importance. Happiness depends on what is entirely a man's own doing, the operation of his mind: if he judges correctly and holds steadfast to truth he will be a perfect being, whom misfortune may strike but will never harm. (Sandbach, 1975, p. 68)

19. NE 1100a 5.
20. DL, VII, 127.
21. Ibid., VII, 120.
22. Cooper, in Engstrom and Whiting (1996), p. 270.
23. This remark has greatly benefited from Annas' discussion of virtue as a skill (Annas, 1993, Chapter 19).
24. E, 41.
25. Attributed to Cleanthes, in DL, VII, 127.

26. Ibid.
27. Long also points out the importance the Stoics attach to aiming rather than achieving a desirable result, 'Virtue is not defined by the consequences in the world which it succeeds in promoting, but by a pattern of behaviour that follows necessarily from a disposition perfectly in tune with Nature's rationality' (Long, 1986, p. 192).
28. On receiving the news of his child's death, Cicero remarked 'I was always aware I had begotten a mortal', Cicero, *Tusculan Disputations*, 3.30, in Nussbaum (1994), p. 363.
29. On being shipwrecked in Athens and losing all his wealth, Zeno pronounced 'It is well done of thee, Fortune, thus to drive me to philosophy', DL, VII, 5.
30. Ibid., VII, 86.
31. Ibid., VII, 94.
32. Seneca, *Letters*, in HP, vol. I, p. 371.
33. The Stoics believed that reason was available equally to men and women, thus avoiding some of the feminist criticisms that have been levelled against Aristotle (for an overview of feminism and Aristotle, see Susan Moller Okin's paper in Crisp, 1996).
34. E, 120.
35. DL, VII, 108.
36. Panaetius, Fragment 96, in HP, vol. I, p. 397.
37. Marcus Aurelius, 5.16, in HP, vol. I, p. 397.
38. Specifically on the difference between Kant and the Stoics on reason and nature, see Cooper, in Engstrom and Whiting (1996).
39. Annas (1993), p. 449.
40. DF, 41.
41. Ibid.
42. Rist (1969), p. 122.
43. This may explain Seneca's admiration for suicide. Seneca most famously praised suicide and in this context we can understand why. Suicide involves recognizing fate and working along with it. It involves taking control of one's life and choosing the time and manner in which to affirm the inevitability of death. For Seneca, contempt for one's body is a sign of freedom and, by extension, suicide is the highest kind of freedom.
44. SVF, vol. III, 191. The Stoics also appeared to have a sense of humour with respect to their views on determinism. Diogenes Laertius relates the following episode: 'The story goes that Zeno was flogging a slave for stealing. "I was fated to steal", said the slave. "And to be flogged", was Zeno's reply', DL, VII, 23.
45. Annas discusses the role of nature in Stoic doctrine in great detail. She comes to the conclusion that the Early Stoics established the content of ethics independently of nature, and later, knowledge of nature served to increase our understanding of ethics, whereas the Later Stoics saw knowledge of the purpose of nature as foundational for ethics, Annas (1993), Chapter 6.
46. DL, VII, 148.
47. See for example DL, VII, 129, which claims that for the Stoics, youths are to be admired because of their natural endowment for virtue.
48. Galen, *On Hippocrates' and Plato's Doctrines*, 5.5.8–26, in HP, vol. I, p. 415.
49. Annas (1993), esp. II. 5.
50. Ibid., p. 178.

51. Ibid., pp. 178–179.
52. G, 816, p. 173.
53. P, 1034 B.
54. Plutarch also has Chrysippus sending the Stoic sage forth to make a profit, ibid., 1043 E.
55. DL, VII, 130.
56. Ibid., VII, 91.
57. P, 1035 F.
58. DL, VII, 91.

6 Kant on luck

1. Williams, in Statman (1993), mainly pp. 36–37.
2. Nagel, in Statman (1993), mainly pp. 64–65.
3. Nussbaum (1986), p. 48. All of the following discussion of Kant takes place in the *Fragility of Goodness*.
4. G 389vi.
5. Rel 6:3.
6. Ibid., 6:44.
7. Allison (1996), p. 120.
8. KrV A554/B582–A555/B583. Allison explains how the first way of considering the action, with regard to its empirical causes, relates to its empirical character, whereas the judgement of blame relates to its intelligible character. More on this distinction later on in this chapter.
9. KpV 5:99–100.
10. Kant seems to use 'anthropology' to mean what we would understand by 'psychology' and he sometimes, like here, uses the two words interchangeably. Kant, G 390x. However, at other times, anthropology is taken to refer to the subjective conditions affecting the exercise of moral laws and the empirical processes by which moral principles are strengthened (see Munzel, 1999, p. 61).
11. Although being conditionally good does not equal being instrumentally good.
12. G 394. This again is similar to the Stoic idea that it is assent to the moral act, rather than the act itself that is of value, although the Stoic position seems more extreme.
13. G 399–400.
14. In deciding to include the following remarks on the intelligible/sensible distinction, I faced a difficult decision. On the one hand, the limited scope of this project does not allow me to pay due credit to the complexity of Kant's theoretical philosophy and the wealth of interpretations and debates in the current literature on it. There are good reasons for not discussing this distinction at all, rather than risking giving the wrong impression of Kant's complex stand on these matters. On the other hand, it seemed to me that the distinction itself underpinned many of my conclusions about Kant on moral luck and I was weary of ignoring it entirely. I hope Kantian scholars will excuse any generalizations and simplifications I have had to make in order to make appropriate reference to the distinction and its role in the Kantian position on moral luck.
15. A 324.

16. Exactly how this should be interpreted will be discussed later.
17. G 411–412.
18. Ibid., 448.
19. In a footnote to the *Metaphysics of Morals*, Gregor observed that '[t]he primary sense of Glück, a component of the German word for "happiness" {Glückseligkeit} is "luck" or "fortune" ' (p. 142, footnote 39).
20. G 408.
21. Writers who have claimed that Kant attaches no importance to the empirical side of human nature include Williams, Foot and MacIntyre.
22. KpV 5:59.
23. Scruton (1982), p. 67.
24. Wood (1999), p. 181.
25. Allison (1990), p. 138.
26. Rescher (2000), p. 15.
27. Allison (1990), p. 32.
28. Rescher (2000), p. 27.
29. Ibid., p. 192.
30. Allison (1990), p. 45.
31. Rel 6:41. This passage is also a good illustration of how 'nature' is used differently with respect to the intelligible self and differently with respect to the sensible self.
32. KrV A555/B583.
33. Rel 6:46.
34. Ibid. 6:47.
35. A 294.

7 Kant on virtue

1. Rel 6:47.
2. MS 383–384.
3. Such writers include John McDowell, Martha Nussbaum, Bernard Williams and Annette Baier.
4. MS 407.
5. See, for example, MS 6:480.
6. Rel 6:48–49.
7. MS 404, see also 432.
8. MS 404 note.
9. Gregor also finds this Kantian criticism of Aristotle unjustified. She argues that although the Aristotelian passage on the mean is concerned with 'deciding how to apply such principles [principles we have already chosen] to situations in which we must act' (p. xviii), Kant wrongly understands it to be concerned with 'choosing one's overriding principles or maxims' (p. xviii) in the first place (in 'Introduction', MS).
10. This remark on the relationship between *eudaimonia* and virtue is made in passing here and I do not examine this relationship anywhere else in this work. Of course, the relationship is complex, central to many accounts of Aristotle and can be interpreted in a variety of ways.
11. KpV 5:72–73.

12. See, for example, MS 6:394 and 6:397.
13. KpV 5:38.
14. For all the above ideas, see KpV 5:76–77.
15. In the MS Kant identifies four 'moral endowments', understood as 'natural predispositions of the mind (*praedispositio*) for being affected by concepts of duty, antecedent predispositions on the side of feeling' (MS 6:399). Although there is no duty to acquire these feelings, there is an obligation to cultivate and strengthen them.
16. See Allison (1996), p. 121. Baxley (2003) seems to hold a similar position when she interprets autonomy as the legislative capacity of the will for creating universally valid laws and autocracy as the executive capacity for observing such laws. The weak-willed man then is autonomous but fails to be autocratic.
17. G 398–399.
18. For a brief account of this standard objection, see Singer (1993), Chapter 14.
19. The main exponent of this line of thought is Williams (1993).
20. Baron (1997), p. 58, 'The relevant contrast shouldn't be between (1) someone who lacks fellow-feeling, love for particular others, the desire to help others, etc. but who has and acts from a sense of duty and (2) someone who has the right desires and affections but lacks a sense of duty. Rather, it should be between (1′) someone who has the right desires and affections and has and acts from a sense of duty and (2).'
21. KpV 5:117–118.
22. G 399.
23. This very helpful distinction is made by Baxley (2003).
24. As an aside, if we were to suppose this interpretation to be correct so that Kantian virtue is similar to Aristotelian continence, it is not clear to me why this is taken to be a criticism of Kant. The gist of certain discussions seems to be that there would be something unsatisfactory with Kantian virtue if it were *merely* continence, but it is not immediately clear to me why that would be the case.
25. See, for example, the MS 6:484, where he discusses how the exercise of virtue proceeds from a hardy spirit and a cheerful one.
26. Munzel (1999), p. 305.
27. Baxley (2003), pp. 577–578.
28. A similar account of inclinations prompting us to action is given in detail in Baron (1995).
29. A similar point is made by Allision against Schiller's account of the inclinations (1990), p. 183.
30. KpV 5:83–84.
31. Munzel (1999), p. 2.
32. A 285.
33. Ibid.
34. MS 389.
35. This is a brief summary of Allison's Incorporation Thesis.
36. Rel 3:35.
37. Munzel (1999), p. 158. Munzel has an extremely detailed and convincing account of all these aspects of Kantian character, from which my very brief remarks have benefited greatly.
38. Munzel (1999), p. 165.

39. MS 397.
40. See, for example, Allison's account of *Gesinnung*, and in particular (1990), p. 139.
41. Of course, as the *Groundwork* clearly illustrates, moral worth is attributed to the agent's maxim for action when he acts from duty alone, and my remark here should not be taken to deny this. The point of this remark is that moral worth, unlike Aristotelian interpretations of the concept, cannot be grounded in the empirical.
42. Rel 6:37.
43. MS 6:392–393.
44. O'Neil, in Crisp (1996), p. 96.

8   Virtue ethics and neo-Kantians: Slote, Hursthouse and Herman

1. Originally published in *Philosophy*, 33 (1958), but also available, amongst other places, in Crisp and Slote (1997) (all references from that edition).
2. Crisp and Slote (1997), p. 31. It is interesting to note that she saw this conception as dominant in Jewish, Stoic and Christian ethics. This is yet another connecting link between the Stoics and Kant, through his influence from Christianity.
3. It also set the scene for thinking of Aristotelianism and Kantianism as rival and conflicting theories.
4. See, for example, articles by Michael Slote, John Cottingham, Michael Stocker and David Wiggins, in Crisp (1996).
5. See, for example, Baron's perplexity as to what virtue ethics actually is, in Baron *et al.* (1997); or Louden's remarks that virtue ethics has had a negative thrust in that it is mainly concerned with criticizing other theories, in Statman (1997).
6. For an overview of virtue ethics, see Trianosky (in Statman, 1997) or Oakley (1996). For attempts to develop a distinctive version of virtue ethics, see the work of Slote (on the centrality of agents), Watson (on the primacy of character in Statman, 1997), Hursthouse (on a nature-based conception of flourishing, in Statman, 1997 and Hursthouse, 1999), Cullity (on the primacy of character and the importance of *aretaic* over *deontic* concepts), among others. Most recently, on a pluralistic account of the virtues, see Swanton (2003).
7. Recently Harman has argued that the results of research in social psychology show that there are no such things as character traits and therefore there is no basis for virtue ethical theories dependent on the concept of 'character traits'. However, his discussion is the result of a misinterpretation of the conclusions and aims of the experiments. See Harman (1999), Athanassoulis (2000) and Chapter 2.
8. Anscombe, in her article, criticizes the work of a great many philosophers, including Mill, Bentham, Hume and Sidgwick, along with Kant. However, it is beyond the scope of this book to discuss her evaluation of all these theories. I concentrate on Kant because he seems to epitomize her conception of law ethics and because renewed interest in his lesser known works has highlighted the weaknesses of Anscombe's criticisms.

9. Anscombe was followed by Williams, MacIntyre, Foot and so on, whose work on the virtues is now considered classic in the modern virtue ethical tradition (a collection of such articles can be found in Crisp and Slote, 1997).

10. The extent of this reliance may range from thinking that everything that needs to be said has been said by Aristotle already (see, for example, Putnam's characterization of virtue ethics as 'what Aristotle did', Putnam, 1988, p. 379), to an acknowledgement that the terms used in virtue ethics were first introduced by Aristotle. Other philosophers such as Plato, the Stoics, Aquinas and Hume may also provide inspiration for virtue ethics (see, for example, Irwin, in Crisp 1996 or Wiggins, in Crisp 1996), but Aristotle's work remains of central importance in the field.

11. See, for example, Oakley (1996) or Trianosky in Statman (1997).

12. Alderman, in Statman (1997), p. 149.

13. Griffin (1996).

14. On the other hand, some virtue ethicists capitalize on the idea that virtue ethics is culture-relative, for example MacIntyre (1985); Cottingham (1994); Crisp (1996).

15. Although this is my interpretation and not anyone's explicit aim.

16. Rosalind Hursthouse seems to hold such a view, see especially Hursthouse (1999).

17. As we shall see, this appears to be Slote's view.

18. See the work of Garrett Cullity.

19. Something like this seems to be Alderman's purpose, in Statman (1997), and plays a role in some of Hursthouse's work, see Hursthouse *et al.* (1998).

20. See Watson, in Statman (1997).

21. See, for example, Simpson and Santas both in Statman (1997).

22. For his earlier work, see Slote (1992) and Baron *et al.* (1997), for his later work, see Slote (2001).

23. Slote (1992), p. 124.

24. Slote, in Baron, Petit and Slote (1997), p. 177.

25. Ibid., p. 178.

26. Ibid.

27. Ibid., p. 216.

28. Ibid., p. 232.

29. Slote often uses direct appeals to intuitions, for example 'resourcefulness and discretion, for example are intuitively regarded as virtues...' or 'I argue that there is intuitive and theoretical reason to...' or '...the counterintuitive implications of utilitarianism in this area stand in stark contrast with the deliverances of a common-sense ethics of virtue', and he describes the theory he is defending as 'intuition-driven' (all in Slote, 1994a).

30. There is a distinction here often appealed to by virtue ethicists between *aretaic* and *deontic* terms. *Deontic* terms like 'right' and 'wrong' are distinguished from *aretaic* terms like 'kind' and 'honest' (see, for example, Cullity, 1995a).

31. Slote (1992), p. 90.

32. Ibid., p. xvi. Incidentally I believe that Slote's definition of a *moral* virtue is highly contentious, but do not discuss this issue further here.

33. Common-sense morality is to be distinguished from common-sense virtue ethics in Slote's writings.

34. See Slote (1992), pp. 119ff.

35. Ibid., p. 121.
36. Ibid., p. 119.
37. Ibid., p. 120.
38. We have already seen that Williams advocates such a move and claims that it reveals a difference between Ancient Greek ethics and modern morality and that there are other commentators who do not support this distinction. See Chapter 1.
39. Such an agent may be removed from society for his own and others' safety, but this is not a moral judgement of blameworthiness.
40. Driver (1994), pp. 510–511. Driver also points out that of course there are non-moral virtues, but it is not clear that they should be accorded the same weight as moral virtues or that the possession of either type of virtue should be evaluated in the same way. Driver (1995) also criticizes Slote for his reliance on motives.
41. See, for example, Feinberg (1969) or Mabbott and Horsburgh (1962).
42. Slote, in Crisp and Slote (1997), p. 259.
43. This discussion is from Dennett (1994).
44. This discussion is reminiscent of a well-known example by James Rachels in his discussion of the moral difference between killing and letting die. Jones and Smith both wish to see their nephew dead in order to inherit a fortune. Smith walks into the bath and drowns the child, whereas Jones happens upon the child as he is drowning and does nothing to save him. Both are equally reprehensible because of their intention to see the nephew dead (Rachels, 1999).
45. Hursthouse (1999), p. 123.
46. Ibid., p. 130.
47. Ibid., see for example p. 160.
48. Ibid., p. 192.
49. Ibid., p. 51.
50. Ibid., p. 74.
51. Ibid., p. 222.
52. Ibid., p. 240.
53. Ibid., p. 226.
54. Ibid., p. 223.
55. Ibid., p. 222.
56. Brad Hooker has an excellent analysis of these two points in Hooker (2002).
57. Ibid., p. 38.
58. Hursthouse (2002), p. 48.
59. Ibid., p. 52.
60. Annas (1993), p. 179.
61. Stohr and Wellman (2002), p. 60.
62. Herman (1993), p. 233.
63. Herman, in Engstrom and Whiting (1996), p. 36.
64. Ibid., p. 36.
65. Herman (1993), pp. 108–109.
66. Ibid., p. 109.
67. Herman, in Engstrom and Whiting (1996), pp. 41–42.
68. Herman (1993), p. 205.
69. Herman, in Engstrom and Whiting (1996), p. 50.

70. Ibid., p. 42.
71. Ibid., p. 43.
72. G 407.
73. MS 6:447.
74. Herman, in Engstrom and Whiting (1996), p. 37.
75. Ibid., p. 55.
76. Slote (1992), p. 51.
77. Rorty (1996), p. 310.

9 Conclusion

1. Williams, in Statman (1993), p. 35.
2. Andre, in Statman (1993).
3. Williams, in Statman (1993), p. 252. This perplexing admission of Williams' leaves us wondering, according to which system of morality is the Gauguin example a genuine example of moral luck?
4. Of course, as with everything, there are some notable exceptions. See for example Hursthouse who points out that although her earlier work adopted a combative style, pitching virtue ethics as a rival to deontology and consequentialism (perhaps as a reaction to the fact that the theory was not very well known or respected and was viewed by some with suspicion), the need for such an approach has now diminished with the theory's growing popularity (Hursthouse, 1999, p. 7).
5. Once again the third part of this distinction, outcome-based, refers to consequentialism, but I will not raise the question of whether this description is viable or useful.

Bibliography

Ackrill, J.L., 'Aristotle on Eudaimonia', in Rorty, A.O. (ed.), *Essays on Aristotle's Ethics* (Berkeley and LA: University of California Press, 1980).

Alderman, H., 'By Virtue of a Virtue', in Statman, D. (ed.), *Virtue Ethics* (Great Britain: Edinburgh University Press, 1997).

Allison, H.E., *Idealism and Freedom* (USA: Cambridge University Press, 1996).

——, *Kant's Theory of Freedom* (USA: Cambridge University Press, 1990).

Andre, J., 'Nagel, Williams and Moral Luck', in Statman, D. (ed.), *Moral Luck* (USA: State University of New York Press, 1993).

Annas, J., *The Morality of Happiness* (New York: Oxford University Press, 1993).

Anscombe, G.E.M., 'Modern Moral Philosophy', in Crisp, R. and Slote, M. (eds), *Virtue Ethics* (USA: Oxford University Press, 1997).

Arrington, R.L., *Western Ethics* (USA: Blackwell, 1998).

Athanassoulis, N., 'Review of Hursthouse's *On Virtue Ethics*', *Ratio*, March 2001.

——, 'A Response to Harman', *Proceedings of the Aristotelian Society*, 2000, Part 2.

Baier, A., 'What Do Women Want in a Moral Theory?', in Crisp, R. and Slote, M. (eds), *Virtue Ethics* (USA: Oxford University Press, 1997).

——, *Postures of the Mind* (Minneapolis: University of Minnesota Press, 1985).

Baron, M.W., Pettit, P. and Slote, M., *Three Methods of Ethics* (Great Britain: Blackwell, 1997).

——, *Kantian Ethics Almost Without Apology* (USA: Cornell University Press, 1995).

Baxley, A.M., 'Does Kantian Virtue Amount to More than Continence?', *The Review of Metaphysics*, vol. 56, March 2003.

Cooper, J.M., 'Eudaimonism, the Appeal to Nature, and "Moral Duty" in Stoicism', in Engstrom, S. and Whiting, J. (eds), *Aristotle, Kant and the Stoics* (USA: Cambridge University Press, 1996).

Cottingham, J., *Philosophy and the Good Life* (UK: Cambridge University Press, 1998).

——, 'Partiality and the Virtues', in Crisp, R. (ed.), *How Should One Live* (USA: Oxford University Press, 1996).

——, 'Religion, Virtue and Ethical Culture', *Philosophy*, vol. 69, 1994.

Crisp, R. and Slote, M., 'Introduction', in Crisp, R. (ed.), *How Should One Live* (USA: Oxford University Press, 1996).

——, 'Modern Moral Philosophy and the Virtues', in Crisp, R. (ed.), *How Should One Live* (USA: Oxford University Press, 1996).

Cullity, G., 'Aretaic Cognitivism', *American Philosophical Quarterly*, vol. 32, no. 4, 1995a.

——, 'Moral Character and the Iteration Problem', *Utilitas*, vol. 7, no. 2, 1995b.

Dancy, J., *Moral Reasons* (Great Britain: Blackwell, 1993).

Dancy, J., Moravcsik, J.M.E. and Taylor, C.C.W., *Human Agency* (Stanford: Stanford University Press, 1988).

——, 'Ethical Particularism and Morally Relevant Properties', *Mind*, vol. XCII, 1983.

Dennett, D.C., 'Reply to my Critics: Luck, Regret and Kinds of Persons', *Philosophical Topics*, vol. 22, nos 1 and 2, 1994.

——, *Elbow Room* (Oxford: Clarendon Press, 1984).

Dent, N.J.H., *The Psychology of the Virtues* (Great Britain: Cambridge University Press, 1984).

——, 'The Value of Courage', *Philosophy*, vol. 56, 1981.

——, 'Virtues and Actions', *The Philosophical Quarterly*, vol. 25, 1975.

Devlin, P., *The Enforcement of Morals* (Oxford: Oxford University Press, 1965).

Dostoyevsky, F., *Crime and Punishment* (1865–6), trans. McDuff, D. (England: Penguin Books, 1991).

Driver, J., 'Monkeying with Motives: Agent-Basing Virtue Ethics', *Utilitas*, vol. 7, no. 2, 1995.

——, 'A Critical Study of Michael Slote's from Morality to Virtue', *Nous*, vol. 28, 1994.

Engstrom, S. and Whiting, J., *Aristotle, Kant and the Stoics* (USA: Cambridge University Press, 1996).

Feinberg, J., *Doing and Deserving* (Princeton: Princeton University Press, 1970).

——, *Moral Concepts* (London: Oxford University Press, 1969).

Foot, P., 'Moral Realism and Moral Dilemma', *Journal of Philosophy*, vol. 80, 1983.

——, *Virtues and Vices* (Oxford: Blackwell, 1978).

Frankfurt, H.G., *The Importance of What We Care About* (Cambridge: Cambridge University Press, 1988).

Griffin, J., *Value Judgement* (Oxford: Clarendon Press, 1996).

Hardy, T., *Jude the Obscure* (1896) (England: Penguin Books, 1994).

Harman, G., 'Moral Philosophy Meets Social Psychology: Virtue Ethics and The Fundamental Attribution Error', *Proceedings of the Aristotelian Society*, 1999, Part 2.

Haybron, D.M., 'Evil Characters', *American Philosophical Quarterly*, vol. 36, no. 2, April 1999.

Herman, B., 'Making Room for Character', in Engstrom, S. and Whiting, J. (eds), *Aristotle, Kant and the Stoics* (USA: Cambridge University Press, 1996).

——, *The Practice of Moral Judgement* (Cambridge: Harvard University Press, 1993).

Hooker, B., 'The Collapse of Virtue Ethics', *Utilitas*, vol. 14, no. 1, March 2002.

Hursthouse, R., 'Virtue Ethics vs. Rule-Consequentialism: A Reply to Brad Hooker', *Utilitas*, vol. 14, no. 1, March 2002.

——, *On Virtue Ethics* (Oxford: Oxford University Press, 1999).

——, 'Applying Virtue Ethics', in Hursthouse, R., Lawrence, G. and Quinn, W. (eds), *Virtues and Reasons: Philippa Foot and Moral Theory* (Great Britain: Oxford University Press, 1998).

——, 'Normative Virtue Ethics', in Crisp, R. (ed.), *How Should One Live* (USA: Oxford University Press, 1996).

Korsgaard, C.M., 'From Duty and for the Sake of the Noble: Kant and Aristotle on Morally Good Action', in Engstrom, S. and Whiting, J. (eds), *Aristotle, Kant and the Stoics* (USA: Cambridge University Press, 1996).

——, 'Aristotle and Kant on the Source of Value', *Ethics*, vol. 96, 1986.

Kultgen, J., 'The Vicissitudes of Common-Sense Virtue Ethics, Part II: The Heuristic Use of Common Sense', *The Journal of Value Inquiry*, vol. 32, 1998.

Levi, D.S., 'What's Luck Got to Do With It?', in Statman, D. (ed.), *Moral Luck* (USA: State University of New York Press, 1993).

Lewis, D., 'The Punishment That Leaves Something to Chance', *Philosophy and Public Affairs*, vol. 18, no. 1, 1989.

Long, A.A., *Hellenistic Philosophy* (Great Britain: Duckworth, 1986).

——, 'Aristotle's Legacy to Stoic Ethics', *Bulletin of the Institute of Classical Studies*, vol. 15, 1968.

Louden, R.B., 'On Some Vices of Virtue Ethics', in Statman, D. (ed.), *Virtue Ethics* (Great Britain: Edinburgh University Press, 1997).

Mabbott, J.D. and Horsburgh, H.J.N., 'Prudence', *Proceedings of the Aristotelian Society*, Supp. vol. 1962.

MacIntyre, A., 'The Nature of the Virtues', in Crisp, R. and Slote, M. (eds), *Virtue Ethics* (USA: Oxford University Press, 1997).

——, *After Virtue* (London: Duckworth, 1985).

——, *A Short History of Ethics* (Great Britain: Routledge & Kegan Paul, 1967).

McConnell, T., 'Moral Dilemmas and Consistency in Ethics', *Canadian Journal of Philosophy*, vol. 8, no. 2, 1978.

McDowell, J., 'Incontinence and Practical Wisdom in Aristotle', in Lovibond, S. and Williams, S.G. (eds), *Essays for David Wiggins*, Aristotelian Society Series, vol. 16 (Oxford: Blackwell, 1996).

——, 'Virtues and Reason', *The Monist*, vol. 62, 1979.

McGinn, C., *Ethics, Evil and Fiction* (Oxford: Clarendon Press, 1999).

Melville, H., 'Billy Budd, Foretopman' (1924), *Billy Budd and Other Stories* (Great Britain: Wordsworth Classics, 1998).

Munzel, G.F., *Kant's Conception of Moral Character: The 'Critical' Link of Morality, Anthropology and Reflective Judgment* (London: University of Chicago Press, 1999).

Nagel, T., 'Moral Luck', in Statman, D. (ed.), *Moral Luck* (USA: State University of New York Press, 1993).

Nussbaum, M., 'Equity and Mercy', *Philosophy and Public Affairs*, vol. 22, 1993.

——, *The Therapy of Desire* (USA: Princeton University Press, 1994).

——, *Love's Knowledge* (Oxford: Oxford University Press, 1990).

——, 'Reply to Seabright', *Ethics*, 1988.

——, *The Fragility of Goodness* (Cambridge: Cambridge University Press, 1986).

O'Neil, O., 'Kant's Virtues', in Crisp, R. (ed.), *How Should One Live* (USA: Oxford University Press, 1996).

——, *Constructions of Reason: Explorations of Kant's Practical Philosophy* (UK: Cambridge University Press, 1989).

Oakeley, H.D., *Greek Ethical Thought* (London: Dent & Sons Ltd, 1925).

Oakley, J., 'Varieties of Virtue Ethics', *Ratio*, vol. 9, 1996.

Plato, *The Republic*, trans. Lee, D. (England: Penguin Books, 1955 [1987]).

Platts, M., *Ways of Meaning* (London: Routledge & Kegan Paul, 1979).

Putnam, R.A., 'Reciprocity and Virtue Ethics', *Ethics*, vol. 98, 1988.

Rachels, J., 'Active and Passive Euthanasia', in Kuhse, H. and Singer, P. (eds), *Bioethics: An Anthology* (Oxford: Blackwell, 1999).

Rawls, J., *A Theory of Justice* (Great Britain: Oxford University Press, 1992).

Reich, K., 'Kant and Greek Ethics', *Mind*, vol. 48, 1939.

Rescher, N., *Kant and the Reach of Reason: Studies in Kant's Theory of Rational Systemization* (Cambridge: Cambridge University Press, 2000).

——, 'Moral Luck', in Statman, D. (ed.), *Moral Luck* (USA: State University of New York Press, 1993).

Rist, J.M., *Stoic Philosophy* (Cambridge: Cambridge University Press, 1969).

Roberts, R.C., 'Virtues and Rules', *Philosophy and Phenomenological Research*, vol. LI, no. 2, 1991.

Rorty, A.O., 'From Exasperating Virtues to Civic Virtues', *American Philosophical Quarterly*, vol. 33, no. 3, July 1996.

——, *Essays on Aristotle's Ethics* (Berkeley and LA: University of California Press, 1980).

Sandbach, F.H., 'Aristotle and the Stoics', *Cambridge Philological Society*, Supp. vol. 10, 1985.

——, *The Stoics* (London: Chatto & Windus, 1975).

Santas, G.X., 'Does Aristotle Have a Virtue Ethics?', in Statman, D. (ed.), *Virtue Ethics* (Great Britain: Edinburgh University Press, 1997).

Scruton, R., *Kant* (Oxford: Oxford University Press, 1982).

Seabright, P., 'The Pursuit of Unhappiness: Paradoxical Motivation and the Subversion of Character in Henry James's Portrait of a Lady', *Ethics*, 1988.

Seidler, M., 'Kant and the Stoics on Suicide', *Journal of the History of Ideas*, vol. 44, 1983.

——, 'Kant and the Stoics on the Emotional Life', *Philosophy Research Archives*, 1981a.

——, 'The Role of Stoicism in Kant's Moral Philosophy', Dissertation, St Louis University, 1981b.

Sherman, N., *Making a Necessity of Virtue* (USA: Cambridge University Press, 1997).

——, *The Fabric of Character* (Great Britain: Clarendon Press, 1989).

Simpson, P., 'Contemporary Virtue Ethics and Aristotle', in Statman, D. (ed.), *Virtue Ethics* (Great Britain: Edinburgh University Press, 1997).

Singer, P., *A Companion to Ethics* (Great Britain: Blackwell, 1993).

Slote, M., *Morals from Motives* (Oxford: Oxford University Press, 2001).

——, 'Agent-Based Virtue Ethics', in Crisp, R. and Slote, M. (eds), *Virtue Ethics* (USA: Oxford University Press, 1997a).

——, 'From Morality to Virtue', in Statman, D. (ed.), *Virtue Ethics* (Great Britain: Edinburgh University Press, 1997b).

——, 'Virtue Ethics, Utilitarianism and Symmetry', in Crisp, R. (ed.), *How Should One Live* (USA: Oxford University Press, 1996).

——, 'Precis of from Morality to Virtue', *Philosophy and Phenomenological Research*, vol. 54, no. 3, 1994a.

——, 'The Problem of Moral Luck', *Philosophical Topics*, vol. 22, nos 1 and 2, 1994b.

——, *From Morality to Virtue* (New York: Oxford University Press, 1992).

——, 'Rational Dilemmas and Rational Supererogation', *Philosophical Topics*, vol. 14, Fall 1986.

Smith, J.C. and Hogan, B., *Criminal Law* (UK: Butterworth, 1992).

Solomon, D., 'Internal Objections to Virtue Ethics', in Statman, D., *Virtue Ethics* (Great Britain: Edinburgh University Press, 1997).

Statman, D., *Virtue Ethics* (Great Britain: Edinburgh University Press, 1997).

——, 'Introduction', *Moral Luck* (USA: State University of New York Press, 1993).

Stohr, K. and Wellman, C.H., 'Recent Work on Virtue Ethics', *American Philosophical Quarterly*, vol. 39, no. 1, January 2002.

Swanton, C., *Virtue Ethics: A Pluralistic View* (Oxford: Oxford University Press, 2003).

Trianosky, G.V., 'What is Virtue Ethics all About?', in Statman, D. (ed.), *Virtue Ethics* (Great Britain: Edinburgh University Press, 1997).

Walker, A.D.M., 'The Incompatibility of the Virtues', *Ratio*, vol. 6, 1993.

——, 'Virtue and Character', *Philosophy*, vol. 64, 1989.

Wallace, R.J., 'Virtue, Reason and Principle', *Canadian Journal of Philosophy*, vol. 21, no. 4, 1991.

Watson, G., 'The Primacy of Character', in Statman, D. (ed.), *Virtue Ethics* (Great Britain: Edinburgh University Press, 1997).

Welsh, I., *Marabou Stork Nightmares* (Great Britain: Vintage, 1995).

Wiggins, D., 'Weakness of Will, Commensurability and the Objects of Deliberation and Desire', *Needs, Values and Truth: Essays in the Philosophy of Value* (Oxford: Blackwell, 1987).

——, 'Truth, Invention and the Meaning of Life', *Proceedings of the British Academy*, vol. 62, 1976.

Williams, B., *Ethics and the Limits of Philosophy* (Great Britain: Fontana Press, 1993).

——, 'Moral Luck', in Statman, D. (ed.), *Moral Luck* (USA: State University of New York Press, 1993).

——, 'Postscript', in Statman, D. (ed.), *Moral Luck* (USA: State University of New York Press, 1993).

——, 'Philosophy', in Finley, M. (ed.), *The Legacy of Greece* (Oxford: Clarendon Press, 1981).

——, 'Ethical Consistency', in Raz, J. (ed.), *Practical Reasoning* (Oxford: Oxford University Press, 1978).

Wood, A.W., *Kant's Ethical Thought* (UK: Cambridge University Press, 1999).

Index

CPSIA information can be obtained at www.ICGtesting.com

226111LV00004B/38/P